COLLINS GEM

BABIES'
Names

**Fourth edition prepared
by Julia Cresswell**

HarperCollins*Publishers*

Julia Cresswell is an authority on first names, and has written a number of books on the subject

HarperCollins Publishers
PO Box, Glasgow G4 0NB

First published 1967
Fourth edition published 1998
   Reprinted twice
This edition published 1999

Reprint 10 9 8 7 6 5 4 3 2 1

ISBN 0 00 472291-4

Printed in Italy by Amadeus S.p.A.

Contents

Using this book

This book is designed to help you choose a name for your baby. Even parents who know what they want to call their child may well want to look at some of the possible forms the name can take, and find out something about its history and meaning. To this end I have crammed in as many names and variants as possible. Variations in name forms have all been cross-referenced, unless they would fall next to the entry in which they can be found. So if you cannot find the name you want in this book, look for the nearest spelling and read the entry there.

Within the entries, names written in LARGE AND SMALL CAPITALS mean that there is another entry for that name in the appropriate alphabetical position elsewhere in the book, where you may find further useful information. Names in **bold type** are alternative forms of spellings of the name at the head of the entry. These are usually much less common forms.

Today's parents have a much wider choice of names than their grandparents did. We have adopted a large number of foreign names, use an ever-increasing number of surnames as first names, and freely invent names or create blends, joining parts of different names to make a new name. I hope this book will help you choose just the right name for your child.

The first edition of this book was compiled in 1967 by Sandra Bance BA Hons, Mary Laird and Charles Wacher, under the supervision of Mr A.G. Hepburn ALA, former Head Librarian of the Mitchell Library, Glasgow, and Mr R. E. Adams BA ALA, of the National Library of Scotland, Edinburgh. Since then I have regularly revised it, and Leslie Dunkling has expanded it to reflect the multi-cultural nature of modern society. Thanks are due to Nicole Müller for advice on Irish names and Will Churchill for help with American ones.

Julia Cresswell
1998

Registering your baby's birth

If you have your baby in a hospital in England or Wales, there is a good chance that your local registrar's office will have a branch there. It is worth taking advantage of this facility, rather than having to cope with a new baby and getting down to the registrar's office later on. If nothing is said at the hospital, ask one of the nurses. Unfortunately, this facility is not available in Scotland where the regulations concerning the registration of births vary slightly from those in England and Wales.

By law, you have to register the birth of your child within 42 days of his or her birth, or within 21 days in Scotland. If you have not used a hospital office, you can go to any registrar's office, although the procedure is slightly simpler if you use your local one, the address of which should be in the phone book. Registration centres round the mother. If the baby's parents are married either parent can register the birth. If they are not married, they can register the birth together if they go to the registrar together, or else the father must get special forms from the registrar's office in advance which, when filled in, will enable his details to go on the birth certificate. Otherwise, the father's details will be left blank, although it may be possible to fill these in later – talk to the registrar about this. There is no need to take the baby with you to the registrar, but only a parent can register the birth; a friend or relative will not do.

At the registrar's you will be asked to give the following information. The place and date of the baby's birth (the time of birth will only be needed if you have twins or more, although in Scotland it is always required). You will also need to state his or her sex, and will be asked for the names you intend to give your child. If the father's details are to go on the form you will need to give his full name, his date and place of birth and his occupation. The mother will be asked to give her full name, her maiden name if she has changed her surname and her place and date of birth. If she wishes, an occupation (current or previous) can be filled in. She has to give her usual address at the time of the birth and, if she is married to the father, the date of marriage will be asked for. She will also be asked for the number of other children she has had.

All this information will be entered into a register, which you should then check carefully – it will be difficult to correct mistakes later – and then sign. You will then be given a free short birth certificate which is all you need. You can also get full copies of the information on the register if you would like to have them, and spare copies of either type of certificate. There is a charge for birth certificates which varies depending on the type you get, but it is always more expensive to get extra copies later than at the time. It is probably worth considering an extra copy so that each parent can have one, or so that one can be sent off with something like an application for a passport and you can still have one to hand.

If you still have not decided on a name for your baby by the time the limit for registration is up, you must still register the birth, but the name can be left blank. You then have up to one year from registration to make up your minds, although in Scotland any correction to the records after registration is likely to attract a fee. If your baby is baptised, the baptismal certificate can be produced at the registrar's office as evidence of the child's name. (Extra names given at baptism can also be added in this way.) Otherwise you need to ask the registrar's office for a Certificate of Naming, and use this to have the names inserted. You can give your child any forenames or surname that you like. In Scotland the registrar has the power to refuse to record a name if he or she deems it to be potentially offensive, although in practice a name is rarely objected to. In England and Wales, the registrar has no right to refuse your choice, although if your choice is too outrageous you may find that you are asked to think of the effect on the child before confirming it is what you want. Modern registrars are trained to be friendly and helpful, and you can always phone your local office for any advice you need; alternatively, contact The General Register Office, Smedley Hydro, Trafalgar Road, Birkdale, Southport PR8 2HH (tel. 0151-4714200) or The Registrar General's Office for Scotland, New Register House, Edinburgh (tel. 0131-334 0380).

Ten points to consider

1. A name that is currently very popular (see pages 370-372) will probably be borne by several children in the same class at school. It is probably best to avoid the top ten names.

2. Listen to the sound of the first name with the surname to avoid falling into the 'Ann Teak' kind of trap.

3. It can help to 'balance' the first name with the surname. If the surname is a common one, such as Smith, a slightly unusual first name is probably a good idea. An unusual surname can be balanced with a more familiar first name.

4. Make sure that the first name, middle name and surname do not form an unfortunate set of initials, such as MAD.

5. Avoid names that begin with the same letter as other members of the family. This can be very inconvenient later on.

6. Remember there is often a difference between what a child is called and what it is named. Make sure you like the pet forms of a name, such as, for example, Rick and Ricky, as well as Richard itself.

7. Even if you intend to call your child by a pet name, it is probably best to use the full form of the name

when you register the birth. This keeps the child's options open. A Catherine, for example, may always be Katie to you, but later in life she may prefer to use a different pet form of her name or the full name.

8. It is probably best to avoid names like Taylor which do not make clear the sex of the child.

9. When you have a name in mind, it could be wise to check with relations and friends that they know how to spell and pronounce it.

10. Inventing a completely new name is dangerous for many reasons; for example, other people may not know how to spell it or pronounce it. There are plenty of well-established names to choose from. A child who has a name other children consider 'odd' may suffer at school.

Aakash *see* **Akash**

Aamena, Aaminah *see* **Amina**

Aaron *m.*

In the Old Testament, Aaron was the brother of **Moses** and the first High Priest of Israel. The traditional interpretation links this name to the Hebrew for 'high mountain', but like Moses, Aaron is probably an Egyptian name of unknown meaning. It is connected with the Arabic names **Harun** and **Haroun**, and has been in use since the Reformation. In the past it was pronounced with a first sound as in 'air', but now it is also found with a short 'a', a pronunciation reflected in the spelling **Ar(r)on**.

Abagail, Abb(e)y, Abbie *see* **Abigail**

Abdullah *m.*

A Muslim name from the Arabic for 'servant of Allah'. The short form **Abdul** also occurs.

Abe, Abie *see* **Abel, Abraham**

Abel *m.*

In the Old Testament, Abel was the second son of **Adam**

and EVE and murdered by his brother Cain. The name may come from a Hebrew word for 'breath', but like so many of the earliest names, its meaning is doubtful. The name has been used in England since before the Norman Conquest. The short forms include **Abe** and **Abie**.

Abigail *f.*

From the Hebrew, meaning 'father rejoiced'. It was the name of one of King David's wives and was much used in England during the 16th and 17th centuries when many Old Testament names were popular. It was so popular for working-class women that it degenerated into a term for a lady's maid and so became unfashionable; but it has now come back into favour. It is sometimes spelt **Abagail** or **Abigal**. The short forms include **Abbie**, **Abb(e)y** and **GAIL**.

Abner *m.*

From the Hebrew words for 'father of light'. In the Bible it is the name of King Saul's cousin, who was commander of the army. In England it came into common use, together with other biblical names, after the Reformation in the early 16th century. It is still found occasionally in North America.

Abraham *m.*

This is the name of the Old Testament patriarch who, for the first 90 years of his life, was called **Abram**, 'high father', but then was told by God that he should be called Abraham, 'father of many nations'. It was used in England regularly after the Reformation and became popular in North America where the abbreviation **Abe**, as in President Abe Lincoln (1809–65), was widely used. Other short forms are **Abie, Ham** and **Bram**.

Absalom *see* **Axel**

Ada *f.*

A name which started life as a pet form for **ADELA**, **ADELAIDE** and **ADELINE**, and so means 'noble'. It was fashionable in Britain in the late 18th and 19th centuries, but is now rare. **Adah** is often confused with Ada, but is in fact derived from the Hebrew word for 'ornament' or 'brightness'.

Adam *m.*

From the Hebrew, meaning 'red', possibly referring either to skin colour, or to the clay from which God formed the first man. The name was adopted by the Irish as early as the 7th century, when *St Adamnan*, 'Little Adam', was Abbot of Iona. It was very common in the 13th century and has been in use ever since, particularly in Scotland. It is currently one of the most popular boys' names. **Adamina** is a rare feminine form.

Adeel *see* **Adil**

Adela *f.*

From the Old German, meaning 'noble'. It was common among the Normans, who brought it to England. One of

William the Conqueror's daughters had this name. It died out but was later revived and became fashionable in the French form **Adèle**. **Addie** or **Addy** is used as a pet form for the names derived from this root (see also **ADELAIDE** and **ADELINE**). Adela can also be spelt **Adella**, which gives us the name **DELLA**, now more popular than its source.

Adelaide *f.*

Derived from the Old German words meaning 'noble and kind'. The name was common for centuries on the Continent but only came to Britain in 1830 when Adelaide of Saxe-Coburg became queen. Adelaide, the capital city of South Australia, was named after this popular queen. **ADA** is sometimes used as a pet form (see also **ALIDA, HEIDI**).

Adeline *f.*

Like **ADELAIDE**, this name is derived from the Old German for 'noble'. It was first cited in England in the Domesday Book and was common during the Middle Ages. After that it disappeared until the Victorian Gothic revival. It is best known from the song *Sweet Adeline*. **ADA** is sometimes used as a pet form, and **Alina** and **Aline**, now used as separate names were also once short forms.

Adella *see* **Adela**

Adil *m.*

An Arabic name meaning 'just, honest'. It is also spelt **Adeel**.

Adnan *m.*

An Arabic name of uncertain meaning. According to tradition, Adnan was the ancestor of the North Arabians.

Adolph

Although Adolph ('noble wolf') and the latinized form of the name, **Adolphus**, have never been common names in this country and received a further set-back with the rise of Adolph Hitler, the short forms **Dolph** and **Dolphus** are sometimes found.

Adrian *m.,* Adrienne *f.*

From the Latin meaning 'man from Adria', and a form of the name of the Roman Emperor *Hadrian*, who built the wall across northern England. It has been used since Roman times; a St Adrian was the first British martyred in the 4th century. Adrian and **Adrien** are now sometimes used as girls' names. **Adriana** is a rare female form, the French Adrienne being more popular. **Adria** and **Adrianne** are also found.

Aeneus, Aengus *see* Angus

Afra *see* Aphra

Agatha *f.*

From the Greek for 'good woman', this was the name of a 3rd-century martyr and saint. The short form is **Aggie**.

Agnes *f.*

From the Greek meaning 'pure'. There was an early Christian martyr called Agnes, whose symbol is a lamb, since the name also sounds very like the Latin *agnus*, 'lamb'. Old forms still occasionally used include **Annis, Annice** and **Annes. Agneta** is the Swedish form and **Inez** is the anglicized form of the Spanish **Inés.** Agnes was popular in Scotland where it also became **Nessie** and **Nessa.** In Wales it became **Nest** and **Nesta. Aggie** is a short form shared with **AGATHA** (see also **INA**).

Ahmad *m.*

This Arabic name is often spelt **Ahmed**. It is one of the names applied to the Prophet Muhammad and means 'more praiseworthy'.

Aidan *m.*

An ancient Irish name which means 'little fire'. It was the name of a 7th-century Irish missionary who founded the monastery of Lindisfarne in Northumbria. The name was revived during the 19th century and is popular at the moment in Ireland. It is sometimes anglicized as **Edan**.

Aiesha *see* **Aisha**

Ailbhe *see* **Elvis**

Aileen *see* **Eileen**

Ailis, Ailish *see* **Alice, Eilis**

Ailsa *f.*
From the Scottish island, Ailsa Craig. First used in Scotland where it can also be a pet form of **ALICE**, it has now spread through Britain.

Aimée *see* **Amy, Esmé**

Ainsley *m. and f.*
A place and surname used as a first name, this comes from the Old English and probably means 'lonely clearing'. It is also spelt **Ainslie**.

Aisha *f.*
From the Arabic meaning 'alive and well' or 'prospering'. A favourite name in the Arab world, originally borne by the third (and favourite) wife of the Prophet Muhammad. In Britain and the USA the name is found in many forms, including **Aiesha**, **Aishah**, **Ayisha**, **Asia**, **Aysh(i)a**, **Ieasha**, **Ieesha**, **Iesha** and **Isha**. H. Rider Haggard used the form **Ayesha** in his novel *She*, where the meaning was given as 'she who must be obeyed'.

Aisling *f.*

The commonest form of a name also found as **Aislinn**, **Isleen** and the phonetic **Ashling**. It is an old Irish name meaning 'a dream, vision' and has been popular in Ireland since the 1960s.

Aithne *see* Eithne

Ajay *m.*

A popular Indian name from the Sanskrit for 'invincible'.

Akash *m.*

This Indian name is sometimes found as **Aakash**. It is from the Sanskrit and means 'the sky'.

Akhil *m.*

An Indian name from the Sanskrit meaning 'whole, complete'.

Akshar *m.*

An Indian name from the Sanskrit meaning 'imperishable'.

Al *see* Alastair, Alexander

Alan *m.*

An old Celtic name of unknown meaning. It has

appeared in various forms from early times. In England it first became popular after the Norman Conquest as **Alain** or **Alein**, the French forms. These developed into Alleyne which is preserved as a surname. Alan, **Allan**, **Allen** and **Alun** (strictly speaking, a Welsh river name used as a first name) are in use today. **Alana**, the feminine form, is also spelt **Allana**, **Alanah** and **Alanna**, and in the USA has developed the form **Alaina** or **Alayna**. The actress **Lana** Turner made the short form well known.

Alastair *m.*

Also spelt **Alasdair**, **Alistair** and **Alister**, this is the Gaelic form of **ALEXANDER**, 'defender of men'. It is shortened to **Al**, **Ali**, **Alli** or **Ally**, **Alec** and **Alick**.

Alban *m.*, Albina *f.*

From the Latin *Albanus*, meaning 'man from Alba' (a Roman town whose name means 'white'), and the name of the earliest British saint. The town of St Albans, where he was martyred, is called after him. **Albin** and **Albinus** are variants which appear occasionally, and Albina and **Albinia**, 'white', are used as feminine forms.

Alberic *see* **Aubrey**

Albert *m.*

An Old German name meaning 'noble and bright'. The Old English form was **Ethelbert**, the name of the Kentish king who welcomed Augustine to Canterbury when he came to convert the Anglo-Saxons to Christianity. This was replaced after the Norman Conquest by the French form, Aubert. Albert became so popular after the marriage of Queen Victoria to Prince Albert of Saxe-Coburg that it became over-used and so went out of fashion. **BERT** and **BERTIE** are short forms. **Alberta**, **Albertina** and **Albertine** are forms of the name used for girls.

Albin, Albina, Albinia, Albinus *see* Alban

Alby *see* Elvis

Aldous *m.*

From the Old German Aldo, meaning 'old'. It has been used in the eastern counties of England since the 13th century and has given rise to various surnames like Aldhouse and Aldiss. **Aldo** is still used in North America. The writer Aldous Huxley (1894–1963) is the best-known British example.

Aldwyn *m.*

This Anglo-Saxon personal name, meaning 'old friend', has been revived in modern times. Some parents prefer the spelling **Aldwin**.

Alec *see* Alastair, Alexander

Aled *m.*

The name of a Welsh river used as a first name. There is a female form **Aledwen**, 'fair Aled'.

Alein *see* **Alan**

Alessandra *see* **Sandra**

Alethea *see* **Althea**

Alex *see* **Alexander**

Alexa *see* **Alexis**

Alexander *m.*

Currently one of the most popular boys' names, this comes from the Greek meaning 'defender of men'. It was made famous in the 4th century BC by Alexander the Great, and was very popular in England in the Middle Ages. **Sandy** is a pet form, particularly in Scotland. **Alex** is the most common of the many short forms, others being **Al**, **Alec**, **Ali**, **Lex**, **Xan** and **Xander**. SACHA is another form of the name.

Alexandra *f.*

The feminine form of ALEXANDER, and like it, currently popular. SANDRA was originally an Italian form, but has become established as a name in its own right. It shares pet and short forms with ALEXANDER, while **Alix** or **Alyx** can be a form of this name or of ALICE. **Alexandria** and **Alexandrina** are also found.

Alexis *f. and m.*

From the Greek word meaning 'helper' or 'defender',

Alexis is the name of one of the great saints of the Orthodox church. Originally a man's name, it is now more frequently used for women. **Alexie** is an alternative form for boys, and **Alexia** and **Alexa** for girls.

Alfred *m.*

From two Old English words, meaning 'elf' (hence 'good') and 'counsel'. It is also a possible development of the Anglo-Saxon name Ealdfrith, meaning 'old peace'. It is sometimes written **Alfrid**. When Alfred was written down in old Latin, the name was spelt **Alured** and developed into **Avery**. **Alf**, **Alfie** and **Fred** are diminutives. There is a feminine form **Alfreda**, and **Elfrida**, although it technically comes from a slightly different name meaning 'elf-strength', is also used as a female version of Alfred.

Algernon *m.*

From a Norman French nickname meaning 'with whiskers'. It was popular in the 19th century but is not much used today. The usual diminutive is **Algie** or **Algy**.

Ali *f. and m.*

When used for boys this is a popular Arabic name meaning 'excellent' or 'noble'. As a girl's name it is usually a pet form of **ALICE** or **ALISON**.

Alia *see* **Ella**

Alice *f.*

From the Old German word for 'nobility'. It originally

had the form **Adelice** or **Adelise**. A number of forms remained popular from the Middle Ages until the 17th century, when it went out of favour. It was revived again in the 19th century together with the variant **Alicia**. Nowadays these have developed additional forms such as **Allice**, **Allyce** and **Alyssa**, **Alysia**, **Alis(s)a**. **ALISON** is a variant. **Alys** is the Welsh form and Irish forms are **Alis**, **Ailis** or the phonetic **Ailish**. **Ali**, **Allie** and **Alley** are used as pet forms, while **Alix** and **Alyx** can be used either as forms of Alice or **ALEXANDRA**.

Alick *see* **Alastair**

Alida *f.*
A Hungarian pet form of **ADELAIDE**, 'noble and kind', which is sometimes found in this country.

Alina, Aline *see* **Adeline**

Alis, Alisa *see* **Alice**

Alison *f.*
Originally a diminutive of **ALICE** that was adopted in the 13th century, this was soon treated as a separate name. It was at one time a particularly Scottish name. Pet forms include those used for **ALICE** and **ELSIE** and it can be found in the forms **Allison** and **Al(l)yson**.

Alissa *see* **Alice**

Alistair, Alister *see* **Alastair**

Alix *see* **Alexandra, Alice**

Allan, Allana, Allen *see* **Alan**

Allegra *f.*
An Italian word meaning 'cheerful, lively', given by the
poet Lord Byron to his daughter and still used
occasionally as a result.

Alley *see* **Alice**

Alli, Ally, *see* **Alastair**

Allice, Allie, Allyce *see* **Alice, Alison**

Alma *f.*
There are many opinions about the origin of this name.
It could be derived from the Hebrew word for 'maiden',
the Latin for 'kind' or the Italian for 'soul'. Most
importantly, the name became very popular after the
Battle of Alma during the Crimean War, and is still
found occasionally.

Aloysius *m.*
This is the Latin form of Aloys, an old Provençal form
of **Louis** (see **LEWIS**). There was a popular Spanish saint

of this name in the 16th century and Roman Catholics continue to use the name in this country. Aloys or Aloyse was the female form of the old name, and is a possible source of **ELOISE**.

Althea *f.*

From the Greek for 'wholesome', this was the Greek name for the marsh mallow plant, still used as a healing herb. It seems to have been introduced to England with various other classical names during the Stuart period, and appeared in the charming lyric by Richard Lovelace *To Althea from Prison*. The similar-sounding **Alethea** (**Alethia**, **Aletia**) comes from the Greek for 'truth'.

Alun *see* **Alan**

Alured *see* **Alfred**

Alvin *m.*

From two Old English names, Alwine, 'friend of all' and Athelwine, 'noble friend'. **Aylwin**, **Alvan**, **Alvyn** and **Alvy** are alternative forms. There is a rare feminine, **Alvina**. The similar-sounding **Alvar** means 'elf army'.

Alys, Alyssa *see* **Alice**

Alyson, Alysson *see* **Alison**

Alyx *see* **Alexandra, Alice**

Amabel *f.*

From the Latin meaning 'lovable'. It has been in use in England in various forms since the 12th century. The short form, **MABEL**, became established as an independent name at an early date.

Amalia *see* **Amelia**

Amanda *f.*

From the Latin for 'deserving love'. It appears first in Restoration plays, where many classical or pseudo-classical names were introduced or fabricated. It has remained in use since then and is still popular. **Mandy** is a pet form also used as a name in its own right.

Amaryllis *f.*

Originally from Greek, probably meaning 'sparkling', and used by Greek poets as a name for a country girl. It served the same purpose for Latin poets, and was introduced to Britain via English poetry in the 17th century.

Amber *f.*

The name of the gemstone, used as a first name. It was not used before this century but has grown in popularity recently.

Ambrin *f.*

From the Arabic for 'ambergris', a substance renowned for its sweet odour. It can also be spelt **Ambreen.**

Ambrose _m._

From the Greek for 'divine'. There was a 4th-century St Ambrose who was Bishop of Milan. The name is found in the Domesday Book and has been used occasionally ever since. The Welsh name **Emrys** is derived from the Latin form of the name. There is a rare feminine form, **Ambrosine**.

Amelia _f._

From an Old German name possibly meaning 'work', its form is perhaps influenced by **Emilia** (see **EMILY**). **Amalia**, **Amalie**, **Amaline** and **Amalita** are forms of the name. It can be shortened to **Milly**.

Amin _m._, Amina _f._

From the Arabic for 'honest', 'trustworthy' or 'reliable'. **Amina**, the feminine form, has always been much used by Muslim families, in honour of Amina bint-Wahab, mother of the Prophet Muhammad. It is sometimes spelt **Aamena**, **Aaminah** or **Amena**.

Aminta _see_ Araminta

Amit _m._

An Indian name from the Sanskrit for 'without limit'. It is also a simplified pet form of names like **Amitbikram** ('limitless prowess') and **Amitjyoti** ('limitless brightness').

Amitabh _m._

A name of the Buddha, from the Sanskrit meaning

'limitless splendour'. The spelling **Amitav** is also used.

Amitbikram, Amitjyoti *see* Amit

Amos *m.*

A Hebrew name, possibly meaning 'he who carries a burden'. It was the name of an Old Testament prophet and was adopted by English Puritans after the Reformation, when saints' names fell out of favour. Popular until the 19th century, it is presently uncommon.

Amrit *f. and m.*

In the Vedic epics of the Hindus, this Sanskrit name refers to immortality or that which confers it, such as the 'water of life, soma juice, nectar, [or] ambrosia'. Amrit can be used for both sexes, although the form **Amrita** can also be used for a girl.

Amy *f.*

From the French, meaning 'beloved'. Sir Walter Scott's novel *Kenilworth*, about Amy Robsart, the tragic wife of the Earl of Leicester, made the name fashionable in the 19th century, and it has been popular again in recent years. **Aimée** is the French original of this name, which can also be found in forms such as **Aime(e)**, **Ami(e)** and **Amye**.

Amynta *see* Araminta

Anaïs *f.*

A French name which comes from the Greek word for 'fruitful'.

Anand *m.,* Ananda *f.*

From the Sanskrit for 'happiness', 'joy' or 'bliss'. It is the name of a god in the *Veda*, sacred book of the Hindus. Variants of the girl's form include **Anandamayi** ('full of joy'), **Anandi** and **Anandini** ('joyful').

Anastasia *f.*

From the Greek meaning 'resurrection'. The name of a 4th-century saint and martyr, it became fashionable in England in the 13th century, though it was usually abbreviated to Anstey or Anstice, which survive today as surnames. It has always been very popular in Russia, and a daughter of the last Tsar of Russia, called Anastasia, is said to have escaped from the massacre in which the rest of her family died in 1918. **STACEY** and **TANSY** started as pet forms of this name. **Nastasia** is a Russian pet form.

Andrew *m.,* Andrea *f.*

From the Greek for 'manly'. Andrew is the name of the Apostle who is patron saint of Scotland, Russia and Greece, and first appears in England in the Domesday Book. It has been used in Britain continuously and has enjoyed particular favour in Scotland. The pet forms include **Andy**, **Dandy** (Scots) and **DREW**, which is also used as an independent name. The Italian form, Andrea, is actually a boy's name in Italy, but is used as a girl's name in this country. The French boys' form, **André**, is likewise sometimes used for girls, although the more correct form **Andrée** is also used. Other female forms include **Andrene**, **Andrena** and **Andreana**, while **Andra** is both a traditional Scots form of the boy's name and used for girls.

Aneirin *see* **Aneurin**

Aneka, Aneke, An(n)ika *see* **Anne**

Aneurin *m.*

This name is traditionally interpreted as the Welsh form of Latin Honorius, meaning 'honourable', and is one of the oldest names still in use is Britain. It also appears in the form **Aneirin**. Short forms are **Nye** and **Neirin**.

Angela *f.*

From the Latin *angelus* originally derived from the Greek word meaning 'messenger', hence our word 'angel'. It is shortened to **Angel** and **Angie**. Other forms of the name include the French **Angelique**, and elaborations such as **Angelica**, **Angelia**, **Angeline** and **Angelina**, as well as spellings with a 'j' instead of a 'g'. Masculine forms of the name died out at the Reformation, but the Italian boy's name **Angelo** and the Spanish **Angel** are now found in the USA.

Angharad *f.*

A Welsh name meaning 'much loved'. It is an important name in early Welsh literature, and has been in use since at least the 9th century. The stress is on the second syllable.

Angus *m.*

From the Gaelic **Aonghas**, meaning 'one choice'. It appears in Irish legend in the form **Aengus** or **Oengus**, but is more common in Scotland. The name became associated with the classical myth of **Aeneas** (which is close to the Irish pronunciation) in the 15th century, and this form was also used.

Anil *m.,* Anila *f.*

The name of the wind-god in the Hindu Vedic epics. It is derived from the Sanskrit meaning 'air' or 'wind'. Anil is the driver of Indra's golden chariot, which is pulled by a thousand horses. **Anila**, the feminine form, is used mainly by Hindu families.

Anish *m.,* Anisha *f.*

A Sanskrit name, one of the thousand borne by the Hindu god Vishnu. Its meaning is possibly 'without a master'.

Anita, Ann, Anna *see* Anne

Annabel *f.*

Together with **Annabelle** or **Annabella,** this is probably from the Latin *amabilis* meaning 'lovable', a variant of AMABEL. It is found in Scotland earlier than ANNE, so it is unlikely to be a form of that name, though it is now sometimes thought of as a compound of **Anna** and the Latin *bella* meaning 'beautiful'. Diminutives include **Bel, Belle** and **Bella**.

Anne *f.*

From the Hebrew **HANNAH**, meaning 'God has favoured me'. The French form Anne or **Ann**, traditionally the name of the mother of the Virgin Mary, was introduced into Britain in the 13th century and the name has enjoyed great popularity since. Anne is currently slightly more popular than Ann, but the form **Anna** is now much more popular than either. Pet forms include **Nan**, **Nanette**, **Nana**, **NANCY** and **Annie**, as well as the variants **Anita**, **Annette** and **Anona** (although this, with its pet form **Nona**, can be Welsh in origin). Ann(e) has often formed part of compounds such as **Mary Ann(e)** or **Annalise**. **Anneke** is the Dutch pet form, more often spelt **Anneka** in this country to reflect the Dutch pronunciation; **Aneke**, **Aneka** and **An(n)ika** are also found. **Anya** is from the Spanish pronunciation of the name and **Anouk** is a Russian form.

Annes, Annice, Annis *see* Agnes

Annette, Annie *see* Anne

An(n)ora *see* Honoria

Anona, Anouk *see* Anne

Anoop *see* Anup

Anthea *f.*

From the Greek *antheos*, meaning 'flowery'. This name seems to have been introduced by the pastoral poets of the 17th century and it has been in use ever since, although it was not until the 20th century that it became very widely known.

Ant(h)ony *m.*, Antonia *f.*

A Roman family name. Its most famous member was Marcus Antonius, the Mark Antony of Shakespeare's *Julius Caesar* and *Antony and Cleopatra*. The name was very popular in the Middle Ages as a result of the influence of St Antony the Great and St Antony of Padua. The alternative and commoner spelling **Anthony** was introduced after the Renaissance, when it was incorrectly thought that the name was derived from the Greek *anthos* meaning 'flower', as in **ANTHEA**. The usual short form is **Tony**, which is also used for the female forms **Antonia** and the French **Antoinette**. Feminine short forms **Toni** and **Tonya** are also found, and **Toinette**, **Net** and **Nettie** are pet forms of Antoinette. **Anton**, a Continental form of the name, is now also used for boys. In the USA **Antonio** (shortened to **Tonio**) and **Antoine** (often in phonetic spellings such as **Antwan** or **Antuan**) are often used.

Anup *m.*

An Indian name, from the Sanskrit meaning 'without comparison'. The spelling **Anoop** is also used.

Anusha *f.*

The name of a star in Hindu astrology.

Anya *see* **Anne**

Aoife *see* **Eve**

Aonghas *see* **Angus**

Aphra *f.*

From the Hebrew word for 'dust'. It is best known from the novelist, playwright and spy Mrs Aphra Behn (1644–89), said to have been the first woman in England to earn her living as a writer. It is also spelt **Afra**.

April *see* **Avril**

Arabella *f.*

A possible variant of **AMABEL**, though it could be derived from the Latin for 'obliging'. It used to be a predominantly Scottish name, particularly in the forms **Arabel** and **Arabelle**. It can be shortened to **Bel, Belle** and **Bella**.

Araminta *f.*

This name appears to have been invented by Sir John Vanbrugh (1644–1726) to use in one of his plays. It may have been influenced by **Aminta** or **Amynta**, an ancient Greek name meaning 'protector'. They all share the short forms **Minta** and **Minty**.

Archibald *m.*

From Old German words meaning 'truly bold'. The Old

English form was used in East Anglia before the Norman Conquest. Thereafter, it was primarily Scottish and was associated particularly with the Douglas and Campbell families. The most usual diminutive is **Archie**, now sometimes given to a child rather than the full name.

Aretha *f.*

Aretha or **Areta** is the Greek word for 'virtue'. It is not a usual name, but has become well known through the singer, Aretha Franklin.

Ariadne *f.*

This is an ancient Greek name meaning 'the very holy one' which probably originally belonged to a goddess. In Greek mythology Ariadne was the daughter of King Minos of Crete and helped Theseus to escape from the labyrinth. The French and Italian forms **Ariane** and **Arianna** are also found.

Ariel *f. and m.*

The name Ariel has two different origins. The masculine form is a Hebrew name, traditionally said to mean 'lion of God', which is popular in Israel and sometimes used in the USA. As a girl's name it has been popular in the USA ever since it was used as the heroine's name in Disney's *Little Mermaid* film and TV series. This name, which is also found in forms such as **Arial** and **Arielle**, presumably owes at least something to Ariel, the airy spirit in Shakespeare's play, *The Tempest*.

Arjun *m.*

A Hindu name from the Sanskrit for 'white' or 'bright'.
It was the name of a famous Pandava prince, son of the
god Indra.

Arlene *f.*

Arlene, **Arleen** or **Arline** is a modern name which
probably comes from the final sounds of such names as
CHARLENE or MARLENE.

Armand, Armin, Arminel, Arminelle
see **Herman**

Arnold *m.*

From the Old German Arnwalt, meaning 'eagle's power'.
It appeared in various forms, both Germanic and French,
in the Middle Ages, but dropped out of use from the
17th century until the late 19th when it had a revival.

Aroon *see* **Arun**

Art *see* **Arthur**

Artemisia *f.*

From the Greek meaning 'belonging to Artemis'.
Artemis was the Greek goddess of wild animals,
vegetation, childbirth and the hunt, comparable to the

Roman **DIANA**. Artemisia was the name of the queen of Caria in the 4th century BC, who built the Mausoleum at Halicarnassus for her husband. She was also celebrated as a botanist and medical researcher. The name was first used in Britain in the 18th century and still survives.

Arthur *m.*

The origin of this name is disputed. Possible sources are the Celtic word for 'bear' and the Roman name Artorius. Whatever its source, its use comes entirely from the fame of its first known bearer, King Arthur. Victorian interest in things medieval made it popular in the 19th century when Queen Victoria gave the name to one of her sons. Over-use in the late 19th and first quarter of the 20th centuries led to a decline, but there are now distinct signs of a revival in popularity. **Art** or **Arty** is used as a short form, particularly in America.

Arun *m.*, Aruna *f.*

An Indian name from the Sanskrit for 'reddish brown', a colour associated with the dawn. It became the name of the mythical personification of the dawn, charioteer of the sun. **Aroon** is an alternative spelling for boys, while for girls **Arumina** is also used.

Asa *m.*

From the Hebrew word meaning 'physician'. It is particularly used in the North of England.

Asha *f.*

An Indian name from the Sanskrit for 'hope, desire, aspiration'.

Asher *m.*

The name of one of the tribes of Israel. It means 'happy'. Although it is an unusual name, there are signs that its use is on the increase, along with other names from the Bible. It is, of course, also a common surname meaning 'ash tree', and some uses may be from this.

Ashish *m.*

A relatively modern Indian name, probably derived from the Sanskrit for 'prayer' or 'benediction'.

Ashley *f. and m.*

A place and surname meaning 'ash field' which has become very popular throughout the English-speaking world. The spelling **Ashleigh** is rather more common for girls, and the variant **Ashlyn(n)** is used as a girl's name in the USA. The related surname **Ashton**, meaning 'ash farm', is also found as a first name for both sexes in the USA.

Ashling *see* Aisling

Ashraf *m.*

A popular Muslim name, from the Arabic for 'more noble' or 'more honourable'.

Asia *see* **Aisha**

Aslam *m.*

A Muslim name, from the Arabic meaning 'safer' or 'sounder'.

Asma *f.*

A popular Muslim name, from the Arabic for 'more eminent' or 'more prestigious'. Asma was the daughter of the caliph Abu-Bakr. She courageously helped the Prophet and her father escape from Mecca when their lives were threatened.

Astrid *f.*

From the Old German words meaning 'god' and 'beauty'. The name of the wife of St Olaf of Norway, it has long been popular in Scandinavia, and has been used in Britain in the 20th century.

Atalanta *f.*

In ancient Greek myth, Atalanta was a very beautiful maiden who wanted to remain single. Since she was a very fast runner, she responded to pressure to marry by saying that she would wed any man who could out-run her, but any losers must suffer death. Many unsuccessful suitors died in the attempt, but she was finally beaten by one man who threw golden apples in her path during their race, and managed to overtake her while she stopped to pick them up. **Atlanta** is also found.

Athene *f.*

This is the name of the Greek goddess of war, crafts and wisdom. In Britain, it has been used occasionally as a girl's name, as has the Roman form of the name, **Athena**.

Athol *f. and m.*

Athol or **Atholl** is the Scottish place name, used as a first name. The place name means 'New Ireland'.

Aubrey *m.*

From the Old German meaning 'elf ruler'. In medieval romance the diminutive **Auberon** was used and Shakespeare adopted it as **Oberon** in *A Midsummer Night's Dream*. The German form, **Alberic**, developed first into Albery and later into Aubrey.

Audrey *f.*

A shortened form of **Etheldreda**, Old English for 'noble strength' and one of the sources of **ETHEL**. St Etheldreda was a 7th-century Anglo-Saxon princess who founded at Ely a religious house which later developed into the cathedral that now stands on the site. She was a popular saint and many churches are still dedicated to her.

Augusta *f.*, Augustus *m.*

From the Latin for 'venerable'. Augustus was a title given to the first Roman Emperor and Augusta is its feminine form. **Augustine**, the name of two important

saints, one of whom converted the English to
Christianity, is another form of the name. It was so
popular in the Middle Ages it developed the shorter
forms **Austin**, **Austyn** and **Austen**. **Augustina** is a
feminine form of Augustine. **Gus** and **Gussie** are pet
forms and this group of names is beginning to become
popular once more.

Aurelia *f.*

From the Latin *aurelius* meaning 'golden'. It has been
used since the 17th century, and recently a short form,
Auriol, **Auriel**, **Oriel** or **Oriole**, has shown some
popularity. The boy's form is **Aurelius**.

Aurora *see* Dawn

Austen, Austin, Austyn *see* Augusta

Ava *f.*

This name is of obscure origin, but probably started life
as a pet form of names beginning Av-. It was made
famous by the film star Ava Gardner, and is more
commonly found in the USA than Britain.

Aveline *see* Evelyn

Averil *f. and m.*

Probably from the Old English *eofor* ('boar') and *hild*
('battle'), which appears as **Everild** and **Everilda** in the

7th century. It was regularly in use until the 17th century, since when it has been less common. Averil is often confused with **AVRIL** which originally was an entirely different name.

Avery *see* **Alfred**

Avis *f.*
The origin of this name, which was popular in England in the Middle Ages, is obscure. It occurred only rarely between the 16th and 19th centuries and was sometimes spelt **Avice**. It is now a rare name.

Avril *f.*
The French for **April**. The name has been popular in the 20th century, mainly for girls born in that month (see also **AVERIL**).

Axel *m.*
The Scandinavian form of the Old Testament **Absalom**. Its probable meaning, 'father of peace', seems ironic for King David's rebellious son. Axel was introduced to the United States by Scandinavian immigrants, and it is more common there than in Britain. There is a rare feminine form, **Axelle**.

Ayesha, Ayisha *see* **Aisha**

Aylmer *see* **Elmer**

Aylwin *see* **Alvin**

Aysha, Ayshia *see* **Aisha**

Azim *m.,* **Azima(h)** *f.*
This Arabic name means 'determined'.

B

Bab, Babs *see* **Barbara**

Babette *see* **Barbara, Elizabeth**

Bailey *f.*

This surname, which comes from the job of steward or bailiff of an estate, has recently been fashionable as a girl's name in the USA.

Bairre *see* **Barry**

Bala *f. and m.*

An Indian name, from the Sanskrit for 'young child'.

Balu *m.*

Originally a pet form of Indian names such as **Balakrishna** or **Balachander**, where the first part of the name derives from a Sanskrit word meaning 'young'. In modern times it is used as a name in its own right.

Barbara *f.*

From the Greek *barbaros*, meaning 'strange' or 'foreign', and associated with St Barbara, a 3rd-century martyr. The name was little used after the Reformation, but in the 20th century it became popular again. Abbreviations include **Bab**, **Babs**, **Barbie** and sometimes **Bobbi**. The variant form **Barbra** was publicized by the singer Barbra Streisand. **Babette** is a French form of the name.

Barnabas *m.*

From the Hebrew meaning 'son of exhortation or consolation', it is best known as the name of the New Testament companion of St Paul. The diminutive, **Barnaby**, is rather fashionable at the moment, more so than the full form. **Barney** is a short form which is also shared with BERNARD.

Barney *see* Barnabas, Bernard

Barry *m.*

The English form of a variety of Celtic names, most prominently **Bairre**, a pet form of the Irish **Finbarr** (**Finnbar**, **Fionnbharr**) meaning 'fair-haired'. Barry can also be spelt **Barrie**, the usual spelling in the name's infrequent use for girls.

Bartholomew *m.*

From the Hebrew, meaning 'son of Talmai', Talmai meaning 'full of furrows'. It was the surname of the Apostle NATHANIEL and was very popular in the Middle Ages when the cult of St Bartholomew was at its height. St Bartholomew's Hospital in London was founded in the 12th century, and a riotous annual Bartholomew Fair held in the city to provide funds for it, was suppressed only in the 19th century. The name is still in use, and has short forms **Bart**, **Barty**, **Bat** and **Tolomey**.

Basil *m.*

From the Greek *basileios*, meaning 'kingly'. It was probably brought to England by the Crusaders, and it has remained in use ever since. Diminutives include **Bas** or **Baz**, **Basie** and **Bazza**, and there are two feminine forms, **Basilia** and **Basilie**. These were common in the Middle Ages, but are hardly ever found today.

Bastian, Bastien *see* Sebastian

Bat *see* Bartholomew

Bathsheba *f.*

This name derives from Hebrew words which mean 'daughter of opulence'. In the Old Testament Bathsheba was the beautiful wife of Uriah and was seduced by King David who arranged to have Uriah die during a battle. Bathsheba married David and became the mother of Solomon. The name was formerly used in Cornwall in the form **Bersaba**, and appears also in its pet form **Sheba**. Bathsheba Everdene is a central character in Thomas Hardy's *Far From the Madding Crowd*.

Baz, Bazza *see* Basil

Bea, Beatty *see* Beatrice

Beata *f.*

From the Latin *beatus* meaning 'blessed' or 'happy'.
It is both a name in its own right and used as a pet form
of BEATRICE.

Beatrice *f.*

From the Latin **Beatrix**, meaning 'bringer of happiness'.
It has strong literary associations. Dante's Beatrice is
probably best known, but Shakespeare also used the
name in *Much Ado About Nothing*. Recently, both forms
of the name have shown signs of returning to popularity,
no doubt helped by the publicity given to it as the name
of one of the Duke and Duchess of York's daughters.
Short forms include **Bea** or **Bee**, BEATA, **Beatty**, **Triss**
and **Trixie**. There is also a Welsh variant, **Bettrys**, and a
Spanish form **Beatriz**.

Becky *see* **Rebecca**

Bee *see* **Beatrice**

Bel *see* **Annabel, Arabella, Belinda,
Isabel**

Belinda *f.*

From an Old German name, the latter part of which
means 'a snake' (see LINDA). The first part of the name is
obscure, but is commonly thought of as representing the
French 'fair'. Its popular use began in the 18th century

when it was used in plays by Congreve and Vanbrugh, and in Pope's poem *The Rape of the Lock*. Short forms include **Bel** and all forms of LINDA.

Bella, Belle *see* Annabel, Arabella, Isabel

Ben *see* Benjamin

Benedict *m.*

From the Latin *benedictus*, meaning 'blessed', and most familiar as the name of St Benedict, founder of the Benedictine Order. It was common in medieval England in the forms **Bennet** and **Benedick**. The latter is the name of a character in Shakespeare's *Much Ado About Nothing*. There are feminine forms **Benedicta** and **Benedetta**, and a Spanish-American form **Benita**.

Benjamin *m.*

From the Hebrew, meaning 'son of the south' or 'right hand', which might imply strength and good fortune. The Old Testament story of Benjamin, son of Jacob, gave the name the added implications of a favoured youngest son. The commonest pet forms are **Ben**, **Bennie**, **Benny**, **Benjie** and **Benjy**. It is currently a very popular name.

Bennet *see* Benedict

Bennie, Benny *see* Benjamin

Berenice *f.*

From the Greek Pherenice, meaning 'bringer of victory'.

It was spread by the imperial conquests of Alexander the Great over Europe and Asia. It was especially popular in Egypt, during the period of Macedonian rule, and its use spread also to the family of Herod of Judea. **Bernice** is a modern form of the name, and **Bunny** is sometimes used as a pet form (see also **VERONICA**).

Bernadette *f.*

The commonest female form of **BERNARD**. Its use has spread due to the fame of St Bernadette of Lourdes, who lived in the mid 19th century and whose visions started the pilgrimages of healing to that town. The Italian **Bernardetta** has been shortened to **Detta**, which can be used as an independent name. **Bernadine** is another form of the name, and **Bernie** the short form.

Bernard *m.*

A Germanic name meaning 'brave as a bear'. It was very popular in the Middle Ages. Two important saints bearing the name were St Bernard of Menthon after whom St Bernard dogs are named, and St Bernard of Clairvaux who inspired the Second Crusade. It has remained in use ever since. The most usual short forms are **Bernie** and **Barney**, which is shared with **BARNABAS**.

Bernardetta *see* Bernadette

Bernice *see* Berenice

Bernie *see* Bernadette, Bernard

Berry *see* **Bertram**

Bert, Bertie *m.*

A pet form of a large number of names including
ALBERT, BERTRAM, BERTRAND, GILBERT, HERBERT,
HUBERT, ROBERT. In all these cases, the '-bert' part of
the name is a Germanic element meaning 'bright'. The
name is sometimes used as a given name, when it may
take the form **Burt**.

Bertha *f.*

From the Old German word *beraht*, meaning 'bright'.
The first famous English Bertha was the wife of King
Ethelbert of Kent who welcomed St Augustine to
England on his mission of conversion. In the Middle
Ages both Bertha and **Berta** were popular, and the name
has been regularly used ever since, although it is rather
uncommon at present.

Bertram *m.*

From the Old German meaning 'bright raven', the
bird associated with the god Odin. The name has been
used in England since the early Middle Ages, and has
the short forms BERT and **Bertie**, and the less common
Berry.

Bertrand *m.*

This name, meaning 'bright shield', is often treated as

the French form of **BERTRAM** and shares with it the short forms **BERT** and **Bertie**.

Beryl *f.*

From the gemstone, whose name is related to the Arabic for 'crystal'. It appeared in the 19th century, and was popular in the early part of the 20th century.

Bess, Bessie, Beth *see* Elizabeth

Betha *see* Bethia

Bethany *f.*

A popular name taken from a New Testament place name, the village where Lazarus lived. The short form **Bethan** is used independently, and is also a short form of **ELIZABETH** which has spread from Wales.

Bethia *f.*

Bethia or **Bethea** can be interpreted in three different ways. It can be thought of as a pet form of **ELIZABETH**, as a use of the Old Testament place name Bethia, or as an English version of a Gaelic name also found as **Betha**, meaning 'life'.

Betsy, Betty *see* Elizabeth

Bettina *f.*

An Italian pet form of **ELIZABETH** which was a popular given name in the 1960s.

Bettrys *see* **Beatrice**

Beulah *f.*

From the Hebrew for 'married'. In the Old Testament Beulah is applied as a place name to Israel, with the explanation, 'as the bridegroom rejoices over the bride, so shall your God rejoice over you'. John Bunyan used the name in *The Pilgrim's Progress* for the 'land of heavenly joy'.

Beverl(e)y *f. and m.*

From an Old English surname meaning 'of the beaver-meadow'. It is shortened to **Bev**, and is now only rarely used for boys.

Bevis *m.*

This is a French name, possibly meaning 'bow', introduced into England at the Norman Conquest. It was popular in the Middle Ages and revived again after Richard Jeffries' *Bevis, The Story of a Boy* was published in 1882.

Bharat *m.*

This was the name of several famous heroes in the Hindu epics, and derives from the Sanskrit for 'being maintained'. India officially became Bharat when it achieved independence.

Bharati *f.*

A Hindu name identified with the goddess of speech and learning.

Bhaskar *m.*

A Hindu name from the Sanskrit for 'the sun'.
Bhaskara, the famous 12th-century Indian astronomer
and teacher, shows an earlier form of the name.

Bhavana *see* Bhavna

Bhavini *f.*

A Hindu name, referring to the goddess Parvati, wife of
the god Siva.

Bhavna *f.*

An Indian name, from the Sanskrit meaning 'wish',
'desire' or 'thought'. The form **Bhavana** is also used.

Bianca *see* Blanche

Bidelia, Biddy *see* Bridget

Bill *see* William

Billie, Billy *f. and m.*

This pet form of the boy's name **WILLIAM** is being used
increasingly as a girl's name particularly in America,
usually in combination to produce names such as **Billie
Jean** or **Billy Joe**.

Birgitta *see* Bridget

Björn *m.*

A Scandinavian name which means 'bear'. The name has become widely known in modern times through the Swedish tennis champion Björn Borg.

Blaise *m.*

From the French, meaning either someone from the Blois region, or derived from the Latin for 'stammerer'. It is also spelt **Blase** or **Blaze**.

Blake *f. and m.*

A surname, from the Old English meaning 'black, dark-complexioned', used as a first name.

Blanche *f.*

This is a French name which was brought to England in the 13th century. It means 'white' or 'fair-skinned'. The Spanish and Italian form **Bianca** was used by Shakespeare, and is now rather more popular than the older form.

Blase, Blaze *see* Blaise

Blodwen *f.*

From the Welsh for 'white flower'. It is rarely found outside Wales. **Blodeuwedd**, 'flower form', is the name of a beautiful but unfaithful woman in Welsh medieval romance, while **Blodyn** or **Blodeyn** is the more simple 'flower'.

Blossom *see* **Fleur**

Bob *see* **Robert**

Bobbi(e), Bobby *f. and m.*

These pet forms of **ROBERT**, **ROBERTA** and **Barbara** are used as names in their own right, and in combinations such as **Bobby Joe**.

Bonnie, Bonny *f.*

A Scots word for 'pretty' used as a name. Like many modern names, it probably owes its spread to its appearance in *Gone with the Wind*.

Boris *m.*

From the Russian word for 'fight'. It has been used in Britain and North America in the 20th century, possibly due to cultural influences such as Moussorgsky's opera *Boris Godunov*, the film actor, Boris Karloff, and the author of *Dr Zhivago*, Boris Pasternak, as well the large number of Slavic immigrants who have come to the West.

Boyd *m.*

From a Gaelic word meaning 'yellow', referring to the colour of the hair. It is the name of a Scottish clan, though the surname can also derive from 'isle of Bute'. Boyd became more widespread outside Scotland after its use in Margaret Mitchell's *Gone With the Wind*.

Bradley *m.*

A surname from the Old English, meaning 'wide meadow', now popular as a first name. **Brad(d)** is a short form.

Bram *see* Abraham

Bran *see* Brenna

Brand *see* Brenda

Brandan, Brandon *see* Brendan

Brandi *f.*

This name, which seems to come from the vocabulary word 'brandy', has been a popular girl's name in the USA for some time. It is also found spelt **Brandy**, **Brandee** and **Brandie**, and probably serves as a feminine form of **Brandon**.

Brannan *see* Brenna

Breanna *f.*

This new name, which has developed in the USA, can either be seen as a blend of the names Bree (a pet form of **Bridget**) and **Anna**, or as a development of **BRIANNA**, a feminine form of **BRIAN**. it is also used in the form **Breanne**, and found in spellings such as **Breeanna** and **Brieanne**.

Bree *see* Bridget

Bren *see* Brenna

Brenda *f.*

Probably a feminine form of the Norse name **Brand**, meaning 'a sword', found in the Shetlands. It was used by Walter Scott in his novel *The Pirate*. However, in practice, it has been used more frequently as a feminine form of BRENDAN.

Brendan, Brandon *m.*

An Irish name meaning either 'with stinking hair', or, according to one authority, from the Welsh word meaning 'prince'. It is most famously found in the 6th-century Irish St Brendan the Navigator, credited in legend with the discovery of America. It is today particularly popular in Ireland, Australia and the USA. The form **Brandan** or **Brandon** has a long history as an alternative form of Brendan, but can also come from an Old English place and surname meaning 'a hill where broom grows'. The name is also spelt **Brandin**, **Brandyn**, **Brenden** and **Brendon**.

Brenna *f.*, Brennan *m.*

Brennan is a pet form of the Irish name **Bren**, which probably means 'tear, sorrow', with **Brenna** a modern feminine form. Since the earliest records this name and **Bran**, 'raven', and its pet form **Brannan** have regularly been confused, and it is not always possible to tell which name has come from which source.

Bret(t) *m.*

From an Old French word meaning 'a Briton' or 'a Breton'. It is currently well used in the USA.

Brian *m.*, Brianna *f.*

A Celtic name, the origin of which is obscure, though it may be derived from words meaning 'hill' or 'strength'. It was known mainly in Celtic areas until the Norman Conquest, when it was introduced to England. Brian Boru was a famous Irish King of the 11th century, who defeated the invading Vikings. The name continued to be popular in England until Tudor times, but after that it disappeared until it was reintroduced from Ireland in the 18th century. Today the spellings **Bryan**, **Brien** and **Brion** are found, and **Bryant** or **Briant**, originally a surname developed from the name Brian, is also found. **Brianna**, **Bryan(n)a** and **Brianne** (**Bryanne**) are used as feminine forms, as is **Bryony**.

Brice *m.*

Brice, possibly meaning 'speckled', is an old Gaulish name, the name of a 5th-century French saint and bishop of Tours, which is now well used in the USA, often in the form **Bryce**. The surname which developed from the first name, **Bryson**, is also found used as a first name.

Bridget *f.*

Brigit was the ancient Irish goddess of poetry whose name meant 'strength'. Her name was borne by 5th-century St Brigit of Kildare, the most revered of the Irish

female saints. The Irish name also appears in the forms
Bri(d)gid and **Bride** (which reflects the Irish pronunciation
of the name, with a long 'ee' sound and no 'g'), with the
diminutives **Bridie**, **Biddy**, **Bree** and the rather elegant
elaboration **Bidelia**. There is also a Swedish saint **Birgitta**
or **Brigitta** whose feast day falls on the same day as
St Brigit's, and her name has influenced the most common
English form of the name, Bridget. **Britt** is a pet form of
the Swedish name.

Brien *see* **Brian**

Brigid, Brigit, Brigitta *see* **Bridget**

Brin *see* **Bryn**

Brion *see* **Brian**

Briony *see* **Bryony**

Britt *see* **Bridget**

Brittany *f.*

The English name of the French region Bretagne.
Brittany began to be used as a name for American girls
in the 1960s, for reasons which are unclear. The sound
of the name rather than its meaning seems to be
important, as it also occurs as **Britanee**, **Britani**, **Britney**
and **Brittney**. In the 1980s a sudden surge in popularity
took it to the top of the American top fifty name charts.

British parents are slowly becoming aware of it, and it is likely to become popular in the late 1990s.

Bronwen *f.*

From the Welsh words meaning 'white breast'. This name has long been popular in Wales where it has strong associations with ancient legend.

Brooke *f. and m.*

The surname meaning 'a brook', used as a first name. The American place name **Brooklyn**, treated as if a blend of Brooke and **Lyn** in forms such as **Brooklynne**, is also occasionally found for girls.

Bruce *m.*

A French surname which came to Britain at the time of the Norman Conquest. Members of the family moved to Scotland where a descendant of one, Robert Bruce, became King of Scots, and was the ancestor of the Stewart or Stuart Kings. Bruce has only been used as a first name since the 19th century, but it proved so popular in Australia that it is almost a nickname for an Australian man. **Brucie** is a pet form.

Bruno *m.*

This is a German name meaning 'brown', probably imported to the UK via the USA where it has been established for longer.

Bryan *see* **Brian**

Bryce *see* **Brice**

Bryn *m.*

A Welsh name, originally describing where someone lived, meaning 'hill'. It can be found as **Brin**, and **Brynmor** ('large hill') is also used.

Bryony *f.*

Bryony, or **Briony**, is the name of the climbing hedgerow plant used as a girl's name. The word comes from ancient Greek and means 'to grow luxuriantly'. It is a rather insignificant plant, although it has pretty berries, and the name probably owes its popularity to the fact that it can be used as a female equivalent to **BRIAN**.

Buck *m.*

Buck was a popular term in the 18th century for a dashing or fashionably-dressed man. It is usually used as a nickname rather than a true first name.

Buddy *m.*

This word for a friend is occasionally used as a first name, but is usually a nickname. The singer Buddy Holly, for example, was christened Charles.

Bunny *see* **Berenice**

Bunty *f.*

This was a traditional name for a pet lamb, which came into use for girls after 1911, when it was featured in a

very successful play called *Bunty Pulls the Strings*.
However, it is used more commonly as a nickname.

Burhan *m.*

An Arabic name meaning 'evidence' or 'proof'.

Burhanuddin *m.*

From the Arabic meaning 'proof of the faith'.

Burt *see* Bert

Byron *m.*

A name more frequently used in America than Britain,
though it honours the English poet Lord Byron
(1784–1824). Byron comes from the word 'byre', which
means a cow-shed or barn. The name may have
originally indicated someone who lived near a barn.

C

Caddy *see* **Caroline**

Cadfael *m.*
A Welsh name, meaning 'battle metal', recently given publicity as the name of the hero of the novels of Ellis Peters.

Cadwallader *m.*
From the Welsh for 'battle chief'; it is one of several names with the Welsh word for battle as its root. It is found in Wales and North America.

Cahal *see* **Carol**

Cai *see* **Caius**

Caitlin *see* **Katharine**

Caius, Gaius *m.*
A Roman first name, meaning 'rejoice', which is still used occasionally. The Welsh name **Cai**, **Kai** or KAY, well known as the name of Sir Kay, King Arthur's foster-brother, is derived from this.

Caleb *m.*
From the Hebrew *kalebh*, meaning 'dog' or 'intrepid'.

It first appeared in England in the 16th century and is now quite fashionable in North America, where it is shortened to **Cale** and can be spelt with a 'k'.

Callie *f.*

Callie or **Cally** was originally a short form of several names, but is now used as a name in its own right. It is an old pet form of **CAROLINE**, or it can come from any name beginning Cal-, particularly those containing the Greek element for 'beautiful', such as **Calliope**, 'beautiful face', the name of the ancient Greek muse of epic poetry, or **Calista**, 'most beautiful'. It is also found spelt **Kally** or **Kalli(e)**.

Callum *m.*

Callum comes from the Latin *columba*, 'a dove'. When the Irish St **Columba** went as a missionary to Scotland in the 6th century, he introduced the name there and it became a typically Scottish name, along with **MALCOLM**, which comes from it. It has recently become increasingly popular in the rest of the UK. It is found spelt **Calum** and **Colum**, while the form **Colm** is particularly popular in Ireland.

Calvin *m.*

From the surname of the 16th-century French religious reformer Jean Cauvin or Chauvin, latinized to Calvinus, and adopted as a first name by Protestants. It may be derived from the Old French *chauve*, 'bald'. It is most commonly found in North America and Scotland, often shortened to **Cal**, and there is a rare feminine form, **Calvina**.

Cameron *f. and m.*

From the Gaelic meaning 'crooked nose'. It is the name of a Scots clan, although its use as a first name has now spread from Scotland. It is a popular boy's name, and is now being used for girls as well.

Camilla *f.*

A name from Roman legend. Camilla was Queen of the Volsci, a great warrior and exceptionally swift runner. The name may be Etruscan, and possibly means 'one who helps at sacrifices'. It was first recorded in Britain as early as 1205 and is still popular at the moment. **Camille** is the French form which can be used for either sex, and **Milla**, **Milly** and **Millie** are used as short forms.

Candice, Candace *f.*

This is an ancient title of the Queen of Ethiopia. It is also spelt **Candis**; **Candy** is a short form.

Candida *f.*

From the Latin meaning 'white'. It was the name of several saints, among them one from Naples whom St Paul is said to have cured. The name was not used in Britain until the early 20th century and its introduction was probably due to G.B. Shaw's play, *Candida*.

Candis, Candy *see* Candice

Cara *f.*

This Italian word meaning 'dear' has come into use as a first name only in the 20th century and is often spelt **Kara** in the USA. Pet forms, used as names in their own right, include **Carissa**, **Carita** and **Carina**. These are found in a number of variant forms such as **Karissa**, **Karena**, **Caryssa** and **Charissa**, and it is not always easy to tell when parents are using forms of Cara, KAREN or CHARIS.

Caradoc *m.*

From the Welsh for 'beloved'. It is common in Wales, but not in other parts of Britain. In the form Caratacus, the name of a Briton who fought against the Romans in the first century, it is one of the earliest recorded British names.

Cari *see* Ceri

Carina, Carissa, Carita *see* Cara

Carl, Karl *m.* Carla, Karla *f.*

These are German forms of CHARLES. The names have been in general use in America most of this century, and from there spread to Britain. The feminines **Carla** or **Karla**, **Carlie** or **Carly** can also be found as forms of the names found under CAROLINE.

Carlo *m.*

This is the Italian form of CHARLES. Like **Carlos**, its Spanish form, it is gaining popularity, especially in the USA.

Carlotta *see* Charlotte

Carlton, Charlton *m.*

These names are both forms of an Old English place name and, later, a surname meaning 'countryman's farm'.

Carly *see* Carl

Carlyn *see* Caroline

Carmel *f.*

From the Hebrew meaning 'garden', and the name of a mountain famous for its lush vegetation near the city of Haifa in Israel. St Louis founded the church and convent on this mountain which, as legend has it, the Virgin Mary and infant Jesus often visited. **Carmen** is the Spanish form of the name, **Carmela** the Italian, and **Carmelita** and **Carmelina** pet forms. Carmen is also the Latin word for song, and some people like to think of it in this sense, hence such modern coinages as **Carmina**, the Latin for 'songs'.

Caro *see* Caroline

Carol *f. and m.*

The female forms of this name, which include **Carole**, **Carola** and **Caryl**, were originally pet forms of CAROLINE or **Carolina**, but are now popular names in their own right. As a boy's name it can be an English form of the Irish **Cathal** or, in its phonetic spelling, **Cahal** ('battle-mighty'). It is also used in central Europe and often spelt **Karol** or **Karel**, deriving from **Carolus**, the latinized form of CHARLES, but it is an uncommon male name.

Caroline, Carolyn *f.*

These names come from **Carolina**, the Italian feminine form of CARLO. The name was introduced into Britain from Southern Germany by Queen Caroline of Brandenburg-Anspach, wife of George II. Both forms have been used steadily since the 18th century. Derivatives are **Carla** (see CARL), **Carlyn**, CAROL, **Carola**, **Carole**. Abbreviations include **Carrie**, **Caddy**, **Caro** and LYN.

Carolus *see* Carol, Charles

Caron *see* Karen

Carrie *see* Caroline

Carwen, Carwyn *see* Ceri

Cary *m.*

A surname which was only rarely used as a first name until it became famous through the film star Cary Grant.

Ultimately, it probably goes back to one of a number of Irish surnames, possibly meaning 'battle-king' or 'dark brown'.

Caryl *see* Carol

Caryn *see* Karen

Carys *see* Ceri

Casey *f. and m.*

This comes from an Irish surname meaning 'vigilant in war'. It can also be a form of the Polish name **Casimir**, 'proclamation of peace'. This has a female form **Casimira**. Both can also be spelt with a 'K'.

Caspar *see* Jasper

Cassandra *f.*

In Greek literature this was the name of a prophetess and princess of Troy. She foretold the truth, but was never believed. The name first became popular in the Middle Ages and has continued in use ever since. It is shortened to **Cassie** and **Cass** and sometimes **SANDRA** or **Sandy**. Cass also occurs as a masculine name, when it may come from an Irish name meaning 'curly-haired'.

Cassia *see* Kezia(h)

Cassie *see* Cassandra

Cassidy *f.*

This is an Irish surname, of unknown meaning, used as a first name, mainly in the USA. **Cassie**, also used as a name in its own right, is a short form it shares with **CASSANDRA**. It is occasionally used for boys.

Cathal *see* **Carol**

Catharine, Catherine, Cathleen, Cathy *see* **Katharine**

Catriona *f.*

A Gaelic form of **KATHARINE**. It was the title of a book by Robert Louis Stevenson, and became very popular in the 19th century as a result of this. **Catrina**, **Katrina** and **Katrine** are other forms of the name, and it becomes **Catrin** in Welsh. **Riona** is an Irish pet form.

Cecil, Cecily *see* **Cecilia**

Cecil *m.*

From the Latin meaning 'blind'. It was the name of a famous Roman clan and was first adopted into English as a girl's name. The popularity of the name in its masculine form only became marked in the 19th century, probably as one of several aristocratic surnames which it was then fashionable to use as first names.

Cecilia *f.*

The female version of **CECIL**. It was the name of a 2nd-century martyr and saint, the patroness of music. The name was first introduced into Britain by the Normans. Variant forms are **Cicely**, **Cecily**, **Sisley**, **Cecil** and the French **Cecile** (used for boys and girls in France). The popular shortened form **Celia** (which can also be derived from another Roman name, Coelia) probably came into fashion as a result of the Celia in Shakespeare's play *As You Like It*. Other abbreviated forms are **Sis**, **Ciss** and **Cissy** or **Sissy** (see also **SHEILA**).

Cedric *m.*

This name seems to have been a creation of Sir Walter Scott's for a character in the novel *Ivanhoe*. Scott is said to have used it by mistake for Cerdic who was the first king of the West Saxons. However, as there is a Welsh name **Cedrych** ('pattern of generosity'), it may well be from this. Cedric became popular with parents as a result of the book *Little Lord Fauntleroy* (1886) by F.H. Burnett whose hero bore that name, and it may well also owe its fall in popularity to its association with the book and its hero's smugly virtuous image. It does, however, show signs of coming back into fashion, particularly in the USA.

Celeste *f.*

From the Latin meaning 'heavenly'. Pet forms, used as names in their own right, are **Celestine**, **Celestina** and **Celesta**.

Celia *see* **Cecilia**

Celina, Céline *see* **Selina**

Cenydd *see* **Kenneth**

Ceri *f.*

A popular Welsh name, sometimes spelt **Keri** to reflect
its pronunciation with a hard 'c'. It comes from the
Welsh word for 'love' as do **Cerian, Cerys** or **Carys** and
Cari. Carwen is 'fair love' and has a masculine form,
Carwyn (see also **KERRY**).

Ceridwen *f.*

This name probably comes from the Welsh words for
'poetry' and 'white, blessed'. It was the name of a Celtic
goddess who was said to inspire poetry and was the mother
of the great poet, **Taliesin** ('radiant brow'). It is pronounced
with a hard 'c' and is generally confined to Wales.

Cerys *see* Ceri

Chad *m.*

The name (of uncertain meaning) of a 7th-century saint
who was Bishop of Lichfield. The name has become
quite popular in America in the 20th century. A famous
holder of the name was the Rev. Chad Varah, founder of
The Samaritans.

Chae *see* Charles

Champak *m.*

The Hindu name of a god, and of a tree bearing yellow flowers.

Chandan *m.*

An Indian name from the Sanskrit for 'sandalwood'. The paste derived from sandalwood is important in Hindu religious ceremonies, when it is used to anoint statues of the gods and to make a mark on the foreheads of worshippers. Chandan occurs as a divine personal name in traditional Hindu texts.

Chandra *f.*, Chander *m.*

An Indian name from the Sanskrit meaning 'the moon'. In the Hindu religion, the moon is a god rather than a goddess, but the name Chandra is nevertheless a popular one for girls. The variant Chander is often used for boys.

Chandrakala *f.*

An Indian name from the Sanskrit meaning 'moonbeams'.

Chandrakant *m.*, Chandrakanta *f.*

From the Sanskrit for 'loved by the moon', referring to a mythical jewel mentioned in classical Hindu texts, supposedly formed by the moon's rays. It is also the name of a white water-lily which blossoms at night.

Chanel *f.*

The name of this famous French perfume has been
taken up as a girl's name in recent years, especially by
Afro-Americans. The perfume was named after
Gabrielle 'Coco' Chanel, whose family name derives
from an Old French word meaning 'wine jar', indicating
an ancestral connection with the wine trade. Chanel is
frequently spelt phonetically, taking such forms as
Shanel, Shanell, **Shanelle** and **Shannel**.

Chantal *f.*

This is a French name which has only been in use since
the beginning of this century. It was the surname of the
16th-century saint, Jeanne-Françoise de Chantal,
meaning 'stone'. It has been popular in the USA,
where it has developed forms such as **Chantalle** and
Chantel(l)e. It is pronounced with a 'sh' sound at the
beginning.

Charis *f.*

From the Greek meaning 'grace'. The 'Ch' is
pronounced as a 'K'. It was first used as a first name in
the 17th century, although in the 16th century the poet
Edmund Spenser in the *Faerie Queen* used the form
Charissa. It has been quite popular in the USA.
Chrissa can be a short form of this or belong under the
CHRISTINE group of names. There is some overlap
between the names under **CERI, CARA** and Charis as they
are pronounced so similarly.

Charity *f.*

From the Latin *caritas*, meaning 'Christian love'. Translated into English as charity, it was adopted when it became the custom for Puritans to name childen after the Christian virtues. The name Charity was shortened to **Cherry**, and is the source of this name. Another abbreviation is **Chattie**, used also for CHARLOTTE.

Charlene *f.*

A feminine form of CHARLES introduced in this century. It may owe something to **Charline**, a Dutch form of CHARLOTTE. **Charleen** and **Sharlene** are also used (see also ARLENE).

Charles *m.*

Originally from the Old German *carl*, meaning 'man'. It was latinized as **Carolus** and then changed by the French to Charles. The Normans brought the name to England, but it did not become popular until its use by the Stuart kings of Britain caused it to be taken up by Royalists in the 17th century and Jacobites in the 18th century. Its popularity has continued ever since. The pet form **Charlie** is now common as the given form of the name. **Chas**, originally a written abbreviation, has now come to be used as a short form. **Chuck** is also used, and in Scotland **Chae** or **Chay**.

Charline *see* **Charlene**

Charlotte *f.*

The French female form of **CHARLES**. It was introduced
into Britain from France in the early 17th century.
Goethe's heroine from the romantic novel, *The Sorrows
of Werther*, and Princess Charlotte, daughter of George
IV, increased its popularity. Abbreviations are **Lottie**,
Lotty, **Totty**, **Charlie** and **Chattie**, and spellings such as
Sharlott have been recorded. It has been one of the most
popular girls' names for a number of years. **Carlotta** is
the Italian form.

Charlton *see* Carlton

Charmaine *f.*

A 20th-century name of rather obscure origin. It may
well be a form of **Charmian**, from the Greek, meaning
'joy'. This was the name of one of Cleopatra's attendants
in Shakespeare's *Antony and Cleopatra*. Strictly speaking,
Charmian should be pronounced with a hard 'c', but the
'sh' pronunciation is also found. Charmaine is sometimes
spelt **Sharmaine**.

Charulata *f.*

An Indian name meaning 'beautiful'.

Chas *see* Charles

Chase *m.*

The rise in popularity of this surname, meaning
'hunter', as a first name in the USA probably owes

much to its use for a character in the 1980s television series *Falcon Crest*.

Chattie *see* Charity, Charlotte

Chay *see* Charles

Chelsea *f.*
This name of a fashionable part of London, which originally indicated a 'landing place (on the River Thames) for chalk or limestone', is also a place name in Australia, where its use as a girl's name seems to have begun. The name was introduced to America by a character in the film *On Golden Pond*, and its popularity was secured by the wide-spread publicity it received through Chelsea Clinton, daughter of US President Bill Clinton, who was named after a Joni Mitchell song. It is now well used in Britain. Spelling variants such as **Chelsie**, **Chelsey** and **Chelsi** are also found.

Cheralyn, Cherilyn *see* Cheryl

Cherie *f.*
The French word for 'darling'. The forms **Sherry, Sheree** and **Sherrie** are phonetic spellings. **Cher** can be the French for 'dear' or a short form of CHERYL. **Cherise** can be regarded either as a development of Cherie, or as a form of **Charisse**, the French form of CHARIS.

Cherry *see* Charity

Cheryl *f.*

This is probably a development of the name **Cherry** (see **CHARITY**). Other forms of the name are **Cheralyn**, **Cherilyn**, **Sheril** and **Sheryl**, and **Cher** can be a short form (see also **CHERIE**). These names came into general use only in the 1940s, but rapidly became popular.

Chester *m.*

A surname taken from the English city, used as a first name. The word comes from the Latin for 'fort'.

Chetan *m.*

An Indian name meaning 'consciousness' or 'awareness'.

Chevonne *see* **Sheena**

Cheyenne *f.*

The name of a famous American Indian nation, of unknown meaning. Cheyenne was first launched as a boy's name in a TV series of that name in the US in the late-1950s. Pronunciation of the name as **Shyann**, in which form it is also found, possibly linked it in parents' minds with the name **ANNE**, suggesting its use for girls. In the USA it continues to grow in popularity.

Chintana *f.*

An Indian name meaning 'meditation'. The form **Chintanika** is also used.

Chip *see* **Christopher**

Chloe *f.*

From the Greek, meaning 'a green shoot', a name given to the goddess Demeter who protected the green fields. It was a popular name in classical literature which was picked up by the Elizabethan poets. It is very popular at the moment. **Chloris**, 'greenish', is another name from Greek myth, and was again associated with fertility. It is sometimes spelt **Cloris**, to reflect the pronunciation of these names with a hard 'c'.

Chris *see* Christabel, Christine, Christopher

Chrissa *see* Charis, Christine

Chrissie, Chrissy *see* Christabel, Christine

Christabel *f.*

This name was first used in Britain in the 16th century, and is thought to be a combination of 'Christ' and the Latin *bella* to mean 'beautiful Christian'. It is not a common name in Britain, although it is sometimes used in memory of the suffragette, Dame Christabel Pankhurst. It is also spelt **Christobel** and abbreviated forms are **Chris**, **Chrissy**, **Chrissie** or **Christie**.

Christel, Christen *see* Christine

Christian *f. and m.*

This name, with its transparent meaning, has been used in Britain since the 13th century. It became more popular after its use by Bunyan for the hero of *Pilgrim's Progress*, but has never been as common as the feminine form, CHRISTINE, although it is currently enjoying some popularity.

Christiana *see* Christine

Christie *see* Christabel, Christopher

Christine *f*

The commonest of the many girls' names meaning 'a Christian'. **Christen** is probably the oldest form, followed by **Christiana**. Others are **Christina**, **Christian(n)e**, a feminine form of CHRISTIAN, the Welsh form **Crystin**, and spellings such as **Krystyna**, **Kristina**, **Krista** and **Kristin**. The German form, **Christel**, may have helped the development of the name CRYSTAL. Short forms are **Chrissie**, **Chrissy** and **Chris** and further variants will be found under the Scottish pet form, KIRSTY. **Chrissa**, **Chryssa** or **Kryssa** can be thought of either as a part of this group or as a short form of **Charissa** (see CHARIS).

Christmas *see* Noel

Christopher *m*

From the Greek meaning 'bearing Christ'. As a first

name it is used in honour of the saint who was believed to have carried the infant Christ to safety across a river. Thus St Christopher became the patron saint of travellers. The popularity of the name in Britain has fluctuated since the 13th century when it was first used, but it is presently a popular choice. The Scottish equivalent of the name was **Chrystal** or CRYSTAL. Abbreviated forms are **Kester**, **Kit**, **Chip** and **Chris**. **Christie** or **Christy** is a pet form particularly used in Ireland.

Chryssa *see* Christine

Chrystal *see* Christopher, Crystal

Chuck *see* Charles

Ciara, Ciaran *see* Kieran

Cicely *see* Cecilia

Ciera, Cieran *see* Kieran

Cilla *see* Priscilla

Cimmie *see* Cynthia

Cindy *f.*

A short form of names such as LUCINDA and CYNTHIA, now used as an independent name. It is also spelt **Cindi** and **Cindie**.

Ciss, Cissy *see* **Cecilia**

Clare, Claire *f*

From the Latin meaning 'clear, famous'. The religious order of the Sisters of St **Clara** or 'Poor Clares', founded in the 13th century, was probably responsible for the rapid spread of the name throughout Europe. The name has been popular for some time. Among the many derivatives are **Claribel** and **Clarinda,** which can be shortened to **Clarrie**.

Clarence *m.*

In the 14th century **LIONEL**, son of King Edward III of England, married the heiress of the town of Clare in Suffolk. He was later created Duke of Clarence, the name Clarence meaning 'of Clare'. This title seems to have been first used as a name in the early 19th century in Maria Edgeworth's novel *Helen*.

Claribel *see* **Clare**

Clarice *see* **Clarissa**

Clarinda *see* **Clare**

Clarissa *f.*

From the Latin meaning 'brightest, most famous'. It was made popular in the 18th century by Samuel Richardson's novel *Clarissa Harlowe*. **Clarice** is an older form of the name. They share the abbreviation **Clarrie** with **Clara**.

Clark *m.*

The surname meaning 'a clerk', used as a first name.
Famous users were the actor Clark Gable and in fiction
Clark Kent, the everyday name for *Superman*. **Clarke** is
also found.

Clarrie *see* Clare, Clarissa

Claud *m.*, Claudia *f.*

From the Roman name, Claudius, itself derived from the
Latin meaning 'lame'. In homage to the Emperor
Claudius, under whom Britain was conquered by the
Romans, the name was used in this country in the 1st and
2nd centuries. Its use soon lapsed in Britain though not
in France where it is spelt **Claude** and used for either
sex, and it was from the French that it was taken and
revived in Britain in the 16th century by the Scottish
family of Hamilton. A derivative is **Claudian**, and the pet
form **Claudie** can be found. The female form, Claudia,
is at the moment rather more popular. Two French
diminutives are also used: **Claudette** and **Claudine**,
a name made famous by the novels of Colette.

Claudius *see* Claud

Claus *see* Nicholas

Clayton *m.*

Clayton, from a place name, later a surname, meaning
'settlement on clay', is enjoying some popularity in the

USA as a boy's name, as is the shorter **Clay**. Both are found spelt with a 'K'.

Clem, Clemmie *see* Clement, Clementina

Clemence, Clemency *f.*

From the Latin for 'mildness'. The name first appeared in Britain in the 13th century. All of the group of names with this meaning are enjoying something of a revival, Clemency in particular.

Clement *m.*, Clementina, Clementine *f.*

From the Latin, meaning 'mild, merciful'. Clement was the name of an early saint and of several popes. Its abbreviated forms are **Clem** and **Clemmie**, which are shared with the feminine forms Clementina and Clementine. Clementine was originally a German form, fashionable during the 19th century, and is now showing signs of returning to popularity. **Clemency** is also used for girls.

Cleo *f.*

A shortened form of **Cleopatra,** from the Greek meaning 'glory of her father'. The famous Egyptian queen of this name died in 30 BC and it did not take long for her name to become a byword for sexual allure and tragic love.

Clidna *see* Cliona

Clifford *m.*

There are several places named Clifford ('ford by the cliff') in Britain, any of which could become a surname. Towards the end of the 19th century the surname came into use as a first name. It is now most often used in its short form **Cliff**. **Clifton**, 'settlement by the cliff', is also found.

Clint *m.*

A short form of **Clinton**, an aristocratic surname meaning 'farm by the river Glyme', used as a first name. The short form has been given fame by the actor, Clint Eastwood.

Cliona *f.*

The name of a beautiful fairy-woman in Irish legend. Her name can also be spelt **Clidna**, **Cliodhna** or **Cliodna**.

Clive *m.*

A surname meaning 'dweller by the cliff' which has come to be used as a first name, probably in honour of Robert Clive, known as Clive of India, who was prominent in the British conquest of India.

Clodagh *f.*

The name of a river in Ireland. It was first used in the 20th century as a first name by the Marquis of Waterford for his daughter. Its use has now spread beyond Ireland.

Cloris *see* Chloe

Clotilda *f.*

An Old German name meaning 'loud battle'. Clotilda was a queen of France in the 6th century who converted her husband, King Clovis (see **LEWIS**) to Christianity. The name is not common.

Clover *f.*

This is the flower name used as a first name. Its spread may have been helped by its use for a character in the *Katy* books by Susan Coolidge. Names such as **Clova** can be interpreted either as a re-spelling of Clover, or as a feminine form of **Clovis** (see **LEWIS**).

Clovis *see* **Lewis**

Clyde *m.*

Clyde is an ancient Scottish river name meaning 'the washer', possibly from the name of a local goddess and used since before the Roman occupation. It became a surname, then a first name.

Cody *f. and m.*

This is said to be an Irish surname meaning 'descendant of a helpful person'. It has been popular in the United States, where it is also a place name and well known as the surname of the Wild West hero, Buffalo Bill Cody. **Codey** and spellings with 'K' have also been recorded. **Codi(e)** is the spelling most often used for girls.

Coinneach *see* **Kenneth**

Colby *m.*

An English place name and surname, now used as a first name in the USA where it grew steadily in popularity in the early 1990s. The name originally indicated a farmstead owned by a Norseman called Koli. **Colton**, however, comes from a place name meaning 'farm by the River Cole'.

Colette *f.*

From a French diminutive of **NICOLA**. It was the name of the 15th-century reformer of the 'Poor Clares' religious order. The name is best known in this country as the pen-name of a 20th-century French writer. It is also spelt **Collette**. The masculine name **Cole** comes from **NICHOLAS**.

Colin *m.*

This has a similar origin to **COLETTE**, for it was a French pet form of **NICHOLAS**. In Scotland, it was also interpreted as coming from the Gaelic word *cailean*, meaning 'puppy' or 'youth'. There are rare feminine forms **Colina** and **Colinette**.

Colleen *f.*

The Irish word for 'girl' used as a first name. The name is not widely used in Britain, but is fairly common in North America and Australia.

Collette *see* Colette

Colm, Colum, Columba *see* Callum

Colton *see* Colby

Con, Conchobar, Conchobhar *see* Conor

Conan *m.*

From the Irish meaning 'hound, wolf'. It is not very common outside Ireland today. The most famous holder of the name was Arthur Conan Doyle, creator of Sherlock Holmes, but the name is probably best known today from the fictional stories and films of *Conan the Barbarian*. Although the fictional character's name is pronounced in the American films with the same sound as in 'cone', in Ireland the name has a short 'o'. It shares its short forms with CONOR.

Conn, Connor, Conny *see* Conor

Connie *see* Constance

Conor *m.*

From the ancient Irish name **Conchobar** or **Conchobhar** meaning 'lover of hounds'. It was the name of one of the great kings in Irish heroic stories, and has long been a popular name in Ireland. Its popularity has spread to the UK, where it is usually spelt **Connor**. It can be shortened to **Con** or **Conny** and sometimes **Conn**, which is also a separate name, perhaps meaning 'wisdom'.

Conn, Connor, Conny *see* Conor

Conrad *m.*

From the Old German words for 'bold counsel'. The name is found mostly in Germany where in the 13th century Duke Conrad was a greatly beloved figure. Objection to his public execution by the conquering Charles of Anjou led to a widespread use of this name in German-speaking states. Examples of it have been found in Britain since the 15th century. **Curt** or **Kurt** is a short form used as an independent name, now used rather more frequently than the full form.

Constance *f.*

Constance and its Latin form, **Constantia**, mean 'constancy'. It became popular in many parts of Christendom after Constantine the Great ordered the toleration of Christianity in the Roman Empire, AD 313. It was introduced into England at the time of the Norman Conquest. The form **Constancy** was used by the Puritans in the 17th century while Constantia became popular in the 18th century. **Constantina** is another form of the name. Constance has been out of fashion since the early part of the century, but there has recently been a sudden surge of interest in its use. Its abbreviation is **Connie**. **Constantine**, the masculine form, comes from the Latin for 'firm, constant'. Three Scottish kings were named Constantine after a Cornish saint who was believed to have converted their ancestors to Christianity in the 6th century. It became popular in England from the 12th to

the 17th centuries, and was the origin of the surnames
Constantine, Considine, Costain and Costin. It is not
widely used in Britain today. The composer **Constant**
Lambert (1905–51) shows an English form of the name.

Cora *see* **Corinna**

Coral *f.*

This name reflects the beauty and value of the substance,
and was popular earlier this century. A French form
which is also in use in Britain is **Coralie.**

Corbin *m.*

Corbin comes from a surname based on the Old French
word for 'raven'. Its spread owes much to the success of
the actor Corbin Bernsen.

Cordelia *f.*

This name first appeared as **Cordeilla** in the 16th-century
chronicles of Holinshed, from which Shakespeare
altered the name to Cordelia for his play *King Lear*. The
name is probably a form of **Cordula**, the name of one of
the virgins martyred with St Ursula. It probably comes
from the Latin word for 'heart'.

Corey *f. and m.*

This is an Irish surname of unknown meaning which has
come to be used as a first name. It has been popular in
the USA for some years. It is also spelt **Cory**, and in

forms such as **Cori** or **Corrie** has been used for girls, especially in combination with other names. Spellings beginning with 'K' are also found.

Corinna *f.*

This name and **Cora** both come from the Greek word *kore* meaning 'girl' or 'maiden', a name given to the goddess **Persephone** who was associated with the coming of spring. The appearance of the name in Ovid's love poetry probably inspired its use among some 17th-century poets, particularly Herrick. The French form **Corinne** is also used. **Corin,** much used in poetry as the name for a love-sick shepherd, is the male form of the name, although it is occasionally also used for girls.

Corisande *f.*

This is a name full of glamour and romance, having been the name of a fair maiden in a medieval romance and a poetic name given to Diane de Poitiers, the beautiful and influential mistress of the 16th-century king, Henry II of France.

Cormac *m.*

This Irish name is of doubtful meaning, although it is sometimes said to mean 'a charioteer'. It appears frequently in Irish legend, but through its prevalence in early Irish history and the Irish Church the name was accepted as having a Christian character in Ireland and remained in steady use. A variant is **Cormick**.

Cornelius *m.*, Cornelia *f.*

From the Latin *cornu* meaning 'a horn', these were the male and female forms of the name of a famous Roman clan. The male version was used in Ireland as a substitute for the native **Conchobar** (see **CONOR**). Its abbreviated forms are **Corney**, **Corny** and **Cornie**. Cornelia is slightly more used, but still uncommon.

Corrie, Cory *see* Corey

Cosmo *m.*

From the Greek *kosmos*, meaning 'order'. It is the name of one of the two patron saints of Milan and was used by the famous Italian family of Medici in the form **Cosimo** from the 14th century onwards. It was the name of the 3rd Duke of Gordon who was a friend of Cosimo III, Grand Duke of Tuscany, and the name was introduced into several other Scottish families. **Cosima** is the feminine form.

Courtney *f. and m.*

An aristocratic surname used as a first name. It comes from **Courtnay**, a French place name, although the name is often interpreted as coming from *court nez*, the French for 'short nose'. It is increasingly popular as a girl's name in the UK.

Craig *m.*

The place and surname meaning 'crag', used as a first name.

Cressida *f.*

Cressida comes from a misreading of the name Briseida, 'daughter of Brisis', who appears in Homer's account of the Trojan War. In the 14th century, the Italian writer Boccaccio used the name, and it was adapted by Chaucer in his verse-novel *Troilus and Criseyde*, the story of Troilus's undying love for the fair Cressida, set against the background of the Trojan War. Shakespeare changed the name to Cressida for his version of the story. Despite the fictional character's faithlessness in love, the name has recently become quite popular. An abbreviated form is **Cressy**.

Crispin, Crispian *m.*

From the Latin *crispus*, meaning 'curled'. The 3rd-century martyrs Crispinus and Crispinianus were the patron saints of shoemakers. Crispin was popular in Britain in the Middle Ages and has recently enjoyed a revival.

Crystal *f.*

While this looks like, and is no doubt mainly used as, another jewel name (see also **AMBER**, **JADE**), the spread of this name may have been helped by **Christel**, the German form of **CHRISTINE**. Crystal is also spelt **Chrystal** and the form **Krystal** has become known through the TV series *Dynasty*. As a man's name it is a pet form of **CHRISTOPHER**.

Crystin *see* **Christine**

Cudbert, Cuddy *see* Cuthbert

Curt *see* Conrad

Curtis *m.*

A surname from the French meaning 'courteous', used as a first name. It has been used more frequently in the United States than in Britain.

Cuthbert *m.*

From the Old English words *cuth* and *beorht*, meaning 'famous' and 'bright'. It was in common use both before and after the Norman Conquest, and was the name of a 7th-century saint and Bishop of Lindisfarne in Northumbria. It sometimes appeared as **Cudbert**, and had the pet form **Cuddy**. The name fell out of use just after the Reformation until the 19th century, when it was brought back by the Oxford Movement. It was a slang term for someone who avoided military service during the First World War, and it may be partly due to this usage that the name is not popular today. The school 'swot' in the *Beano*'s Bash Street Kids is called Cuthbert Cringeworthy.

Cy *see* Cyril, Cyrus

Cybill *see* Sybil

Cynan *m.*

This is a Welsh name based on the word *cyn*, meaning

'chief' or 'outstanding'. It can also be found spelt **Cynin** or **Cynon**. There are a number of other Welsh names formed from this word, including **Cynyr**, which means 'chief hero'.

Cynthia *f.*

One of the titles of the Greek goddess Artemis, Cynthia means 'of Mount Cynthus', reputedly one of her favourite places. It first became known as a name through its use by the Latin poet Propertius, and it was later popular among Elizabethan poets. Mrs Gaskell's character in her novel *Wives and Daughters* brought it back into favour during the late 19th century. Pet forms include CINDY, **Cindi** or **Cindie** and the rare **Cimmie**.

Cyprian *m.*

From the Latin *Cyprianus*, meaning 'from Cyprus'. It was the name of a Christian martyr of the 3rd century.

Cyra *see* Cyrus

Cyril *m.*

From the Greek *kyrios*, meaning 'lord'. There were two saints of this name in the 4th and 5th centuries, and it was a 9th-century Saint Cyril who took Christianity to the Slavs, and devised the Russian Cyrillic alphabet. The name was first used in England in the 17th century, but did not become common until the 19th century. The name shares the abbreviation **Cy** with CYRUS, and has been recorded spelt **Syril**. There is a rare feminine form **Cyrilla**.

Cyrus *m.*

A Greek form of the Persian word meaning 'sun' or
'throne'. This is the name of the founder of the Persian
Empire in the 6th century BC, as well as a number of
other Persian kings. It was first used in Britain in the
17th century among Puritans, probably in honour of the
fact that the Emperor Cyrus allowed the Jews to return
to Palestine from their Babylonian captivity. They took it
to North America, where the short forms are **Cy** and
Cyro. There is a feminine form, **Cyra**.

D

Daffodil *f.*

One of the less common flower names, but it is still found from time to time.

Dafydd, Dai *see* David

Daisy *f.*

Possibly a 19th-century pet name for **MARGARET**, a pun on *marguerite*, the French word for daisy. However, there is no reason why it should not have come into use as a simple flower name, and few people today would use it otherwise.

Daithi *see* David

Dakota *f. and m.*

The name of this American Indian nation is now being regularly used in the USA. Its use can be compared to that of **CHEYENNE**.

Dale *f. and m.*

The Old English for 'valley'. At first more common as a girl's name, it is now more frequently used for boys. There are a number of other place names starting with the same sound, such as **Dalton**, **Dallas** and **Dallin**, that may owe their use as boys' names to the popularity of Dale.

Damaris *f.*

The Greek name in the New Testament of an Athenian woman converted by St Paul. This led to its adoption by Puritans in the 17th century. It is probably a form of a Greek name meaning 'heifer'.

Damhnait *see* Dymphna

Damian, Damien *m.*

From the Greek, meaning 'tamer'. There have been four saints called by this name. It was little used in this country before this century, but became popular in the 1970s.

Damon *m.*

From the Greek, meaning 'to rule' or 'guide'. In Greek legend, Damon and Pythias were inseparable friends, famous for their willingness to die for each other.

Dan *see* Daniel

Dana *f and m.*

As a boy's name this comes from the surname, the Old English word for a Dane, and is sometimes found in the form **Dane**. The female name is either a Scandinavian girl's form of **DANIEL**, or, in Ireland, taken from the pagan fertility goddess, Dana or Ana.

Dandy *see* **Andrew**

Daniel *m.,* **Danielle** *f.*

Daniel is the Hebrew name of an Old Testament prophet, meaning 'God has judged'. It was found in England before the Norman Conquest, but only among priests and monks. It became more widespread in the 13th and 14th centuries. In Ireland and Wales it is often found as a version of the Irish **Domhnall** (see **DONALD**) and Welsh **Deiniol**, meaning 'attractive, charming'. Its shortened forms are **Dan** and **Danny**. For girls, **Danielle** is the most common form, but **Daniel(l)a** and **Danette** are also used.

Daphne *f.*

From the Greek for 'bay tree, laurel'. In classical mythology, it was the name of a nymph whom the god Apollo loved. She called on the gods for help to escape his attentions, and was changed by them to a laurel. The name was a traditional name for dogs until the turn of the century, when it became quite common as a girl's name.

Darcy *f. and m.*

Darcy can be either from a French surname meaning someone from a place called Arcy, hence the form *d'Arcy*, or an Irish surname meaning 'descendant of the dark one'. For girls it often takes the form **Darcey** or **Darci(e)**.

Daria *f.*, Darius *m.*

Darius was the name of the 6th-century BC king of the Persians who was defeated by the Athenians at Marathon. The name means 'protector'. Daria is the feminine form.

Darian, Darien *see* Dorian

Darlene *f.*

This appears to be a modern invention, made up of the first syllable of one of the names beginning 'Dar-', or perhaps from 'darling', with the -ene ending that is popular with newly created names such as **CHARLENE** and **Raelene**.

Darrel(l) *f. and m.*

Also spelt **Dar(r)yl**, this is another surname used as a first name. In this case the surname comes from a French village, the village name meaning 'courtyard, open space'. Originally mainly a boy's name, its spread as a girl's name may owe something to Enid Blyton's use of her second husband's surname, Darrell, for the heroine of her *Malory Towers* school stories.

Darren *m.*

A surname of unknown meaning used as a first name. It seems to have been introduced in the 1950s and become popular in the 1960s. **Darran** is also found.

Darryl, Daryl *see* Darrell

Darshan *m.*

An Indian name from the Sanskrit meaning 'to see'.
Darshan refers to being in the presence of, or being
near enough to touch and see with one's own eyes, a
holy or revered person. It is thought to bestow spiritual
enrichment on the observer.

David *m.*

The Hebrew name of the second king of Israel in the
Old Testament, meaning 'beloved'. This name absorbed
the Celtic **Daithi**, meaning 'nimbleness' (the 'th' is
pronounced 'h'), and became very popular in Wales and
Scotland. The patron saint of Wales is a 6th-century
David. There were Scottish kings of this name in the
10th and 14th centuries. The name did not appear in
England before the Norman Conquest, but it was a
common medieval surname in the variant forms Davy,
Davit and Deakin. Short forms are **Dave**, **Davy**, **Davie**,
and in Wales **Dafydd** becomes **Dai** or **Taffy**, the latter
being an English nickname for a Welshman.

Davida, Davina *f.*

These Scottish female forms of **DAVID** are found from
the 17th century, but were not much used until about
thirty years ago, when they started to become more
popular. They are sometimes shortened to **Vida** and
Vina, and **Davita** and **Davinia** are also found.

Davie, Davy *see* **David**

Dawn *f.*

This name came into use in the late 19th century.
Aurora, the name of the Greek goddess of dawn, had
been in vogue slightly earlier and the English translation
was probably a literary invention.

Dean *m.*

A surname, meaning 'valley', adopted as a first name. It
seems to have become popular in the United States first,
but has been widely used in the UK since the 1960s.
Deana or **Dena** is a feminine.

DeAndre *m.*

One of the names that was highly fashionable among
Afro-American families throughout the 1980s. The
prefix 'De-' was regularly attached to other names,
leading to new forms such as **DeAngelo**, **DeJuan**,
DeMarco or **DeMarcus**, **DeMario**, **DeShawn** and
DeWayne. For the meanings of these names, look under
the entries for the names which follow the 'De-' prefix.

Deanna, Deanne *see* **Diana**

Dearbhail *see* **Dervla**

Deb *see* **Dev**

Debdan *see* **Devdan**

Deborah *f.*

A Hebrew name meaning 'bee', and the name of a prophetess and poet in the Old Testament. It was first used by Puritans in the 17th century. **Debbie** or **Debby** is a common abbreviation which is sometimes used independently. **Debra** is a modern spelling of the name.

Declan *m.*

The name of an early Irish saint associated with Ardmore. It has recently been popular with Irish parents.

Dee *f. and m.*

This is usually a nickname, given to anyone with a name beginning with the letter 'D', but is occasionally found as a given name. Compounds such as **Deedee** also occur.

Deepak *m.,* Deepika *f.*

An Indian name from the Sanskrit meaning 'little lamp'. It is one of the descriptive names applied to Kama, god of love. The spelling **Dipak** is also used for boys.

Deiniol *see* **Daniel**

Deirbhile *see* **Dervla**

Deirdre *f.*

The Irish name of a character in Irish and Scottish legend, possibly meaning 'raging' or 'sorrowful'. The name became popular after the late 19th-century Celtic revival, and is now enjoying another major revival in Ireland. It often takes the form **Deidra** in the USA.

DeJuan *see* **DeAndre**

Del, Dell *see* **Delbert, Derek**

Delbert *m.*

This name has been in use since at least the beginning of the 20th century. It is probably formed on the pattern of several surnames such as **Delroy** ('of the king') and **Delmar**, ('of the sea') which are also used as first names, keeping the 'Del-' part and adding '-bert' from the many Germanic names which end in this suffix. The short forms **Del** or **Dell** are also used as first names, and can be pet forms of **DEREK**.

Delia *f.*

This name is derived from Delos, the legendary birthplace of the Greek moon goddess Artemis and a name sometimes given to her. It was popular with pastoral poets in the 17th and 18th centuries.

Delilah *f.*

This is the name borne by the well-known biblical

character who betrayed Samson to the Philistines. It derives from a Hebrew name meaning 'coquette' or 'flirt'. It was also the title of a song popularized by Tom Jones, but this failed to persuade many parents to make use of it.

Della *f.*

Originally a short form of **ADELA**, this is now well established as a name in its own right.

Delmar, Delroy *see* Delbert

DeMarco, DeMarcus, DeMario *see* DeAndre

Demelza *f.*

A place name, meaning 'the hill-fort of Maeldaf', used as a first name in Cornwall. It became more widely known through its use in the *Poldark* books and TV series.

Demetrius *m.*

This is an ancient Greek name which means 'follower' or 'devotee of **Demeter**', the Greek pagan goddess of corn and agriculture whose name in turn means 'earth mother'. It was the name of a highly successful general who died in 286 BC. In the form **Demetrios**, it is the name of a Greek saint and as **Demitrus** it is found in the Bible. **Dimitri** or **Dmitri** is the form the name takes in Russia, where it has been long established. **Demetra**, which can be shortened to **Demi**, is the commonest form of the names for girls. Demetrius was a name little used by English speakers until fairly recently, when it became popular in the United States among Afro-American families because it began with the fashionable 'De-' prefix (see **DEANDRE**).

Den *see* **Denis**

Dena *see* **Dean**

Denholm *m.*

A place name, meaning 'island valley', used as a first name. The similar **Denham**, 'home in a valley', is also used.

Denis *m.*, **Denise** *f.*

A development of Dionysos who was the Greek god of wine and revelry. Denis or **Dennis** is the French form and the name of the patron saint of France. It occurs in England from the 12th century on. In Ireland it has long been used as a substitute for the Irish **Donnchadh** (see **DUNCAN**). **Den** and **Denny** are short forms. Denise, the female form, is also from French. **Dion** (*m.*) and **Dionne** (*f.*) can either come from Dionysos or be a separate name from the same root, connected with the word for 'a god', while **Dione** can be thought of either as a variant of Dionne, or as the name of another character from Greek

mythology whose name means 'divine queen'. These are
growing in popularity (see also **DWIGHT**).

Denzil *m.*

In the form **Denzell**, this is an old Cornish surname
derived from a place-name.

Deo *see* Dev

Deodan *see* Devdan

Derek, Derrick *m.*

From the Old German **THEODORIC**, meaning 'people's
ruler'. It occurs in the 15th century but has only become
popular in the last century. Its fall from favour between
these two periods is attributed to a notorious 17th-
century hangman of that name. Variants recently revived
are **Deryk, Deric** and the Dutch form **Dirk**, popularized
by the actor Dirk Bogarde. Pet forms are **Derry**, **Rick**,
Rickie and **Del** or **Dell**.

Dermot *m.*

This is the anglicized spelling of **Diarm(a)it** or
Diarm(a)id, the Irish name possibly meaning 'free from
envy', or 'free man'. The legendary character who bore
this name eloped with **GRAINNE** who was betrothed to
FINN. Finn pursued the lovers for a long time and finally
brought about Dermot's death.

Derrick, Derry *see* Derek

Dervla *f.*

This is the phonetic form of **Deirbhile**, an old Irish name which means 'daughter of the poet'. It is best known through the travel writer, Dervla Murphy. It also occurs as **Dervila**, reflecting the Irish pronunciation. The similar-looking **Dearbhail**, which can be anglicized **Derval** or **Dervilia**, meaning 'daughter of Fal' (a figure in Irish legend), is also very popular at the moment in Ireland.

Deryk *see* Derek

Des, Desi *see* Desmond

DeShawn *see* DeAndre

Désirée *f.*

A French name meaning 'desired'. It has been in use since the beginning of the Christian era in the Latin form **Desideria**, originally for a long-awaited, much-desired child. The French boy's name **Didier**, 'longing', shortened to **Didi**, would be the male equivalent.

Desmond *m.*

From the Irish *Deas-Mumhain*, meaning '(man) of Desmond', i.e. Munster. It was originally used as a surname in Ireland. Later it became a first name, and came to England in the late 19th century. **Des** and **Desi**, **Desy** or **Dezi** are short forms.

Destiny *f.*

This vocabulary word has recently become popular as a girl's name in the USA.

Detta *see* Bernadette

Dev *m.*

An Indian name from the Sanskrit meaning 'god'. Deva is also the term used to address royalty, Brahmins and priests. Dev becomes **Deb** or **Deo** in different parts of India.

Devdan *m.*

This Indian name is from the Sanskrit and means 'gift of the gods'. The forms **Debdan** and **Deodan** are used in some parts of India.

Devnet *see* Dymphna

Devon *f. and m.*

This name appears to be the name of the English county, but American parents usually stress it on the second syllable. Its use was probably suggested when 'De-' became a fashionable prefix for names among Afro-American families, as in **DEANDRE**. The alternative spelling **Devin** is frequent and forms such as **DaVon** are also found.

DeWayne *see* DeAndre, Duane

Dezi *see* Desmond

Dhanishta *f.*

An Indian name that derives from the Sanskrit for 'star'.

Di *see* **Diana**

Diamond *f.*

The name of this precious stone has only recently found favour with Afro-Americans. It was rarely used when other jewel names, such as BERYL, PEARL and RUBY were popular at the start of the 20th century.

Diana *f.*

The Latin name of the Roman goddess, equivalent to the Greek, **Artemis**. She was associated with the moon and virginity. She was also the goddess of hunting and protector of wild animals. Its use as a first name dates from the Renaissance, when the French form **Diane** is also first found. **Di** is the commonest short form, as seen in the popular nickname for the Princess of Wales. Despite her immense popularity the name is not widely used, although it was given to rather more babies than usual in the months following her death in 1997. The actress **Deanna** Durbin introduced a different form of the name, and the form **Deanne** is also found, while Diane has developed forms such as **Dianne** and **Dyan(ne)**. DINAH is a separate name.

Diarm(a)id, Diarm(a)it *see* **Dermot**

Dick, Dickie, Dickon *see* **Richard**

Didi, Didier *see* Desirée

Diego *m.*

This popular Spanish name is well used in the USA. It is a form of **JAMES**, through the intermediary forms Tiego and Tiago, from Sant Iago, 'Saint James'.

Dieudonné, Dieudonnée *see* Donata

Digby *m.*

A place and surname, meaning 'the settlement by the dike', used as a first name.

Dilip *m.*

The name of several kings in the Hindu epics. It is probably derived from the Sanskrit words which mean 'protecting Delhi'. An alternative form of the name is **Duleep**.

Dilys *f.*

From the Welsh, meaning 'perfect, genuine'. The name became current in Wales in the 19th century, and is now no longer confined to Wales. **Dilly** is a short form.

Dimitri *see* Demetrius

Dinah *f.*

From the Hebrew, meaning 'lawsuit' or 'judged'. It was the name of one of Jacob's daughters in the Old

Testament. It came into use in the 17th century and was a favourite name in the 19th century, when it often confused with **DIANA**. Nowadays it is often spelt **Dina**.

Dinsdale *m.*

A place and surname used as a first name. It means 'settlement surrounded by a moat'.

Dion, Dione, Dionne, Dionysos
see **Denis**

Dipak *see* **Deepak**

Dirk *see* **Derek**

Divya *f.*

An Indian name derived from the Sanskrit for 'divine lustre'.

Djamila *see* **Jamila**

Dmitri *see* **Demetrius**

Dodie, Dodo, Doll, Dolly *see* **Dorothy**

Doireann *see* **Doreen**

Dolores *f.*

This name was originally a short form of the Spanish *Maria de los Dolores*, or 'Mary of the Sorrows', after the feast of the 'Seven Sorrows of Our Lady'. Spain uses other names from titles of the Virgin: **Mercedes** (Our Lady of the Mercies) and **Montserrat**, from Our Lady of Montserrat, a famous monastery. Dolores became popular in North America about 1930. Pet forms are LOLA, **Lolita** and **Lo**.

Dolph, Dolphus *see* Adolph

Domhnall *see* Daniel, Donald

Dominic *m.*, Dominique *f.*

From the Latin *dominicus* meaning 'of the Lord'. It probably became more widespread on account of St Dominic, founder of the Order of Preachers known as the Black Friars early in the 13th century. Until this century it was almost exclusively a Roman Catholic name, but is now widely used. **Dominick** is also found, and the name can be shortened to **Dom**. **Dominique**, from the French, is now the most popular form for girls, although **Dominica**, the original Latin feminine form, is sometimes used.

Donald *m.*

From the Irish **Domhnall** or **Donal(l)** (the second reflecting the pronunciation, with a long 'o' as in 'doe') meaning 'world mighty'. It was the name of a number of medieval Irish kings. This became Donald in Gaelic. Common short forms are **Don** and **Donny**. Various forms of the name were coined in the Highlands to turn

Donald into a girl's name, of which **Donalda** and **Donella** have been the commonest.

Donata *f.*

This name is far more often used than its male equivalent, **Donatus** or **Donat**, both Latin for 'given [by God]'. The Old French equivalent was **Dieudonné(e)**, which is still very occasionally found.

Donella *see* Donald

Donna *f.*

This is the Italian word for 'lady'. It has been popular as a first name in the 20th century, particularly in North America. **Madonna**, 'My Lady', in use in the USA by the 1930s, comes from the same word.

Donnchadh *see* Denis, Duncan

Donny *see* Donald

Donovan *m.*

An Irish surname, meaning 'dark brown', used as a first name. It gained publicity as the name of a popular singer from the 1960s.

Dora *f.*

Originally this name was a short form of **DOROTHY** and **THEODORA**, but it is now a name in its own right. It came into use at the beginning of the 19th century. A pet form is **Dorrie**, shared with other names like **DOREEN** and **DORIS**.

Dorcas *f.*

From the Greek for 'gazelle'. In the New Testament it was used as a Greek translation of the Aramaic **TABITHA**, the name of the woman raised from the dead by St Peter. The name was later used to describe groups of women who made clothes for the needy.

Doreen *f.*

From the Irish **Doireann**, a name sometimes found in English spelling as **Dorren**. Its origin is rather obscure, but in Irish mythology it is the name of at least two supernatural beings. A short form is **Dorrie,** and the name can also be spelt **Dorinne**.

Dorian *f. and m.*

The ancient Greek people known as Dorians came from Doris in the north, but later dominated southern Greece. The best-known group were the Spartans. The word was introduced as a first name in Oscar Wilde's *The Picture of Dorian Gray* (1891). Like so many boy's names, it is now used as a girl's name as well. It is now also spelt **Dorien** or **Dorrien** and for girls **Dorianne** and **Doriana**. Forms such as **Darian** and **Darien** can be seen as either a form of this name, or a blend of such names as **DARIUS** and **DARREN**.

Dorinda *f.*

This name was invented in the 18th century as a poetic variation of **DOROTHY** and **DORA**. Many other forms,

like **BELINDA** and **Clarinda** (see **CLARE**), were invented at
this time.

Dorinne *see* **Doreen**

Doris *f.*

The name of a sea nymph in Greek mythology, possibly
meaning 'bountiful', and also a term for a woman
member of the **DORIAN** people of Greece. In classical
literature it was used as a poetic name for a lovely
woman. It came into common use at the end of the 19th
century and was popular into the 1930s. A short form is
Dorrie.

Dorothy, Dorothea *f.*

From the Greek meaning 'gift of God'. The name is
found in Britain from the end of the 15th century and
has been in use ever since. In the 16th century, it was
abbreviated to **Doll(y)**, and was so popular that the toy
became known as a doll, Doll being such a likely name
for a baby. In Scottish dialect, a doll is sometimes called
a **Dorrity**. Later short forms are **DORA**, **Dot**, **Dottie**,
Dodo, **Dodie** and **Thea** (see also **THEODORA**).

Dorren *see* **Doreen**

Dorrie *see* **Dora, Doreen, Doris**

Dorrien *see* **Dorian**

Dorrity, Dot, Dottie *see* **Dorothy**

Doug, Dougie *see* **Douglas**

Dougal, Dugal(d) *m.*

From the Irish *dubh ghall*, meaning 'dark stranger', a name given to the Danish Vikings. It was a common first name in the Scottish Highlands, and while it still has strong Scottish associations, it now has a more general use.

Douglas *m.*

From the Gaelic *dubh glas*, meaning 'black stream'. It was first a Celtic river name, then the surname of a powerful Scottish family famous for its strength and bravery in fighting, and then from about the late 16th century a first name for both girls and boys. It is now restricted to boys. **Duggie** and **Doug(ie)** are pet forms.

Drew *m.*

From the Old German **Drogo**, meaning 'to carry' or 'to bear', a name which was brought to Britain by the Normans and later became a surname. This surname, which like any other, can also be used as a first name, may also come from two other sources: as a short form of **Andrew**, probably the commonest form of Drew as a first name, and from an old French word for 'lover'. Parents wishing to use this name may take their choice. It has recently been used occasionally for girls.

Drusilla *f.*

A feminine form of the Latin Drusus, a Roman family name, possibly meaning 'firm'. It occurs in the New

Testament and was adopted in the 17th century by the
Puritans. It is still used occasionally, mainly in
North America.

Duane, Dwayne *m.*

An Irish surname, probably meaning 'black', used as a
first name. Pop star Duane Eddy made the name better
known in the 1950s. More recently it has developed
exotic variants such as **DeWayne** or **Du'aine**.

Dudley *m.*

Originally a surname derived from the place of that
name in Worcestershire. Robert Dudley, Earl of
Leicester, was the favourite of Queen Elizabeth for many
years. Like other aristocratic names it was adopted for
general use as a first name in the 19th century. **Dud** is
used as a short form.

Dugal(d) *see* Dougal

Duggie *see* Douglas

Duke *see* Marmaduke

Dulcie *f.*

Dulcie is a name coined in the 19th century from the
Latin *dulcis*, meaning 'sweet'. There was an earlier name,
Dulcibella ('fair and sweet'), which in popular speech
became Dowsabel. Dulcie was very popular in the early

years of this century, but now has an old-fashioned ring to it.

Duleep *see* Dilip

Duncan *m.*

The Scots form of the Irish **Donnchadh** (pronounced *don*-ne-ha, the 'h' ideally the sound in Scottish 'loch'), meaning 'brown'. It was the name of two Scottish kings and at one time was almost entirely confined to Scotland, although this is no longer the case.

Dunstan *m.*

From the Old English words *dun*, meaning 'hill' and *stan*, meaning 'stone'. It was the name of a famous 10th-century Archbishop of Canterbury. It appears from time to time before the Reformation, and was revived by the Oxford Movement in the 19th century.

Durga *f.*

The name of the Hindu goddess, the wife of **SHIVA**, when depicted in her terrifying form. Durga is from a Sanskrit word for 'inaccessible'.

Dustin *m.*

Best known from the actor Dustin Hoffman, this name has recently been very popular in the USA. It may be from a place name meaning 'dusty', or could be a form of **Thurstan**, a Norse name meaning 'Thor's stone', i.e. an altar dedicated to the thunder god Thor.

Dwayne *see* **Duane**

Dwight *m.*

Originally an English surname, which may go back to the same source as **DENIS**. The use of this name as a first name in the United States probably arose from respect for Timothy Dwight, President of Yale University (1795–1817). US President Dwight D. Eisenhower gave a wider circulation to the name.

Dyan, Dyanne *see* **Diana**

Dylan *m.*

This is the name of a legendary Welsh hero, son of the sea god, possibly meaning 'son of the wave'. It was rare outside Wales, but the Welsh poet, Dylan Thomas, made it more familiar to the general public. The singer, Bob Dylan, often referred to by his second name, took his stage name from the poet and has increased its use.

Dymp(h)na *f.*

The anglicized form of the Irish **Damhnait**, the name of an Irish virgin martyr. It means 'fawn, little deer'. The English form is pronounced with a 'pf' or just 'p' in the middle, the Irish name something like 'dav-nit' and is often spelt **DEVNET**.

E

Eachan *see* **Hector**

Eadan *see* **Etain**

Eamon(n) *see* **Edmund**

Earl *m.*
From the noble title, in Old English meaning a
'nobleman' or 'chief'. This has been used as a first name
in the last hundred years, mainly in North America.
Erle is a variant spelling, as in the author Erle Stanley
Gardiner.

Earnest *see* **Ernest**

Eartha *f.*
From the Old English *eorthe*, meaning 'earth'. A famous
modern example is the singer and actress Eartha Kitt,
but the name is rare outside the southern US, where
Ertha and **Erthel** are also found.

Ebenezer *m.*
From the Hebrew meaning 'stone of help'. In the Old
Testament it is the name of a stone which Samuel called
Ebenezer, in memory of the triumph of the Jews over the

Philistine army and in thanks for God's help. It was first used as a first name in the 17th century among the Puritans. It is now used mainly in North America, with the shortened form **Eben**.

Ebony *f.*

The name of an intensely black wood which symbolizes blackness, Ebony began to be used by Afro-American parents in the 1970s. It reached a peak of popularity in the 1980s after the song *Ebony and Ivory* by Paul McCartney and Stevie Wonder, but then began to fade. Its other spellings include **Ebbony**, **Eboney**, **Eboni**, **Ebonie** and **Ebonnee**.

Ed, Eddie *see* Edgar, Edmund, Edward

Edan, Edana *see* Aidan, Edna

Edgar *m.*

From the Old English meaning 'fortunate spear'. Owing to the popularity of King Edgar, King Alfred's grandson, the name continued in use after the Norman Conquest, but it faded out at the end of the 13th century. It was then used by Shakespeare in *King Lear*, and revived with other Old English names by 18th-century writers of fiction. Its popularity in the 19th century probably stems from its use for the hero of Scott's novel *The Bride of Lammermoor*. It is now a fairly unusual name, sometimes shortened to **Ed** or **Eddie**.

Edie *see* Edith

Edina *see* Edna

Edith *f.*

From the Old English name Eadgyth, meaning 'fortunate war'. There were at least two English saints of that name in the 10th century. The name survived the Norman Conquest and was probably adopted by the Normans and used to replace several English names. Edith was in use throughout the Middle Ages, after which it became rather rare, but it returned to favour in the 19th and early 20th centuries. Often shortened to **Edie**, it has a rare form, **Editha**.

Edmund *m.*

From the Old English Eadmund, meaning 'happy protection'. It was the name of two kings of England and of two saints. **Edmond** is the French form which was used from the late Middle Ages. **Eamon(n)** is the Irish form. It was well used in the 19th century, then went rather out of fashion but is now steadily coming back into use. Shortened forms are **Ed**, **Eddie**, **Ted** and **Teddy**.

Edna *f.*

One source of this name may be **Edana**, a feminine form of the Irish name **Edan**, meaning 'fire' (see **AIDAN**). It has also been connected with a shortened form of **Edwina** (see **EDWIN**), via **Edina**. In addition the name occurs twice in the Apocrypha and its Hebrew meaning is probably 'rejuvenation'. The modern use of it may stem from the popularity of the novelist Edna Lyall in the late 19th century.

Edward *m.*

From the Old English meaning 'fortunate guardian'. Edward the Confessor established its popularity in England and ensured its survival after the Norman Conquest. It was further strengthened by the accession of Edward I, after which there was an Edward on the English throne for over a hundred years, and it has remained in use ever since. The short forms **Ned** and **Ted**, together with **Neddy** or **Teddy**, have been used since the 14th century, but **Ed** and **Eddie** are the more common abbreviated forms found today.

Edwin *m.,* Edwina *f.*

From the Old English meaning 'fortunate friend'. This was the name of the first Christian king of Northumbria in the 7th century. The name survived the Norman Conquest and became popular in the 18th century. There has recently been an increase in the number of parents choosing it for their child, particularly as a second name. Edwina is a 19th-century female form.

Effie *see* Euphemia

Egbert *m.*

From the Old English meaning 'bright sword'. This was the name of the first king of a united England and of a 7th-century Northumbrian saint. It enjoyed some degree of popularity in the 19th century, but is now rarely found.

Eibhlin *see* Evelyn

Eileen *f.*

An Irish development of **EVELYN**. Like other Irish names it spread throughout Britain at the beginning of the 20th century. **Eily** is a short form. It is not uncommon to find it spelt **Aileen**.

Eilis, Ailis *f.*

In theory Eilis, sometimes spelt **Eil(l)ish** to reflect its pronunciation, is an Irish form of **ELIZABETH**, and Ailis (**Ailish**) an Irish form of **ALICE**, but in practice many users do not distinguish between the two.

Eithne *f.*

A name prominent in Irish legend and history, being used by a goddess, a number of queens and no less than nine saints. It means 'kernel' which in old Irish poetry is a term of praise. Modern variants include **Ethne, Ethna, Aithne** and the phonetic **Enya.**

Ekata *f.*

An Indian name from the Sanskrit meaning 'unity'.

Elaine *f.*

An Old French form of **HELEN**, which occurs in medieval literature. It came into general use through the popularity of Tennyson's *Idylls of the King* (1859), which is based on Malory's *Morte d'Arthur* and which includes the story of *Lancelot and Elaine*. There is also a Welsh name **Elain**, meaning 'fawn'.

Eleanor *f.*

Eleanor and **Elinor** are French forms of HELEN which have been used in this country since the Middle Ages. **Eleanora**, the Italian form which gives us LEONORA, is also found, as is **Elena**. Eleanor is shortened to **Ellie** (currently very popular as a given name), ELLA, ELLEN, NELL and NORA.

Elfrida *see* Alfred

Eli *m.*

From the Hebrew meaning 'elevated'. It was the name of the high priest in the Old Testament who looked after the prophet Samuel when he was given to the Temple as a baby. It was used as a first name in the 17th century and is also a shortened form of ELIAS, **Eliza** (see ELIZABETH) and **Elihu**, which means 'God is the Lord'.

Elias, Elijah *m.*

From the Hebrew meaning 'Jehovah is God'. Both forms were very common in the Middle Ages, along with the diminutives **Ellis** and **Eliot(t)** or **Elliot** which became surnames, and are now used as first names.

Elihu *see* Eli

Elinor *see* **Eleanor**

Eliot *see* **Elias**

Elissa *m.*

A name by which Dido, Queen of Carthage, was known,
but in modern use it is probably a pet form of
ELIZABETH. The Austrian-Italian film actress Elissa
Landi (whose full name was Elizabeth Zanardi-Landi),
was well known in the 1930s.

Elizabeth, Elisabeth *f.*

From the Hebrew *Elisheba*, meaning 'oath of God' or
'God has sworn'. The present form developed from the
Greek **Elisabet** through the Latin **Elisabetha** to
Elizabeth. In Britain the 'z' form is usual, on the
Continent the 's' is used, although in the Authorized
Version of the New Testament; the name is spelt
Elisabeth. It was first used by members of the Eastern
Church, then found its way across Europe to France,
where it developed the form **ISABEL(LE)**. This was also
the usual medieval form in England. Elizabeth became
common about the end of the 15th century, and its later
popularity in England stemmed from the long reign of
Elizabeth I. Among the many pet forms are: **Bess(ie)**,
Betsy, **Betty**, **Beth** (with **Bethan** in Wales, see **BETHANY**),
Eliza, **Lizzy**, **Liz**, **Liza**, **Libby** and the Scottish **Elspeth**,
Elspie and **Elsie**, which are now used independently.
The German **ELSA**, **Elissa**, **Lisa**, **Liese** or **Liesel**, the

Italian **BETTINA**, and the French **Elise**, **Lisette** and **Babette**, are also used in Britain.

Elke *f.*

A German pet form of the name **ALICE**. It is found in a slightly different form used by the singer **Elkie** Brooks.

Ella *f.*

A name used by the Normans probably derived from the Old German **Alia**, meaning 'all'. It can also be a pet form of **Isabella** (see **ISABEL**), **ELLEN** or **ELEANOR** and is currently an increasingly popular choice for parents (see also **LUELLA**).

Ellen *f.*

An older English form of **HELEN**, now used independently, and also a short form of **ELEANOR**. In the past it has been especially popular in Scotland and Ireland and is now showing signs of wider popularity.

Ellie *see* **Eleanor**

Elliot(t), Ellis *see* **Elias**

Elmer *m.*

This is a surname which comes from both the Old English Ethelmer, 'noble and famous' and Ethelward, 'noble guard'. It became a first name in the USA in

honour of two brothers with the surname Elmer who
were prominent in the American War of Independence.
Aylmer is another form of the name. While **Elma** is
actually a short form of **Wilhelmina**, a German feminine
of **WILLIAM**, it can also be used as a female form of
Elmer.

Eloise *f.*

Currently, the more popular version of the name known
to history as **Heloise**. Abelard and Heloise were two
famous and tragic 12th-century lovers, and Heloise was
renowned for her beauty, intellect and faithfulness in
love. The name can be spelt **Heloïse** or **Eloïse** and
sometimes occurs as **Eloisa**. Experts do not agree on its
origins: some say it is an Old German name perhaps
meaning 'helmet power'; others say it comes from the
same source as **LEWIS** by way of an old southern French
name **Aloys** or **Aloyse** (see **ALOYSIUS**).

Elsa, Elsie *f.*

One source of Elsa is the Old German for 'noble one',
but both names are also used as abbreviations of
ELIZABETH, and Elsie is sometimes a short form of
ALISON. Elsie was originally Scottish and is the more
common form in Britain. Elsa is the heroine in Wagner's
opera *Lohengrin*, which made the name popular in the
19th century.

Elspeth, Elspie *see* Elizabeth

Elton *m.*

A surname, probably meaning 'Ella's settlement', used as a first name. The singer, Elton John, effectively began its first-name use.

Eluned *f.*

This Welsh name, seldom used outside Wales, is connected with the word for 'idol'. The short form **Luned** is the origin of LYNETTE.

Elvira *f.*

A Spanish name, probably introduced by the conquering Visigoths in the Dark Ages. Its meaning is not clear. It has been used occasionally since the beginning of the 19th century. It is perhaps best known as the name of the ghost in Noël Coward's play, *Blithe Spirit*.

Elvis *m.*

A name that was almost unknown until given world fame by Elvis Presley. It is probably a version of the name of the Irish saint **Ailbhe** (a name which in Irish can be used for either sex, and which is pronounced 'alva') or **Alby**, which is found in Wales in the form St Elvis. Although Presley was not the first member of his family to bear the name, modern uses are all thanks to him.

Emanuel *m.*

From the Hebrew meaning 'God with us'. It was the name given to the promised Messiah by the prophet

Isaiah in the Old Testament. It was introduced as a first name by the Greeks in the form **Manuel**. This is also the Spanish form. **Manny** is used as a pet form, and there is a feminine, **Em(m)anuelle**.

Emer *f.*

Emer (pronounced with a long 'ee' at the beginning) is currently one of the more popular Celtic names in Ireland. In legend it was the name of the woman loved by Cuchulainn, the great hero of the Ulster cycle of legends. She is described as having the following six desirable gifts: those of beauty, voice, sweet speech, skill with the needle, wisdom and chastity. It is occasionally found as **Emir**.

Emerald *see* **Esmeralda**

Emily *f.*

From the Latin Aemilius, the name of a Roman family. Boccaccio, the 14th-century Italian writer, used **Emilia**, popularizing this form in the Middle Ages, and Chaucer borrowed it in the form Emelye. The name has persisted since then, becoming very common as Emily in the 19th century, when it was sometimes shortened to **EMMA**. Nowadays, these two names are among the most popular girls' names. **Milly** is a pet form. It may be the popularity of Emily that has led to signs of an increased use of the masculine form **Emil** or **Emile** for boys. **Emmeline** is an old French pet form.

Emir *see* **Emer**

Emlyn *m.*

A common Welsh name, possibly derived from the Latin Aemilius, also the source of **EMILY**, but which is more likely to be from a Welsh place-name.

Emma *f.*

A shortened form of Old German compound names beginning *ermen* meaning 'universal', as in the name *Ermyntrude*, 'universal strength'. It was introduced to England by Emma, daughter of Richard I, Duke of Normandy. The English form was Em(m), and this was used until the mid-18th century, when the original form was revived. Jane Austen's novel *Emma* (1816) has also been influential. Today, Emma is one of the commonest girls' names. **Emmy** is a pet form, and Emma is also used as a short form of **EMILY**.

Emmeline *see* **Emily**

Emmy *see* **Emma**

Emrys *see* **Ambrose**

Ena *f.*

This name can come from a number of sources. It can be a short form of any name ending with '-ina' or '-ena', or an English form of **EITHNE**, but its popularity in the last century came from the affection for Queen Victoria's daughter, Princess Ena, who became Queen of Spain. Her name came from neither of these sources, but was due to a misreading of her intended name 'Eva' at her christening.

Enid *f.*

This is a Welsh name, meaning 'life, soul', that came into use in England in the 19th century through Tennyson's Arthurian poem, *Geraint and Enid* in *Idylls of the King* (1859).

Enoch *m.*

From the Hebrew, meaning 'trained, skilled' or 'dedicated'. It was the name of an Old Testament patriarch and was adopted in the 17th century by the Puritans. It is now rare, although a well-known modern example is the politician, Enoch Powell.

Enya *see* **Eithne**

Eoan, Eoghan *see* **Eugene**

Eoin *see* **John**

Ephraim *m.*

From the Hebrew meaning 'fruitful', an Old Testament name that was revived in the 17th century by the

Puritans. It is seldom used in England, but is still found in North America. **Eph** is a short form.

Eppie *see* **Euphemia**

Erasmus *m.*

From the Greek, meaning 'beloved, desired', and the name of an early Christian martyr. The Dutch scholar and religious reformer Desiderius Erasmus (1465–1536) made the name famous, although it was used in Britain before his influence was felt. **Erastus** comes from the same root. The short form **Rastus** is better known in Britain and in North America, but the name is rare.

Eric *m.*, Erica *f.*

From Scandinavia; the second syllable means 'ruler', the first is doubtful but may mean 'ever'. The name was brought to Britain by the Danes about the 9th century. Possibly Dean Farrar's book *Eric or Little by Little* was responsible for its popularity with 19th-century parents. Erica, the feminine form, is now sometimes identified with the Latin botanical name for heather. Both forms are sometimes spelt with a 'k' instead of 'c'. Short forms are **Rick**, **Rickie** or **Ricky**.

Erin *f.*

From the Gaelic *Eireann*, a poetical term for Ireland. It is a modern name, particularly popular in the USA and Australia.

Erle *see* **Earl**

Ermyntrude *see* **Emma**

Ernest *m.*

From the Old German, meaning 'vigour' or
'earnestness'. It is sometimes spelt **Earnest**. It was
introduced by the Hanoverians in the late 18th century
and was common in the 19th century. Oscar Wilde's play,
The Importance of Being Earnest (1899) increased its
popularity. **Ernestine**, the female form, like Ernest, is
not very common today. Shortened forms are **Ern** and
Ernie.

Errol *m.*

Probably a surname used as a first name, although it is
not certain whether the surname is a development of
Eral, a medieval form of **HAROLD**, or whether it is a
variant of **EARL**.

Ertha, Erthel *see* Eartha

Esmé *f. and m.*

Probably from the French for 'esteemed', but is now
usually treated as synonymous with the French **Aimée**,
meaning 'beloved' (see **AMY**). It passed from France to
Scotland in the 16th century, and then much later
to England. It is now more often used as a girl's name, in
which case it can also take the forms **Esmée** and **Esma**.

Esmeralda *f.*

The Spanish for 'emerald'. The 19th-century French writer Victor Hugo used it for the heroine in his novel *The Hunchback of Notre Dame*, and it has occasionally been used since in Britain and France. The English form **Emerald** is also found, as is the form **Esmeraldah.**

Esmond *m.*

From the Old English *east* and *mund*, meaning 'grace' and 'protection'. This name was never common and fell out of use in the 14th century. Its modern use probably dates from Thackeray's novel *The History of Henry Esmond* (1852). It is nowadays rather rare.

Ess, Essie, Essy *see* Esther

Essylt *see* Isolda

Estella *f.*

A blend of the Latin *stella* and the French *étoile*, 'star'. It was a French name given by Dickens to the main female character in *Great Expectations*, and has been used since. **Estelle** is another form. It sometimes shares the shortened forms of **ESTHER** (see also **STELLA**).

Esther *f.*

In the Old Testament, this name is the Persian equivalent of a Hebrew word meaning 'myrtle'. It was frequently used in the form **Hester** and appears in England in the 17th century, adopted by the Puritans. It can also be spelt **Ester**. Shortened forms include **Essy**, **Essie** and **Ess**, with Hester becoming **Hetty**.

Etain *f.*

In Irish legend, *The Wooing of Etain* is the story of the love of the fairy Princess Etain of the Fair Hair for a mortal man. This tale was retold in an opera called *The Immortal Hour* first performed in 1914. The opera was a great success at the time, and led to a use of the name outside Ireland. In Ireland the name is usually **Etan** or **Eadan** and pronounced 'ad-an'.

Ethan *m.*

This is a Hebrew name meaning 'firmness', which occurs several times in the Old Testament. It is more popular in the United States than in Britain.

Ethel *f.*

Not originally an independent name, but developed in the 19th century as a shortening of various Anglo-Saxon names beginning with the root 'Ethel-', from *aethel*, meaning 'noble' (see **AUDREY**).

Ethelbert *see* **Albert**

Etheldreda *see* **Audrey**

E

Eugene *m.*, Eugenie *f.*

From the Greek meaning 'well-born'. In North America the masculine form is usually abbreviated to **Gene**. The Celtic names **Eoghan** (pronounced 'eoh-un') or **Eoan** ('ohn'), and their Scots form **Ewan**, **Ewen** or **Euan** have traditionally been interpreted as forms of Eugene, although sometimes confused with **Eoin**, a form of **John**. However, some would claim that they are a native Celtic name meaning 'born of the yew'. **Eugenie**, the French feminine form, came into use from the French Empress Eugénie (1826–1920) who spent the last 50 years of her life in England. **Eugenia** is also used for girls.

Eunice *f.*

From the Greek, meaning 'happy victory'. The name is mentioned in the New Testament and was adopted by the Puritans in the 17th century. In Greek it is pronounced as three syllables, with a hard 'c' and the final 'e' sounded, but modern users soften the 'c' if they use the three-syllable pronunciation or more often use the pronunciation indicated by the phonetic spelling **Unice**.

Euphemia *f.*

From the Greek, meaning 'fair speech' or, by implication, 'silence'. It occurs as **Eufemia** and **Euphemie** from the 12th century. Later it became confined to Scotland, where it is still found, usually abbreviated to **Effie** (very popular at the beginning of the century), **Eppie** or, occasionally, **FAY** or **PHOEBE**.

Eustace *m.*

From the Greek meaning 'rich in corn' and hence 'fruitful' generally. Because of the two saints Eustachius, this name was in use in Britain before the Norman Conquest and was popular from the 12th to the 16th centuries. **Eustacia**, the female form, was used in the 18th and 19th centuries but is now rare. A short form, **STACEY** (or **Stacy**), is now a name in its own right.

Eva *see* Eve

Evadne *f.*

This is a Greek name of uncertain meaning. It was used occasionally in the early part of the 20th century but became better known recently because of the character of Evadne Hinge of the Hinge and Brackett comic duo.

Evaline *see* **Evelyn**

Evan *m.*

This is a Welsh form of **JOHN**, the anglicized form of the Welsh spelt variously **Iefan**, **Ifan** or **Ieuan**. In Scotland it is also an anglicized form of the Irish **Eoghan** (see **EUGENE**).

Evangeline *f.*

From the Greek meaning 'bringer of good news', the same word that gives us 'evangelist'. It was first introduced by Longfellow for his poem *Evangeline* (1847), and still tends to have a rather literary flavour. **Evangelina** is also found.

Eve *f.*

From the Hebrew meaning 'life', and in the Old Testament this is the name of the first woman. **Eva** is the Latin form, Eve the English. It was in use in Britain even before the Reformation, when Old Testament names were not generally popular. In Ireland it was used as a substitute for the earlier Gaelic **Aoife** (pronounced 'ee-fa'), meaning 'radiant', currently a very popular name. The pet form of Eve is **Evie** and **Evita** is a Spanish pet form (see also **ZOE**).

Evelyn *f. and m.*

When the Normans conquered Ireland they brought with them a girl's name **Aveline**, meaning 'wished for (child)'. It was adopted by the Irish in the form **Eibhlin** (pronounced either with the 'bh' as a 'v', or silent, giving **EILEEN**), which in turn was anglicized **Eveline** or **Eveleen** and later developed forms such as **Evaline**, **Evelena** and **Evelina**. It was also adopted as a surname, usually spelt Evelyn, and around the 17th century the surname started to be used for boys. The boy's form is usually spelt Evelyn; all spellings are used for girls.

Everard *m.*

From the Old German for 'brave boar'. The name was brought to Britain by the Normans and was fairly common in England in the 12th and 13th centuries and has been used occasionally ever since. In Scotland, it became **Ewart**. The surname **Everett** comes from Everard, and is also used as a first name.

Everild, Everilda *see* Averil

Evie, Evita *see* Eve

Ewan, Ewen *see* Eugene

Ewart *see* Everard

Ezekiel *m.*

From the Hebrew meaning 'may God strengthen'. It is the name of an Old Testament prophet, and was used from the 17th century in Britain. It is still current in North America and is beginning to re-appear here. **Zeke** is the usual short form.

Ezra *m.*

From the Hebrew meaning 'help', Ezra is the name of the author of one of the books of the Old Testament. It was adopted as a first name by the Puritans in the 17th century. The name is no longer common, but a well-known example from the 20th century is the American poet, Ezra Pound.

F

Fabian _m._

From the Latin family name Fabianus, possibly meaning 'bean-grower'. There was a pope of this name and a St Fabian in the 3rd century, and there is a record of the name's use by a 13th-century sub-prior of St Albans. There is little other evidence of it until the 16th century, but its use as a surname shows that it was known previously. The Roman general **Fabius**, known as the 'delayer' for his tactics of awaiting the right moment to achieve his ends, was the inspiration for the socialist Fabian Society, founded in 1884. A female form, **Fabienne**, comes from the French **Fabien**. Spanish forms are **Fabio**, and **Fabiola** for girls.

Fahimah _f._

A Muslim name from the Arabic for 'discerning' or 'intelligent'.

Faisal _see_ **Faysal**

Faith _f._

One of the Christian virtues used as names after the Reformation. It was formerly used for both sexes, but is now a girl's name. **FAY(E)** or **Fae** is a short form.

Fallon *f.*

This is an English form of the Irish surname 'O Fallamhain', or 'leader'. It was made known as a first name by a character in the TV series *Dynasty* and came into limited use in the USA and Britain as a result, but does not seem to have established itself.

Farah *f.*

From the Arabic meaning 'joy, cheerfulness'. **Farrah** is also found. American actress Farrah Fawcett claimed that her parents were unaware that Farah existed when they invented her first name.

Farall *see* **Fergal**

Farhanah *f.*

A Muslim name from the Arabic for 'joyful' or 'delighted'.

Farrell *see* **Fergal**

Fatima *f.*

This is an Arabic name which means either 'chaste' or 'motherly'. It was the name of the Prophet Muhammad's favourite daughter, the only one of his children to have children of her own. It has been popular in the USA with Black Muslims. It is also occasionally used in a Christian context in honour of Our Lady of Fatima.

Faustine *f.*

Fausta and **Faustus** were names given to his twin

children by the ancient Roman dictator, Sulla. The names mean 'fortunate' and Sulla had always considered himself particularly blessed with good luck, taking the nickname **FELIX**. **Faustine** is the French form of the name. Although the two girls' names are sometimes used, the legend of Dr Faustus, who sells his soul to the Devil, has made it difficult to use the boy's name.

Fawn *f.*

The word for a young deer used as a first name.

Fay *f.*

A short form of both **FAITH** and **EUPHEMIA**, and also an old form of the word 'faith'. In addition it is an old version of the French word for 'fairy' found in the name of the Arthurian enchantress Morgana le Fay. It was in use by 1872, at least in fiction. It is also spelt **Faye**.

Faysal *m.*

This Arabic name indicates one who decides between right and wrong, a decision-maker or a judge. This has been a royal name in modern times, borne by kings of Iraq and Saudi Arabia. The name is also found as **Faisal** and **Feisal**.

Feargus *see* **Fergus**

Fedelm, Feidhelm *see* **Fidelma**

Feisal *see* **Faysal**

Felice, Felicia *see* Felix

Felicity *f.*

From the Latin *felicitas*, meaning 'happiness'. It was the name of two saints and was used by the Puritans in the 17th century.

Felix *m.*, Felicia *f.*

From the Latin meaning 'happy, lucky'. Felix was widely used in the Middle Ages and had a fairly strong hold in Ireland, where it was used to replace the Irish **Phelim**. It is currently enjoying a revival in popularity. The female form, Felicia, has a long history of use and was also very popular in the Middle Ages. **Felice** was a variant form.

Fenella *f.*

A Gaelic name meaning 'white-shouldered'. The name became known in Britain in the 19th century as a result of Sir Walter Scott's novel *Peveril of the Peak*. The Irish form of the name is **Finola** or **Fionnuala** (pronounced 'Fin-noola'), which can be shortened to **Nola** or **Nuala**. Some years ago the Scottish form was the more popular choice, but this has probably now been overtaken by the Irish.

Ferdinand *m.*

From the Old German for 'brave journey'. Never a popular name in Germany, it was common in Spain, especially in the forms Fernando and Hernando. Short forms are **Ferd, Ferdie** and occasionally **Nandy**. At the moment the name is being used slightly more often than before.

Fergal *m.*

This is an Irish name meaning 'valorous'. The surnames **Farrell** and **Farall**, which come from it, reflect the Irish pronunciation.

Fergus *m.*

Fergus or **Feargus** come from the Irish words for 'man' and 'strength'. It is a fairly common first name in Scotland and Ireland and is also used in the North of England. **Fergie** is a short form.

Fern *f.*

The plant name used as a first name.

Ffion *f.*

Ffion is the Welsh word for the foxglove flower, and a word used in poetry to describe the cheek of a beautiful girl.

Fi *see* **Fiona**

Fidelma *f.*

The more usual form of the Irish name **Fedelm** or **Feidhelm** (in modern Irish, pronounced 'fed-elm'). Its meaning is not clear, but several of the early women who bore the name were famous for their beauty.

Fifi *see* Josephine

Finbar, Finnbar, Fionnbharr *see* Barry

Finch *see* Raven

Fingal *m.*

This is the name given to the Scottish legendary hero
(the equivalent of the Irish **FINN**), who figures in the
18th-century Ossianic poetry. He was a mighty warrior,
a defender of the underdog and righter of wrongs.
Fingal's Cave is named after him. The name means
'blond stranger' and was a term used of the Vikings.

Finn *m.*

Finn or **Fionn** is an Irish name meaning 'white, fair' or
can also be used as a pet form of **Finbar** (see **BARRY**).
Finn Mac Coul (Finn mac Cumaill) is a great hero of
Irish mythology and folklore. He was chosen to lead the
Fenians (an elite armed troop) because of his
truthfulness, wisdom and generosity, but he was also of
great physical strength. However, all these qualities were
not enough to prevent Finn's fiancée **GRAINNE** from
running away with his companion, **DERMOT**. **Finnian** or
Finian comes from the same root, and was the name of
a 6th-century British saint; **Fintan** means either 'white
ancient one' or 'white fire'.

Finola *see* Fenella

Fintan *see* Finn

Fiona *f.*

From Gaelic, meaning 'fair, white'. It was first used in the 19th century by William Sharp as a pen name (Fiona Macleod). He modelled it on the Irish man's name **Fionn** or **FINN**. It was long thought of as a particularly Scotish name, but is now used throughout the English-speaking world. **Fi** is the short form.

Fionn *see* Finn

Fionnuala *see* Fenella

Flann *m.*

This is an Irish name meaning 'red' that would have started life as a nickname. **Flannan** started as a pet form of this.

Flavia *f.*

A Roman family name, which probably meant something like 'golden or tawny-haired'. See also **FULVIA.**

Fleur *f.*

The French word for 'flower'. It was first used as a name in the 20th century, in John Galsworthy's series of novels, *The Forsyte Saga.* The English equivalents **Flower** and **Blossom** are also found.

Flip *see* **Philip**

Flo, Floy *see* **Florence**

Flora *f.*

From the Latin meaning 'flower'. Flora was the Roman goddess of flowers and the spring. The male equivalent names **Florent** and **Florian** are now little used in Britain but are found on the Continent.

Florence *f.*

From the Latin name Florentius, derived from the word meaning 'blooming'. In the Middle Ages, Florence was used as often for men as for women, but it has since ceased to be used as a man's name. Florence Nightingale was named after the town in Italy where she was born, and her fame popularized the name in the 19th century. Abbreviated forms are **Florrie**, **Flossie**, **Floy** and **Flo**.

Florent, Florian *see* Flora

Florrie, Flossie *see* Florence

Flower *see* Fleur

Floyd *see* Lloyd

Forrest *m.*

This is the word 'forest' in its surname form. It was originally used as a first name in the southern US in the late 19th century, when it was fashionable to name boys after Confederate generals – in this case, General Nathan Bedford Forrest. The name continues to be used sporadically in Britain as well as the USA. It is sometimes found as **Forest**.

Frances *f.*

This name derives from **Francesca,** the feminine form of the Italian *Francesco* (see **FRANCIS**). It was first used in Italy in the 13th century, about the same time as the French form **Françoise** began to appear. **Francine** is another French form. Frances was not used in Britain until the 15th century, and it became popular with the English aristocracy at the time of the Tudors. The short forms are **Fanny**, **Fran**, **Francie** and **Frankie**.

Francis *m.*

From the Latin meaning 'little Frenchman'. The name became popular in Europe in the 13th century because of St Francis of Assisi. The Italian word *Francesco* was the saint's nickname, his Christian name being Giovanni, the Italian form of **JOHN**. It was given to him in his worldly youth because of his love of fashionable French things. It was first used in Britain in the 15th century. **Fran** is a short form along with **Frank** and **Frankie**. Frank can be used as an independent name.

Françoise *see* Frances

Frank, Frankie *see* Frances, Francis

Franklin *m.*

From medieval English and meaning 'free'. A franklin was a man who owned land in his own right but was not a noble. A famous modern user was Franklin D. Roosevelt, the 32nd US President.

Fraser, Frazer *m.*

A Scottish surname of unknown meaning, used as a first name.

Frea *see* Freya

Fred, Freddie, Freddy *see* Alfred, Frederick

Freda *see* Frederick, Winifred

Frederick *m.,* Frederica *f.*

From the Old German, meaning 'peaceful ruler'. It is also found with such spellings as **Frederic** and **Frederik**. Common abbreviations are **Fred**, **Freddie** and **Freddy**, also used as independent names. The female form is **Frederica**, the origin of the names **Freda**, **Frida** or **Frieda** (the last two influenced by the German form, **Friede**).

Freya *f.*

The name of the ancient Norse goddess of beauty, love and fertility. It can also be found as **Frea** or spelt the Swedish way **Freja**.

Frida, Frieda *see* Frederick

Fulvia *f.*
The feminine form of a noble Roman family name
meaning 'tawny-haired'. See also **FLAVIA**.

G

Gabriel *m.,* Gabrielle *f.*

From Hebrew, containing the elements 'God', 'man' and 'strength', and possibly implying the phrase 'strong man of God' or 'God is my strength'. In St Luke's Gospel, Gabriel is the Archangel who announces to Mary that she is to bear the baby Jesus. The name has been used infrequently since the Middle Ages for boys, outside Ireland, where it can be shortened to **GAY**. **Gabrielle** or the Italian **Gabriella**, the female forms, are much more common. A short form is **Gaby**.

Gaea *see* Gaia

Gaenor *see* Jennifer

Gaia *f.*

In Greek myth **Gaea** or Gaia is the earth goddess, the universal mother, probably once the most important divinity. Her name is occasionally found used as a first name, usually with 'green' or feminist overtones.

Gail *f.*

Originally a pet form of **ABIGAIL**, now widely used as a name in its own right. The spellings **Gale** and **Gayle** are also found.

Gaius *see* **Caius**

Galal, Galil, Galila *see* **Jalal**

Gale *see* **Gail**

Ganesh *m.*

A title of the Hindu god **SHIVA**, and the name of his elder son, derived from the Sanskrit for 'lord of the hosts'. It is customary to appease Ganesh at the beginning of Hindu ceremonies.

Gareth *m.*

From the Welsh meaning 'gentle'. This name was used by the 15th-century writer Malory in his *Morte d'Arthur*, and later by Alfred Tennyson, the 19th-century poet, in his version of Malory's story, *Gareth and Lynnette*. It was due to the latter that the name was revived in this century. **Garth** and **GARY** or **Garry** can be used as short forms.

Garfield *m.*

A surname meaning 'spearfield' in Old English, used as a first name, probably after J.A. Garfield (1831–81), 20th president of the USA. The cricketer Sir Garfield (Gary) Sobers is a well-known holder of the name, and also shows its short form.

Garret, Garrett *see* **Gerard**

Garth, Garry *see* **Gareth**

Gary *m.*

While this can be used as a short form of both **GARETH**
and **GARFIELD**, its use as an independent name owes
much to the film star Gary Cooper (1901–61). He was
born Frank James Cooper, and chose his stage name
from the American town of Gary. **Garry** is also found,
reflecting the usual pronunciation, although Gary
Cooper pronounced his name to rhyme with 'airy'.

Gaspar, Gaspard *see* **Jasper**

Gaston *m.*

A French name, originally spelt Gascon and meaning a
man from the region of Gascony. It is a common French
first name which has been used occasionally in Britain.

Gauri *f.*

This name is from the Sanskrit for 'white', and was
applied to the wife of the Hindu god **SHIVA** when she
had acquired a fair complexion after meditating in the
snows of the Himalayas.

Gavin *m.*

The name of Sir **Gawain**, King Arthur's famous nephew,
was Gauvin in Old French, and from France was
adopted in Scotland as Gavin. Originally confined to

Scotland, the name is now found throughout the English-speaking world.

Gay(e) *f.*

This name is simply the adjective meaning happy and lively, and its use dates from this century. Since the adoption of the word 'gay' by the homosexual community, few parents have used the name.

Gayle *see* Gail

Gaynor *see* Jennifer

Geena *see* Gina

Geeta *see* Gita

Gemma *f.*

The Italian word for 'gem'. Its modern use is probably due in part to the Italian saint Gemma Galgani (1875–1903), canonized in 1940. For a long time it was rarely used but in the 1980s it became one of the most popular in the country. It is also spelt **Jemma**.

Gene *see* Eugene

Genevieve *f.*

A French name possibly meaning 'lady of the people'. It is found in Latin records as **Genovera** and **Genoveva**.

St Genevieve is the patron saint of Paris; she saved the city from the Huns in the 5th century by cool thinking, courage and prayer. The name has been used in Britain since the 19th century. French pet forms are **GINA**, **Ginette** and **Veva**.

Geoffrey, Jeffrey *m.*

From the Old German *Gaufrid* the second half of which means 'peace', but the meaning of the first half is unclear. Geoffrey or Jeffrey was popular between the 12th and 15th centuries in England resulting in many surnames e.g. Jeffries, Jeeves, Jepson. It fell from favour from the 15th until the 19th century, when it was revived. **Geoff** and **Jeff** are common abbreviations.

George *m.*

From the Greek for 'farmer'. The famous St George is said to have been a Roman soldier who was martyred in Palestine in AD 303. In early Christian art many saints were represented as trampling on dragons, as a symbol of good conquering evil. This may be an explanation of how the legend of St George and the dragon originated. In the Middle Ages, St George was closely associated with knighthood and chivalry, and after 1349, when Edward III of England founded the Order of the Garter and put it under St George's protection, he became the patron saint of England. Despite this, the name was not much used until the Hanoverian succession in 1714 brought a line of four Georges to the throne. It is currently popular with parents. **Geordie** is a Scottish and

North Country pet form which is used as a nickname for Tynesiders.

Georgina *f.*

Georgina and **Georgia** are the most common female forms of **GEORGE**, both a popular choice at the moment. They were first used in Britain in the 18th century, when George became popular. The form then was **Georgiana**, which is still sometimes used. Other feminine forms of George are **Georgette** and **Georgine**.

Ger, Gerry *see* Gerald, Gerard

Geraint *m.*

This is a very old Welsh name, a variant form of the Latin Gerontius, which is in turn derived from a Greek word meaning 'old'. The 19th-century poet Alfred Tennyson used the old Welsh story of Geraint and Enid in his *Idylls of the King*, and it was from this that the name's modern use has stemmed. The real-life hero on which the fictional character is based died in battle about AD 530.

Gerald *m.*

From the Old German, meaning 'spear rule'. It was used in England from the 11th to the 12th century and was probably introduced by the Normans. The name flourished in Ireland due to the influence of the Fitzgerald ('Sons of Gerald') family, the powerful rulers of Kildare. It was probably from Ireland that the name returned to England in the late 19th century. Shortened forms are **Ger**, **Gerry** and **Jerry**.

Geraldine *f.*

Geraldine started life as a poetic nickname used by the 16th-century Earl of Surrey, in a poem praising the beauty of Lady Elizabeth Fitzgerald. Geraldine therefore means 'one of the Fitzgeralds'. It shares short forms with **GERALD**.

Gerard *m.*

From the Old German, meaning 'spear-brave'. It was brought to Britain by Norman settlers and was very common in the Middle Ages. The surnames **Gerrard** and **Garret(t)** are derived from it, and these were the most common medieval pronunciations of the name, although it is not always possible to distinguish between forms of Gerard and **GERALD**. **Ger**, **Gerry** and **Jerry** are its short forms.

Germaine *f.*

Several early saints bore the name, which probably indicated someone who came from Germany, in the way that **FRANCIS** indicated a Frenchman. Germaine is little used in English-speaking countries, but has been made well known by the writer and academic Germaine Greer. *Jermain(e)* is a form of the French **Germain**, which is quite popular in the USA, and is also found as **Jermyn**.

Gerry *see* Gerald, Geraldine, Gerard

Gertrude *f.*

From the Old German for 'strong spear'. The name
came to Britain in the Middle Ages from the
Netherlands, where a saint of that name was popular.
It was much used in the 19th and earlier 20th centuries,
but is not often chosen by parents now. Pet forms are
Gert or **Gertie**, and **Trudi**, **Trudie** or **Trudy** come from
a German pet form of the name.

Gervais, Gervase *m.*

From the Old German meaning 'spear vassal' or 'armour
bearer'. The name was first used among English
churchmen of the 12th century in honour of the 1st-
century martyr St Gervase. It spread to the general
public, giving rise to the surname **Jarvis**. Gervais is the
French spelling.

Geunor *see* Jennifer

Ghislaine *f.*

This is an Old French name, related to GISELLE and
meaning 'pledge, hostage'. It has only come to be used
in Britain comparatively recently. It is also found in the
forms **Ghislane** and **Ghislain**, although in France this
last form is used for boys. It is pronounced with a hard
'g' and the 's' is silent.

Gianna *f.*

A short form of the Italian name **Giovanna**, feminine of **Giovanni**, or **John**. Use of Gianna is currently increasing in the USA. Other short forms of Giovanna include **Gina**, **Giannina** and **Vanna**.

Gib *see* **Gilbert**

Gideon *m.*

From the Hebrew, now generally thought to mean 'having a stump for a hand', although the traditional translation was 'a hewer'. It is the name of an Old Testament Israelite leader who put the forces of the Midianites to flight. The name was adopted at the Reformation and was a favourite among the Puritans who took it to North America where it is still in use.

Gigi *f.*

This name became well known in 1958, when the novel *Gigi* by the French writer Colette was made into a successful musical film. In the book Gigi is the pet form of **Gilberte**, the French feminine form of **Gilbert**.

Gilbert *m.*

From the Old German meaning 'bright hostage'. The Normans brought the name to England and it was common in medieval times, when St Gilbert of Sempringham (died 1189) was much admired. Shortened forms are **Gib**, **Gilly**, **Bert** and **Bertie**.

Giles *m.*

According to legend, St Giles was an Athenian who took his name, Aegidius, from the goatskin that he wore. He left Greece in order to escape the fame that his miracles had brought him, and became a hermit in France. There the name became Gilles. The name is first recorded in England in the 12th century, but it was not popular. It has been suggested that this may be because of St Giles's association with beggars and cripples, of whom he is the patron saint. However, recent years have seen an increase in its popularity. It is sometimes spelt **Gyles**.

Gillian *f.*

This name, which is an English rendering of the Latin name JULIANA, was so common in the Middle Ages that its short form **Gill** was used as a general term for a girl, as Jack was for a man. It was revived in the 20th century and once again became very popular. A variant form is **Jillian**, and **JILL**, the abbreviated form, is now given as an independent name. **Jilly** is also found.

Gilly *see* Gilbert

Gina *f.*

A short form of such names as **GEORGINA** and **Regina** (see **QUEENIE**), now used as an independent name.

In France, Gina and **Ginette** are pet forms of
GENEVIEVE and it is also a short form of the Italian
GIANNA. **Geena** is also found.

Ginette *see* Genevieve, Gina

Gini, Ginny *see* Virginia

Giovanna, Giovanni *see* Gianna

Giselle *f.*
From the Old German meaning a 'pledge' or 'hostage'.
Gisèle has for a long time been a common French name,
and the English form Giselle and the latinized **Gisela**
have been used in Britain (see also **GHISLAINE**).

Gita *f.*
An Indian name from the Sanskrit meaning 'song'.
Geeta is a popular alternative spelling.

Giulia *see* Julia

Giulietta *see* Juliet

Gladys *f.*
This is the anglicized form of **Gwladys**, which means

'ruler'. It is recorded in Wales as early as the 5th century, but only moved into the mainstream of names in the 19th century. In the earlier part of this century it was very popular, but in recent decades it has become less fashionable. It is often shortened to **Glad**.

Glen(n), Glyn(n) *f. and m.*

These are both forms of Celtic words for 'a valley'. In the last forty years they have become popular names throughout the English-speaking world. **Glenna** and **Glenne** are also found for girls.

Glenda *f.*

This is a Welsh name meaning 'holy and good'.

Glenice, Glenis *see* Glenys

Glenn, Glenna *see* Glen

Glenys *f.*

From the Welsh meaning 'holy'. It is spelt in a variety of ways, including **Glen(n)is**, **Glennys** and **Glenice** (see also **GLYNIS**).

Gloria *f.*

This is Latin for 'glory' or 'fame'. The name seems to have been coined by George Bernard Shaw (1889) in his play *You Never Can Tell*. It was very common in the first half of the 20th century.

Glyn(n) *see* Glen

Glynis *f.*

From the Welsh for 'a little valley', and thus related to GLEN and **Glyn**. It can be spelt **Glinys**, and is often confused with **GLENYS**.

Gobind *see* Govind

Godfrey *m.*

From the Old German meaning 'God's peace'. It was brought to Britain by the Normans.

Gopal *m.*

This Indian name can be taken to mean 'a devotee of Krishna'. It derives from the Sanskrit words meaning 'cow-protector', indicating a cowherd, but the name was applied to Krishna in medieval devotional texts. In southern India the name is sometimes given as **Gopalkrishna**.

Gordon *m.*

Originally a Scottish place name from which the local lords took their name, it then became the name of a large and famous clan. It was rarely used as a first name until

1885, when the dramatic death of General Gordon at
Khartoum gave the name immense popularity.

Govind *m.*, Govindi *f.*

This Indian name is similar to **Gopal**, deriving from
the Sanskrit words which mean 'cow-finding', a
reference to a cowherd, but the 12th-century *Song of
Govind* associated the name firmly with Krishna.
Sikhs often make use of the form **Gobind** for boys.

Grace *f.*

The vocabulary word, originally used in its religious
sense. This name existed as **Gracia**, the Latin form, in
the Middle Ages but did not become common until the
Puritans adopted Grace along with other Christian
qualities as a name. The pet form **Gracie** is sometimes
given as a separate name, and forms from other
languages, such as **Gracia**, **Graciela**, **Gratia** and **Grazia**
are also found.

Graham *m.*

Like **GORDON**, this was originally a place name which
developed into a family name, particularly on the
Scottish/English border. At first restricted to this area,
it gradually came into general use as a first name.
Graeme and **Grahame** are also found.

Grainne, Grania *f.*

In Irish and Scottish legend, Grainne was a princess

betrothed to **FINN**, the famous chieftain. However Grainne preferred **DERMOT** and eloped with him. The story of Finn's pursuit of the couple and Grainne's suicide after Finn brought about Dermot's death is an important subject in Irish literature. Grania is the anglicized form of the name, reflecting the pronunciation 'grahn-ya'.

Grant *m.*

A surname from the French for 'tall, large' used as a first name. It seems to have come to this country from the USA, where its use may have been connected with the popularity of General Ulysses Grant, the 18th President. But as it is a common Scots surname there is no reason why the name would not have developed independently in the UK.

Gregory *m.*

From the Greek meaning 'watchman'. The name first came to Britain through St Gregory the Great, the pope who sent St Augustine to England. It was in common use from the Norman Conquest, when most Latin names were introduced, until the Reformation when, because of its association with the papacy, it fell out of favour. Gregour was the usual medieval form, which is still found as **Gregor** in Scotland, and hence the surname MacGregor. The most common shortened form is **Greg**.

Greta *f.*

A Swedish abbreviation of **MARGARET**. It was rare in

England until the 20th century, when the fame of the film actress Greta Garbo led to some parents using it. **Gretel** and **Gretchen** are the German forms.

Griffith *m.*

From the Welsh name **Gruffud** or **Gruffydd**, meaning 'lord' or 'strong warrior'. It has always been fairly popular in Wales, and was the name of several Welsh princes. **Griff** is a pet form.

Griselda *f.*

From the Old German, the meaning is disputed but possibly 'grey battle-maiden'. Chaucer told the story of *Patient Griselda* in the *Canterbury Tales*, which encouraged its use by parents who wanted meek and virtuous daughters. **Grizel** is an old Scots form which is little used nowadays, and **Zelda** which has had a mild fashion, started as a short form.

Gruffud, Gruffydd *see* Griffith

Guendolen *see* Gwendolyn

Guenevere, Guinevere *see* Jennifer

Gulab *f.*

A Hindu flower name, from the Sanskrit for 'rose'.

Gus, Gussie *see* Augusta

Gustav *m.*

An Old Norse name which means 'Gautr's staff'.
Gustav was the name of several Swedish kings and is
still used by American families of Swedish descent.
The French form of the name was borne by the writer
Gustave Flaubert, while the composer Gustav Mahler
was Austrian.

Guy *m.*

From the Old German Wido, the meaning of which is
uncertain, possibly 'wide' or 'wood'. Wido became
Guido in Latin records and Guy was the French form
introduced to Britain by the Normans. Apparently the
medieval clergy identified the name with the Latin **Vitus**
meaning 'lively', hence the disease St Vitus' Dance is
known in France as *la danse de Saint Guy*. St Vitus was a
Sicilian martyr who was invoked for the cure of nervous
ailments. The name fell out of use after Guy Fawkes'
gunpowder plot in the 17th century. It was revived in
the 19th century with the help of Walter Scott's novel,
Guy Mannering.

Gwen *f.*

The pet form of several names, such as **GWENDOLYN**,
which come from the Welsh word meaning 'white'.
Gwen and **Gwenda** (a pet form, which can also mean

'fair and good') are now used as separate names and have spread to the rest of Britain.

Gwendolyn, Gwendolen, Guendolen *f.*

From the Welsh meaning 'white circle', probably a reference to the ancient moon-goddess. The name occurs frequently in Welsh legend. Its wide range of spellings also include **Gwendoline** and **Gwendolyne**. It was a popular name at the beginning of the century, but is not much used now.

Gwenfrewi *see* Winifred

Gwenhwyfar *see* Jennifer

Gwill, Gwilym *see* William

Gwladys *see* Gladys

Gwyn *m.*

From the Welsh meaning 'white' or 'blessed'. This name has been anglicized as **Wyn** or **Wynne**. Its use is mainly confined to the Welsh. **Gwynfor** or **Wynfor** is Gwyn with the word for 'great' added to the end.

Gwyneth *f.*
From the Welsh meaning either 'fair maiden' or
'happiness'. **Gwyn** is the pet form.

Gyles *see* **Giles**

H

Hadrian *see* **Adrian**

Hal *see* **Henry**

Haley *see* **Hayley**

Ham *see* **Abraham**

Hamish *m.*
The anglicized form of **Seumas** (see **SEAMAS**), the Gaelic form of **JAMES**. This name became popular in the second half of the 19th century and is still used, mostly in Scotland.

Hamzah *m.*
The name of the Prophet Muhammad's uncle, probably from the Arabic for 'lion'. It is also spelt **Hamza**.

Hana *f.*
From the Arabic for 'bliss' or 'happiness'.

Hani *m.*
A Muslim name from the Arabic for 'joyful' or 'delighted'.

Hank *see* **Henry**

Hannah *f.*

From the Hebrew meaning 'God has favoured me'. In the Old Testament it was the name of Samuel's mother. The Greek form of this, **Anna** (see **ANNE**), was used at first. Hannah was not adopted in England until after the Reformation. It is currently one of the most popular girls' names.

Hans *m.*

The equivalent of **JOHN** in north European countries including Germany, the Netherlands and Sweden. It is ultimately a contracted form of the Latin Johannes.

Harald *see* **Harold**

Hari *m.*

This Indian name occurs frequently in classic Hindu texts and is often applied to Vishnu or Krishna. It derives from a Sanskrit word which indicates a yellow-brown colour.

Harold *m.*

From the Old Norse, meaning 'army-power'; **Harald** is the original Scandinavian form. It was used in the Middle Ages, but went out of fashion until it became popular again in the 18th century. It is not much used at the moment. It shares the abbreviation **Harry** with the name HENRY.

Haroun *see* **Aaron**

Harriet *f.*

A female form of HENRY, derived from **Harry**, which was the usual form of the name Henry in the Middle Ages. The name was very popular in the 18th and 19th centuries and has recently been popular again. Short forms are **Hattie** or **Hatty.**

Harrison *m.*

A surname meaning 'son of Harry', used as a first name. It was popular in the last century and has once again come to be well known thanks to such users as the actor, Harrison Ford.

Harry *see* **Harold, Henry**

Harsha *f.*

A Hindu name derived from the Sanskrit for 'happiness'.

Harun *see* **Aaron**

Harvey *m.*

From the French meaning 'battle-worthy'. It was common until the 14th century, and had a slight revival in the 19th. Its modern use as a first name may be due in part to its widespread use as a surname.

Hasan *m.*

One of the most popular Muslim names, derived from the Arabic for 'handsome' or 'good'. Al-Hasan was the Prophet's grandson. Similar names derived from the same Arabic word are **Hasin**, **Hassan**, **Husayn**, **Husni**, **Hussain** and **Hussein**.

Hattie, Hatty *see* **Harriet**

Havelock *see* **Oliver**

Hayden *m.*

This name is destined to become well used by American parents in the 1990s. It appears to be a form of **Haydn**, a name used (especially in Wales) in honour of the Austrian composer Franz Josef Haydn. As a first name, it is also spelt **Haydon**. The surname Haydn in its turn derives from the Old German word for 'heathen'.

Hayley *f.*

From a surname meaning 'hay field'. This name came into use in the 1960s, after the success of the film actress, Hayley Mills, and has since become very popular. It is also spelt **Haley** and **Haylie**.

Hazel *f.*

One of the plant names adopted as a girl's name in the 19th century.

Heather *f.*

This is one of several plant names first used in the 19th century. Since heather is a feature of northern Britain, the name became especially popular in Scotland and is now popular in the USA. **Heath**, another name for the same plant, is also used for both sexes.

Hector *m.*

From the Greek meaning 'hold fast'. It was the name of the Trojan hero who was killed by the Greek Achilles and took quite a strong hold in Scotland, where it was used as an equivalent for the quite unconnected Gaelic name **Eachan**, which means 'a horseman'.

Heena *see* **Hina**

Heidi *f.*

This name is a pet form of the German version of **ADELAIDE**. It has come into use in the English-speaking world thanks to the popularity of Johanna Spyri's *Heidi* stories.

Helen *f.*

From the Greek meaning 'the bright one'. The popularity of this name in Britain was due originally to the 4th-century St **Helena**. She was the mother of Constantine the Great and was supposed to have been the daughter of the ruler of Colchester, the Old King Cole of nursery rhyme. When she was over eighty she made a pilgrimage to the Holy Land where she was believed to have found the true cross of Christ. The name is first found as **Elena** and then ELAINE and ELLEN. The 'H' was not used until the Renaissance, when the study of classical literature brought Homer's story of the Trojan war and the beautiful Greek queen Helen to public notice. **Lena** is a contraction and NELL is a pet form. **Ilona** is a Hungarian form.

Helga f.
From the Norse, meaning 'holy'. It has occasionally been used in Britain but is more common in North America, where it was introduced by Scandinavian immigrants (see also OLGA).

Heloise, Heloïse *see* Eloise

Hema f.
An Indian name which derives from the Sanskrit for 'golden'.

Henri *see* Henry

Henrietta f.
The female form of HENRY. It was introduced into this

country in the 17th century by Henriette Marie, Charles I's French wife. The full form gave way to the abbreviated **HARRIET**, but was revived in the 19th century. Abbreviations are **Etta**, **Ettie** and **Hetty**.

Henry *m.*

From the Old German, meaning 'home ruler'. The Latin Henricus became **Henri** in France. **Harry** was, in fact, the original English form of Henri, used until the 17th century and often abbreviated to **Hal**. Today, Harry is used as the pet form of Henry and increasingly as a name in its own right. **Hank** is a pet form more common in the United States.

Herbert *m.*

From the Old German for 'bright army'. It seldom appears before the Norman Conquest, after which it became quite common. It was revived at the start of the 19th century and became quite popular again towards the century's end, due in part to the fashion for using aristocratic surnames as first names. **Herb**, **Herbie** and **BERT** or **Bertie** are short forms.

Herman *m.*

A Germanic name meaning 'soldier'. The French form of the name is **Armand**, and the old English form **Armin** or **Arminel**, which along with **Arminelle** can also be used as a feminine name.

Hermione *f.*

From the Greek meaning 'daughter of Hermes'; in Greek mythology Hermione was the daughter of Menelaus and **HELEN**. Hers is a tragic story, and it was Shakespeare's use of the name in *A Winter's Tale* that gave rise to its use in modern times. He used another form, **Hermia**, in *A Midsummer Night's Dream*, and this has also been found occasionally.

Hester *see* **Esther**

Hetty *see* **Esther, Henrietta**

Hew *see* **Hugh**

Hilary *f. and m.*

From the Latin meaning 'cheerful'. The original Latin forms **Hilaria** and **Hilarius** are very occasionally found, and the writer **Hilaire** Belloc used the French form. Hilary, or **Hillary**, was once quite usual as a boy's name, but is now rarely used except for girls.

Hilda *f.*

From the Old English word for 'battle'. There was an Anglo-Saxon St Hilda, a woman of outstanding ability who founded an abbey at Whitby in the 7th century. When the names of Anglo-Saxon saints were revived in the 19th century Hilda became popular but is now often felt to be rather old-fashioned.

Hillary *see* **Hilary**

Hina *f.*

A Hindu name meaning 'henna', the dye used to colour the hair and fingernails. It is also found as **Heena** and **Henna**.

Hiram *m.*

From the Hebrew, meaning 'brother of the high one', and the name of an Old Testament king of Tyre. It was a favourite 17th-century name and was taken at that time to North America where it still flourishes.

Holly *f.*

A plant name used as a first name, currently popular on both sides of the Atlantic.

Honoria *f.*

From the Latin meaning 'reputation' or 'honour'. The Latin forms **Honora**, Honoria and **An(n)ora** were predominant until the Reformation, when the Puritans adopted the abstract virtue names and used **Honour** and **Honor**. They were then used both as masculine and feminine names. In the 19th century the Latin forms were revived (see also **NORA**).

Hope *f.*

This Christian virtue was adopted as a first name in the 17th century, in the same way as **FAITH** and **CHARITY**.

It was especially popular among Puritans at this time, who used it for both sexes. It is now only used for girls, and is becoming quite popular.

Horace, Horatio *m.*

From the Roman clan named Horatius of which the famous **Horatius** who defended the bridge was a member. The fame of the name is also due to the Latin poet Horace. Horatio seems to have come from Italy to England in the 16th century, and has been kept alive by the fame of Nelson, although Horace is the form more likely to be found today. **Horatia** is a rare feminine form.

Howard *m.*

Like other aristocratic family names, this was adopted as a first name by the general public in the 19th century. The origin of the surname is disputed. It may be from the Old German meaning 'heart-protection' or the French for 'worker with a hoe', or even from the medieval official, the 'hogwarden', who superintended the pigs of a district. **Howie** can be used as a short form.

Hubert *m.*

From the Old German meaning 'bright mind'. This name was popular in the Middle Ages, probably as a result of the fame of St Hubert of Liège, the patron saint of huntsmen. It was not much used from the 16th to the 18th centuries, after which it was revived to some extent, but it has since gone out of fashion again. **BERT** is the short form.

Hugh, Hugo *m.*

From the Old German meaning 'heart' or 'soul'. It appears frequently in the Domesday Book. It was further strengthened by the popularity of St Hugh, Bishop of Lincoln in the 14th century. Hugo is the Latin form. **Hew** and **Huw** are Welsh forms of the name; **Hughie** and **Huey** are used as pet forms.

Humayra *f.*

This name was given by the Prophet Muhammad to his wife **AISHA**. Its meaning is unclear.

Humphrey *m.*

From the Old German meaning 'peace'. This name was originally spelt with an 'f', the 'ph' coming in when it was equated with the name of the obscure Egyptian saint, Onuphrios, in order to Christianize it.

Hunter *m.*

The Old English vocabulary word used as a first name, this is another surname that has come to be used as a boy's name.

Husayn, Husni, Hussain, Hussein
see **Hasan**

Huw *see* **Hugh**

Hywel *m.*

A Welsh name meaning 'eminent'. It has become well
known through the actor Hywel Bennett.

I

Iain, Ian *see* **John**

Ianthe *f.*

This is an ancient Greek name meaning 'violet flower'. It has a strong literary flavour, having been used by a number of poets including Byron and Shelley. It is still quietly but steadily used.

Ibrahim *m.*

The Arabic form of ABRAHAM.

Ida *f.*

From the Old German, meaning 'hard work'. The name was introduced by the Normans, and lasted until about the middle of the 14th century. In the late 19th century it was revived by Tennyson for the name of the heroine of his poem *The Princess*, which Gilbert and Sullivan subsequently took as a basis for the operetta *Princess Ida*. These uses led to a revival of the name at the end of the 19th century.

Idris *m.*

This is a Welsh name meaning 'fiery lord'. In Welsh legend, Idris the Giant was an astronomer and magician, who had his observatory on Cader Idris.

Ieasha, Ieesha, Iesha *see* Aisha

Iefan *see* Evan

Ieuan, Ifan *see* Evan

Ifor *see* Ivor

Ignatius *m.*

Ignatius or **Inigo** is a Latin name, derived originally from a Greek name of obscure origin, possibly meaning 'fiery'. It took root mainly in Russia and Spain and was carried further afield by the Jesuits whose founder was Inigo Lopez de Recalde, better known as St Ignatius of Loyola.

Ike *see* Isaac

Ilona *see* Helen

Imelda *f.*

Imelda is probably the Italian form of the Germanic name **Irmhilde** 'universal battle'. It is the name of a rather obscure saint, and had a certain popularity in Ireland in the middle of the century.

Imogen *f.*

First appearing in Shakespeare's *Cymbeline*, this name is thought to be a misprint of the name Innogen which appears in Shakespeare's source for the story. It may be derived from the Greek meaning 'beloved child'. It is quite popular at the moment.

Ina *f.*

This name can come from three different sources. It is an Irish form of **AGNES**, a form of the name **ENA**, and can also be a pet form of first names ending '-ina', such as **Christina** and **GEORGINA**.

Inderjit *m.*

An Indian name from the Sanskrit meaning 'conqueror of the god Indra'. The spelling **Indrajeet** is also used.

India *f.*

This is one of the most recent names to become fashionable. It was the name of a character in *Gone with the Wind*, but its popularity is more likely to be due to the interest, particularly since the 1970s, in Indian culture and religion.

Indira *f.*

An Indian name associated with the goddess Lakshmi, wife of Vishnu. Usually derived from a Sanskrit word meaning 'beauty', but possibly connected with **INDRA**.

Indra *m.*

The name of the god of the sky and rain in Hindu tradition. The meaning of the name is uncertain, but may be connected with the Sanskrit for 'raindrop'.

Indrajeet *see* **Inderjit**

Inés, Inez *see* **Agnes**

Ingrid *f.*

From the Old Norse, meaning 'Ing's ride'. In Norse mythology Ing was the god of fertility and crops who rode a golden-bristled boar. It is a common name in Scandinavia and was made famous in this country by the Swedish film star, Ingrid Bergman (1915–82). **Ingeborg** ('Ing's fortress') and **Inga**, the short form of these two names, are also found occasionally.

Inigo *see* **Ignatius**

Iola *f.*

The Latin form of a Greek name meaning 'dawn cloud'. In Greek mythology Hercules fell in love with a princess **Iole**. The name is rare in Britain.

Iolanthe *see* **Yolanda**

Iona *f.*

This is the name of the Scottish island used as a first name. The island seems originally to have been called Ioua, 'yew-tree island', but at some point the 'u' was misread as 'n' and so the island got its present name. The name's popularity has been increasing in recent years. **Ione** ('eye-oh-nee') is not the same name, but a Greek name connected with the word 'violet'.

Ior *see* Ivor

Ira *m.*

A name from the Old Testament meaning 'watchful'.
The name was used by the Puritans, who took it over to
America where it is now much more common than in
Britain. The song-writer Ira Gershwin was a famous
bearer of the name.

Irene *f.*

The name of the goddess of peace and also of one of the
seasons in ancient Greece. Although the name was used
earlier in other parts of Europe, it did not appear in
England until the late 19th century. The abbreviation
Renie is sometimes used and it can also be found in the
form **Irena**. Irene is pronounced in two different ways:
in the Greek way with three syllables and the final 'e'
pronounced, and the usual modern way with only two
syllables.

Iris *f.*

Although this name is usually associated with the flower,
it comes from the Greek word for 'rainbow', after which
the flower was named because of its bright colours.
In Greek mythology Iris carried messages from the gods
to men, across the rainbow which was her bridge. It was
not used in England before the 19th century.

Irma *f.*

This was originally a German name meaning 'universal'.

It has only been used in this country since the beginning of the last century.

Irving *m.*

Irving or **Irvine** are Scottish place names which were used first as surnames and then as first names.

Isa *see* Isabel

Isaac *m.*

From the Hebrew meaning 'laughter'. It was the name given by **SARAH**, wife of **ABRAHAM**, to the son born in her old age. The name is popularly believed to have been chosen by Sarah because she laughed when she was told that she would conceive. The name appears in Britain in the Middle Ages and came to be regarded as a specifically Jewish name. It came into general use in the 16th and 17th centuries, when it was spelt with a 'z' as in **Izaak** Walton, the author of *The Compleat Angler*. In the mid-17th century the 's' spelling came into fashion, as in Sir Isaac Newton, the great scientist. **Zak** or **Ike** are used as pet forms.

Isabel(le), Isobel *f.*

These are variant forms of **ELIZABETH** which developed in medieval France. Elizabeth became Ilsabeth and then Isabeau, and finally **Isabelle**. Up to the end of the 17th century at least, the derivatives Isabel(le) in England, Isobel in Scotland and the Gaelic **Iseabail**, sometimes spelt phonetically as **Ishbel**, were interchangeable with

Elizabeth. **Isa** and **Bel** or **Belle** were the common short forms. The Latin **Isabella** and **Bella** were used from the 18th century.

Isadora *see* Isidore

Isaiah *m.*

From the Hebrew meaning 'Jehovah is salvation', and the name of the great Old Testament prophet. It was first used by the 17th-century Puritans and is rather rare today in Britain, although quite popular in North America.

Iseabail *see* Isabel

Iseult *see* Isolda

Isha *see* Aisha

Ishbel *see* Isabel

Ishmael *see* Ismail

Isidore *m.*, Isidora *f.*

From the Greek, possibly meaning 'gift of Isis'. There were two Spanish saints of this name. The scandal caused by the private life and dancing style of **Isadora** Duncan (1878–1927) made the feminine form of the name well known.

Isla *f.*

A Scots island name, used as a girl's name in Scotland since the 1950s. It has now spread to other parts of Britain. The 's' is silent, as in 'island'.

Isleen *see* Aisling

Ismail *m.*

This is the Arabic form of **Ishmael**. Arabs are sometimes known as Ismailites, 'descendants of Ismail'.

Isobel *see* Isabel

Isolda *f.*

From Old Welsh **Essylt** meaning 'fair one'. It was a common name in medieval times because of its place in the tragic legend of **TRISTAN** and Isolda. **Iseult** was the Norman form which became Isolda in Latin, Isot(t) in Middle English. Isolda or **Isolde** had a brief revival in the 19th century owing to the popularity of Wagner's opera *Tristan and Isolde*. It is also spelt **Yseult(e)** and **Ysolde**.

Israel *f.*

From Hebrew, although its meaning is disputed; the most likely translation is 'may God prevail'. In the Old Testament Jacob was named Israel after his struggle with the angel of God. The name was first adopted by Christians after the Reformation.

Ivan *m.*

The Russian form of **JOHN**, found occasionally in Britain.

Ivo *m.*

From the Old German meaning 'yew'. It was common in Brittany in the form **Yves**, and was brought to Britain at the time of the Norman Conquest. It has been used occasionally since.

Ivor, Ifor *m.*

Ifor is a Welsh name which means 'lord', and Ivor is the anglicized spelling. It was originally **Ior**, but was probably influenced by the Breton version, **Yves**, which became **Ivo** and was brought over by the Normans.

Ivy *f.*

This is a plant name which came into use in the 19th century. Because ivy clings so firmly, the name may have been used to indicate faithfulness.

Izaak *see* Isaac

J

Jacaline *see* **Jacqueline**

Jack *m.*

Originally the pet form of **JOHN**, this is now a very popular name in its own right. In the Middle Ages **JAN** evolved from John, and then developed the pet form Jankin, later shortened to Jack. **Jock** is a traditionally Scottish form. Jack shares the pet form **Jake**, now a name in its own right, with **JACOB**. **Jackson**, a surname meaning 'son of Jack', is also found as a first name.

Jackalyn, Jackie, Jacky *see* **Jacqueline**

Jacob *m.*

The meaning of this Hebrew name is uncertain. In the Old Testament, it was the name of Isaac's younger son, who tricked his brother Esau out of his inheritance. This explains the popular interpretation of the name as 'he supplanted'. There were two Latin forms, Jacobus and Jacomus. Jacob came from the former and **JAMES** from the latter. Jacob has survived as a first name because translators of the Bible kept this form for the Old Testament Patriarch, although they called the two New Testament apostles James. **Jacoba**, **Jacobine** and **Jacobina** are rare feminine forms. **Jake** is an abbreviation shared with **JACK** and now a popular choice as a name in its own right.

Jacqueline *f.*

Jacqueline and **Jacquetta** are French feminines of **Jacques**, the French equivalent of **JAMES** and **JACOB**. Both were introduced into this country in the 13th century, and have been in use ever since. Jacqueline, with its pet forms **Jacky**, **Jacki(e)** or **Jacqui**, is found in a very wide range of spellings which include **Jackalyn**, **Jacaline**, **Jacquelyn** and **Jaqueline**.

Jade *f.*

The name of the precious stone used as a first name. Although the names of precious stones have been in use as girls' names since the last century, this one seems only to have come into use in the 1970s and has been popular again recently.

Jai *see* Jay

Jaimal *see* Jamila

Jake *see* Jack, Jacob, Jesse

Jalal *m.,* Jalila *f.*

An Arabic name which means 'glory' or 'greatness'. A similar name is **Jalil**, meaning 'honoured' or 'revered'.

Jalila is the feminine form of both. The names are also found as **Galal**, **Galil** and **Galila**.

Jaleesa *f.*

Also spelt **Jalisa**, this is a popular and apparently newly formed name, blending the 'Ja-' of names like **JANE**, **JANET** and **JACQUELINE** with the sound of **Lisa**. It was introduced in 1988 through a character in the TV comedy show *A Different World*. Afro-American parents immediately responded to the name with great enthusiasm.

Jalil *see* Jalal

Jalisa *see* Jaleesa

Jamal, Jaimal *see* Jamila

James *m.*

This name has the same root as **JACOB**. It became established in Britain in the 12th century when pilgrims started to visit the shrine of St James at Compostella in Spain. At that time the name was more common in Scotland. With the accession of James VI as the first king of both Scotland and England in 1603, the name became more popular in England. It was unfashionable in the 19th century, but is now probably the most used boy's name. The pet forms are **Jim**, **Jimmy** and **JAMIE**. The Irish form is **SEAMAS** and the Scots **HAMISH**.

Jamie *f. and m.*

This pet form of **JAMES** was originally a Scottish form but has since spread throughout the English-speaking world and become popular in its own right. Since at least the 1960s it has also been used as a girl's name, particularly in the United States.

Jamila *f.,* Ja(i)mal *m.*

An Arabic name meaning 'beautiful'. The name is popular in the male and female forms in the Arab world and with Black Muslims in the USA, where it is also spelt **Jamil** and **Jamel**. It is also used in France, where it can be found as **Djamila**.

Jan *f. and m.*

The female version is a common pet form of **JANET**. The male form is a form of **JOHN** in a number of European languages such as Dutch and Polish and is then pronounced 'yan'. It is also the old English pronunciation of John, still used in the West Country.

Jane *f.*

This is now the commonest female form of **JOHN**. It comes from the Old French form Jehane. It was very rare before the 16th century, the medieval female forms of John being **JOAN** and **JOANNA**. An early example was Jane Seymour, third wife of King Henry VIII of England and mother of Edward V. Since Tudor times the name has been in and out of fashion. At the moment it is freely used as a second name, but rarely as a first unless in some combination like Sarah Jane. It can also be spelt **Jayne**. The commonest pet forms are **Jenny** and **Janey** or **Janie** (see also **JANET**). **Jancis** seems to be a combination of Jane with **FRANCES** or **Cicely**. Other elaborations include **Janice** or **Janis**; **Jana**, a form found in a variety of other languages; and **Janelle** (see also **SHEENA**, **SIAN**).

Janene *see* Janine

Janet *f.*

This was originally derived from **Jeanette**, the French pet form of **JEAN**. It was first used in Scotland. **Janette** and **Janetta** are also found, and **Net**, **Nettie**, **Netta** and **Jan** are pet names. A Scottish pet form is **Jessie** (see also **SHEENA**).

Janey, Janice, Janie, Janis *see* Jane

Janine *f.*

Like **JANET**, this name comes from a pet form of **Jeanne**, the French form of **JEAN**. It is also spelt **Jannine** and **Janene**, and the latinized **Janina** is also used.

Jaqueline *see* Jacqueline

Jared *m.*

A biblical name meaning 'to descend' and connected

with **JORDAN**. It was used in the past by the Puritans but had become very rare until the mid-1960s when it became popular in the United States and Australia. It is also found in the forms **Jarred**, **Jarod** and **Jarrod**, although some of these forms may be influenced by similar surnames. **Jaron** is also used.

Jarvis *see* Gervais

Jasmine *f.*

A flower name also found in its normal botanical form, *Jasmin*. The word comes from Persian, and the name is also used in the Persian form **Yasmin**, with variants such as **Yasmine** and **Yasmina**. It is currently growing in popularity.

Jason *m.*

This name was adopted in the 17th century when biblical names became popular, because it is the traditional name for the author of Ecclesiasticus. It has been a popular name in recent years, when parents probably associated it more with the Greek hero Jason, who won the Golden Fleece. A short form, **Jace**, is sometimes used.

Jasper *m.*

Gaspar or **Caspar** (**Kaspar**) is the traditional name of one of the three kings or wise men of the Christmas story. It may mean 'keeper' or 'bringer of treasure'. **Gaspard** is the French form and Jasper the English.

Jawahir *f.*

An Arabic name which means 'jewels'.

Jay *f. and m.*

This name derives most probably from a short form of any name beginning with a 'J', but it could also be from a surname, originally a nickname referring to the bird and the noise it makes, indicating that the holder was a chatterer. It is sometimes spelt **Jaye**. As an Indian name for boys, Jay is derived from the Sanskrit word for 'victory'. It can also be spelt **Jai**.

Jayne *see* **Jane**

Jean *f.*

This name started as a Scottish form of **JANE** or **JOAN** derived from the Old French Jehane. The diminutive **Jeanette** is also found (see **JANET**). The commonest pet forms are **Jeanie** and **Jenny**.

Jed *m.*

A short form of the biblical name **Jedidiah**, which means 'beloved of the Lord'. It is much more common in the United States than in the UK.

Jeff, Jeffrey *see* **Geoffrey**

Jem *see* **Jeremy**

Jemima *f.*

From the Hebrew meaning 'dove' or 'handsome as the day', and the name of one of Job's daughters in the Old Testament. First used in the 17th century by Puritans, it was very popular in the 19th century and is used steadily today. **Mima** is a pet form.

Jemma *see* **Gemma**

Jennifer *f.*

An old Cornish form of **Guenevere**, from the Welsh meaning 'white ghost', and the name of King Arthur's wife. It was practically obsolete until its 20th-century revival. It spread rapidly, and was very popular in the 1950s and '60s. **Jenny** or **Jenni** is the pet form, shared with **Jane** and **Jean**. **Gaenor**, **Geunor** and **Gaynor** are other forms of Guenevere, which is also spelt **Guinevere** and in Wales, **Gwenhwyfar**. **Jenna**, another Cornish version, has recently become more popular.

Jenny *see* **Jane**, **Jean**, **Jennifer**

Jeremy *m.*

From the Hebrew, meaning 'may Jehovah exalt'. **Jeremiah** was the Old Testament prophet who wrote the Book of Lamentations. The traditional English form is Jeremy, which appears from the 13th century onwards, although in the 17th century, the two forms **Jeremias** and Jeremiah were more common. **Jerry** is a short form, which is shared with **GERALD**, and **Jem** and **Jez** are also used. **Jer(r)ell** is a recent variant.

Jermain(e) *see* Germaine

Jerome *m.*

From the Greek *Hieronymos*, meaning 'holy name'.
This name is pre-Christian in origin, but soon became popular with the early Church. St Jerome translated the Bible into Latin in the 4th century, and was an important religious influence in the Middle Ages.
The name appears in England in the 12th century as Geronimus, which gradually gave way to the French form Jerome.

Jerry *see* Gerald, Geraldine, Gerard, Jeremy

Jess *see* Jesse, Jessica

Jesse *m.*

From the Hebrew meaning 'God exists', and in the Old Testament, the name of King David's father. It was adopted in the 17th century by the Puritans who took it to America where it has been commoner than in the UK. Jesse James, the outlaw, and the politician Jesse Jackson are probably the best known examples. **Jess** is a short form, and **Jake** a pet form shared with **JACOB**. The name is sometimes spelt **Jessie.**

Jessica *f.*

The source of this name is much debated, but it may well have been invented by Shakespeare for his play *The Merchant of Venice* in which Shylock's daughter is called Jessica. It is shortened to **Jess** or **JESSIE** (also a Scottish pet form of **JANET**), which is sometimes spelt **Jessye**. It is very popular at the moment.

Jessie *f.*

This is a Scottish diminutive of **JANET** but is often used as a separate name. It is fairly common in the literature of the 18th and 19th centuries, and is also a pet form of **JESSICA**.

Jessye *see* **Jessica**

Jesus *see* **Joshua**

Jethro *m.*

From the Hebrew meaning 'abundance' or 'excellence'. In the Bible it is the name of **MOSES**' father-in-law. It has been used as a first name since the Reformation.

Jill *f.*

A pet form of **Jillian** or **GILLIAN**, often given as a separate name (see **JULIANA**).

Jillian, Jilly *see* **Gillian, Juliana**

Jim, Jimmy *see* **James**

Jinny *see* **Virginia**

Jo *see* **Joseph, Josephine**

Joan, Joanna *f.*

This is the oldest female form of **JOHN** and is a
contraction of **Johanna**, the Latin feminine form of
Johannes. The name came over from France as Jhone
and Johan in the second half of the 12th century, but by
the 14th century Joan was the established form. By the
mid-16th century it was so common that it became
unfashionable, and **JANE** superseded it. It was revived at
the beginning of the 20th century. **Joni** is the pet form.
Joanne was a later development of the name. **Juanita** is
the Spanish pet form, which can be shortened to **Nita**.

Job *m.*

From the Hebrew meaning 'hated' or 'persecuted'.
Jobey, **Jobie** or **Joby** are pet forms of the name.

Jocelyn, Jo(s)celin *f. and m.*

These names seem to be derived from several different
names which have come together over a period of time
to form one name. The most important source is
probably from the Latin meaning 'cheerful, sportive'.
There is also a possibility that it is derived from an Old
German name meaning 'little Goth'. A further derivation

has been traced from the name **Josse**, 'champion', a form of **Jodoc**, the name of an early Breton saint which also gave us **JOYCE**. Jocelyn is the usual form for boys, although the name is now rarely masculine.

Jock *see* Jack

Jodi(e), Jody *see* Judith

Jodoc *see* Jocelyn

Joe *see* Joseph, Josephine

Joel *m.*
From the Hebrew, meaning 'Jehovah is God' and the name of one of the minor Old Testament prophets. It was adopted by the Puritans, like many other biblical names, after the Reformation. **Joelle** is a form of the name for girls.

Johan *see* John

Johanna *see* Joanna

John *m.*
From the Hebrew, meaning 'the Lord is gracious'. Its earliest form in Europe was the Latin Johannes, which was shortened to **Johan** and **Jon** before becoming John.

However, in France the name became Jean, and both forms of the name were introduced into the British Isles, which resulted in two groups of names developing. Thus the Johannes-form gives us the Gaelic **Ian** and **Iain**, **Ieuan** and **EVAN** in Welsh, and **Eoin** ('oh-n') in Irish, while the Jean-form gives **SEAN** or **Shane** in Irish and **Sion** in Welsh. Since the 16th century, John has been one of the commonest boys' names in Britain (see also **IVAN**, **JACK**).

Joisse *see* Joyce

Jolyon *see* Julian

Jon *see* John, Jonathan

Jonah, Jonas *m.*

From the Hebrew meaning 'dove'. The Old Testament story of Jonah and the whale was very popular in the Middle Ages and because of this the name was common. It continued to be used occasionally until the 19th century, when it became rare probably because of the association of the name with bad luck. Jonas is the Greek form of the name and is now the more common of the two.

Jonathan *m.*

A Hebrew name meaning 'the Lord has given'. In the Old Testament, Jonathan was the son of King Saul and

it was his great friendship with David that gave rise to
the expression 'David and Jonathan' to describe two
close friends. The name came into use at the time of the
Reformation, and it is popular today. The short form,
Jon, is often used as a separate name and the name is
sometimes spelt **Jonathon**.

Joni *see* Joan

Jordan *f. and m.*
Jordan was quite a popular name in the Middle Ages
when it was given to children baptized with water from
the River Jordan brought back by pilgrims to the Holy
Land. It has recently been revived as a first name and is
currently a popular choice for boys. The name of the
river means 'to descend or flow' and comes from the
same word that gives us the name **JARED**.

Jos *see* Joseph, Josiah

Joscelin *see* Jocelyn

Joseph *m.*
From the Hebrew meaning 'the Lord added' (i.e. to the
family). In the Old Testament it was the name of Jacob
and Rachel's elder son who was sold into slavery in
Egypt. In the New Testament, there are Joseph, the
husband of Mary, and Joseph of Arimathea, who is
believed to have buried Jesus and whom legend connects

with Glastonbury and the Holy Grail. The name was not often used until the 17th century, when Old Testament names were adopted by the Puritans, and Joseph became a favourite. **Joe** and **Jo** are common abbreviations and well used as names in their own right, and **Jos** is also found.

Josephine *f.*

Josephine is the French female form of **JOSEPH**. It was Napoleon's first wife, the Empress Josephine, who started the fashion for the name in Britain and France. **Josepha** and **Josephina** are less common forms of the name. Pet forms are **Jo(e)** and **Josie**, and in France Josephine has the pet form **Fifi**.

Joshua *m.*

From the Hebrew meaning 'the Lord saves'. In the Old Testament Joshua succeeded Moses and finally led the Israelites to the Promised Land. The name was not used in England before the Reformation. **Josh** is a short form. **Jesus** is the Greek form of the name, popular as a first name with Spanish speakers.

Josiah *m.*

From the Hebrew meaning 'may the Lord heal'. The 18th-century potter, Josiah Wedgwood, in whose family the name is still used, is possibly the best known British bearer of the name. **Josias** is an alternative form of the name, and **Jos** a short form.

Josie *see* **Josephine**

Josse *see* **Jocelyn, Joyce**

Joy *f.*

This is the vocabulary word used as a first name. It occurs as early as the 12th century but then disappears, to be revived in the 19th century.

Joyce *f. and m.*

In the Middle Ages when this name was most common it usually had the form **Josse**. A 7th-century saint from Brittany, who also gave us the name JOCELYN, was the cause of the name's popularity. One of its French variants was **Joisse**, and it was from this that the name's final form was derived. Joyce was little used after the Middle Ages until the general revival of medieval names in the last century. It is now very rare as a man's name.

Juanita *see* **Joan**

Jude *m.*

The Hebrew form of this name is **Yehudi**, which was rendered as **Judah** in the Authorized Version of the Old Testament. **Judas** Iscariot bore the Greek form, and because of him Jude was not used by Christians until the Reformation. The name is still used occasionally, but is best known through Thomas Hardy's novel *Jude the Obscure* and the Beatles' song *Hey Jude*. It means 'praise'.

Judith *f.*

From the Hebrew meaning 'a Jewess', and in the Apocryphal Book of Judith the name of the resourceful woman who saves the Israelites by letting the enemy general think he was seducing her, and then cutting off his head with his own sword. The short form **Judy** is often given independently, while the pet forms **Jody** and **Jodi(e)** are now the most common form of the name.

Jules *see* **Julian**

Julia *f.*

Julia is the feminine form of **Julius**, which came to England from Italy as **Giulia** in the 16th century. It did not become common in Britain until the 18th and 19th centuries. **Julie** is the French form. Julia was popular in the middle of this century, then fell out of favour, but is now coming back into use.

Julian *m.*

Julianus was a Roman family name which meant 'connected with the family of **Julius**'. Julius probably comes from the same root that gives the Latin word for 'god', but in Roman times the family believed that it referred to the soft growth of hair that forms a boy's first sign of a beard, as this was the state of development that a founding member of the clan had reached when he first distinguished himself in battle. The most famous of numerous saints of this name was St Julian the

Hospitaller, who devoted himself to helping poor travellers. The name came to Britain in the Latin form, which was anglicized as **Julyan**, and in the North of England as **Jolyon**. **Jules**, the French form of Julius, is also used as a short form of Julian.

Juliana *f.*

This is the feminine form of **JULIAN**. It was a popular name in the Middle Ages, when the name normally took the form Julian, still occasionally used for girls. The variant forms **GILLIAN** and **JILL** were among the commonest girls' names from the 12th to the 15th centuries. The name subsequently dropped out of use but was revived in the 18th century. The short form **Julie** is shared with **JULIA** (see also **LIANNE**).

Julie *see* Julia, Juliana

Juliet *f.*

This is a short form of the Italian **Giulietta**, the diminutive of **JULIA**. Its use nowadays is probably the result of the influence of Shakespeare's *Romeo and Juliet*. **Juliette** is a French form sometimes used in Britain.

Julius, Julyan *see* Julian

Junayd *m.*

An Arabic name meaning 'warrior'. It also occurs as **Junaid**.

June _f._

This is simply the name of the month which, like **APRIL**, has been used as a girl's name in the 20th century.

Juno _see_ **Una**

Justin _m.,_ Justine _f._

From the Latin meaning 'just'. These were uncommon names until thirty years ago when they came back into fashion. **Justina** is an old feminine form.

K

Kai *see* **Kay, Caius**

Kalli(e), **Kally** *see* **Callie**

Kamal *m.*, Kamala *f.*
In India this name derives from the Sanskrit, where it means 'pale red' but it is specifically associated with the lotus flower. Kamala, the feminine form, is one of the goddess Lakshmi's names in classical Hindu texts, where it is also a name of **SHIVA**'s wife. In the Arab world Kamal is from an Arabic word which means 'perfection'.

Kamil *m.*, Kamila(h) *f.*
From the Arabic meaning 'complete' or 'perfect'.

Kanisha *f.*
A modern variation of **TANISHA**, much used in the early 1990s by Afro-American parents, with whom names beginning with a 'k' sound have recently been fashionable. It is sometimes spelt **Quanisha**.

Kanta *f.*
An Indian name meaning 'beautiful' and 'desired'.

Kara, Karena, Karissa *see* **Cara**

Karel *see* **Carol**

Karen *f.*
A Scandinavian form of **KATHARINE** which was only introduced into this country in the 1930s. Variants include **Karan** and **Karin**, **Karyn**, **Caryn**, **Caron** and **Karyna**, although some of these could be analyzed as belonging to **CARA** (see also **KEREN**).

Karenza *see* **Kerensa**

Karin *see* **Karen**

Karl, Karla *see* **Carl**

Karyn, Karyna *see* **Karen**

Kashif *m.*
An Arabic name which means 'discoverer'.

Kasia *see* **Kezia(h)**

Kasimir, Kasimira *see* **Casey**

Kaspar *see* **Jasper**

Katharine, Katherine, Catharine, Catherine *f.*

A name of unknown meaning, but from an early date associated with the Greek *katharos* meaning 'pure'. The name came to England in the early 12th century when crusaders brought back the legend of St Katharine of Alexandria. She was an Egyptian princess who was tortured and put to death in the early 4th century for her learned defence of Christianity. There are a number of further spellings for the name, of which **Kathryn** is one of the most frequent. The most common short forms are **Kate**, **Kitty**, **Katie**, **Cathy** and **Kay**, all of which are used as independent names. The Irish forms, **Kathleen** and **Cathleen**, are now used throughout Britain, while *Caitlin* is an older Irish form which has recently become popular. The Irish pronounce it with the sound of 'cat', but the American pronunciation is reflected in the spelling **Katelyn(n)**. **Kathlyn** is a variant of Kathleen. Russian **Katarina**, **Katia** or **Katya** and **Katinka** are occasionally found (see also **Catriona**, **Karen**).

Katrina, Katrine *see* **Catriona**

Katya *see* **Katharine**

Kay *f. and m.*
A pet form of names beginning with a 'K', such as

KATHARINE. It has been used as a first name for the last hundred years, and can also be spelt **Kai** and **Kaye** (see also CAIUS). Blends such as **Kaylyn** are also found.

Kayla *f.*

This name has been immensely popular in the USA since 1990. It appears to link with **Michaela**, but that name is rarely used, especially by American parents. It is more likely to be a variant of KAYLEIGH, especially in the relaxed pronunciation of rural western states such as Montana, where use of Kayla seems to have begun in the 1970s.

Kayleigh *f.*

This name suddenly became popular in the 1980s, although it had been around for some years. It is also spelt in forms such as **Kayley** and **Kaylee**. While it can be interpreted as derived from an Irish surname, it is more likely to be a modern creation, used at a time when LEE was popular, as were a number of similar-sounding names beginning with 'K' such as KYLIE and KELLY. **Keeley** is either a variation of this name or of Kelly.

Keir *m.*

Keir is a Scottish surname used as a first name. It came into use out of respect for James Keir Hardie (1856–1915), who was generally referred to as Keir Hardie, the first man to be elected as a Labour MP.

Keiran *see* Kieran

Keisha *f.*

Another of the names beginning with a 'K' sound which have recently proved so popular with Afro-Americans (see also **LAKEISHA**). Keisha is probably a similar adaptation of **AISHA**, or **Iesha** as it is frequently spelt by Black American Muslims.

Keith *m.*

This is a first name from Scotland which has spread throughout the rest of Britain. It was originally a surname which was taken from the Scottish place name, probably from the Gaelic meaning 'wood' or 'windy place'.

Kelly *f. and m.*

A modern first name which has rapidly become very popular. It is an Irish surname which means 'warlike' used as a first name. At first mainly a boy's name, it is now more usual for girls. **Kelley** is also found (see also **KAYLEIGH**, **KYLIE**).

Kelsey *f. and m.*

The surname, which in turn comes from an Old English name meaning 'ship-victory', used as a first name. It is more common for girls than boys.

Kelvin *m.*

This is the name of the river which flows through

Glasgow, used as a first name. The river's name possibly means 'narrow water'.

Kendall *f. and m.*

The surname, which can have various sources, used as a first name. Another surname, the similar-sounding **Kendrick**, is also used for boys, and from it a feminine form, **Kendra**, has evolved.

Kenneth *m.*

This is the English form of the Gaelic **Coinneach**, meaning 'handsome', and equivalent to modern Welsh **Cenydd**. It is basically a Scottish name which became popular when Kenneth MacAlpine became first King of Scotland in the 9th century, uniting the Picts and the Scots. From there it gradually spread over Britain. It is often shortened to **Ken** or **Kenny**.

Kent *m.*

This is the surname taken from the English county used as a first name. It first became popular in the United States. The county name is an ancient one, meaning 'border' from its position on the coast.

Kentigern *see* **Mungo**

Kenton *m.*

This is taken from a surname, derived from a common

place name meaning 'royal manor', and now used as a first name.

Keren *f.*

Although some modern uses of this may be as a form of **KAREN**, this is an ancient name, a short form of the Old Testament **Kerenhappuch**, one of the beautiful daughters of **JOB**. The name means 'horn (container) of kohl'. It has also been found in the form **Kerena** and **Ker(r)yn**.

Kerensa, Kerenza *f.*

A Cornish name meaning 'affection, love'. It is also found as **Karenza.**

Keri *see* Ceri

Kerry *f. and m.*

The Irish county name used as a given name. It is a modern name, apparently first used in Australia usually for boys, but it is now in general use, mainly for girls. It is also found as **Kerri**. Its spread may have been helped by the Welsh name **CERI**, pronounced in the same way.

Keshia *see* Kezia

Kester *see* Christopher

Ketan *m.,* Ketana *f.*

An Indian name meaning 'home'.

Kevin *m.*

From the Irish meaning 'handsome birth'. The name was very popular in Ireland on account of St Kevin, a 6th-century hermit and abbot of Glendalough. It is now widely used across the English-speaking world.

Kezia(h) *f.*

The Hebrew word for the spice cassia, and the name of one of JOB's beautiful daughters in the Bible. The form **Keshia** also occurs, with short forms **Kezie**, **Kizzie** and **Kissie** or **Kissy**. **Cassia** and **Kasia** have also been recorded, with the latter also a Polish pet form of KATHARINE.

Khadija *f.*

A Muslim name from the Arabic meaning 'premature child'. Khadiya bint-Khuwaylid, the first wife of the Prophet Muhammad, was the mother of all his children. The name is also spelt **Khadeeja**, **Khadeejah** and **Khadijah**.

Kiara *f.*

This is another name which is currently popular among Afro-American families. It probably adapts 'tiara', making use of the fashionable 'k' sound. See also KIERAN. The similar **Kiana** is also found.

Kieran *m.*, Ki(e)ra *f.*

This is a form of the Irish name **Ciaran**, meaning 'dark-

haired'. It was the name of 26 Irish saints and in the last two or three decades it has become increasingly popular. It is sometimes spelt **Cieran**, **Keiran** or **Kieron**.
Ciara (see also **SIERRA**), **Ciera**, **KIARA** and Ki(e)ra are used for girls.

Kim *f. and m.*

Probably from Old English *cynebeald*, meaning 'royally bold', developing through the surname Kimball. Rudyard Kipling's hero in the novel *Kim* (1901) used a shortened form of his true name, Kimball O'Hara, showing the use of the surname as a first name. More recently the name has been commoner for girls. **Kym** is also found.

Kimberl(e)y *f.*

Another possible source of the name **KIM**. Kimberley is a diamond-mining town in South Africa, and the association with jewels seems to have encouraged its use. It spread rapidly after its first use in the 1940s. There was also a brief fashion for Kimberley as a boy's name at the turn of the century, no doubt commemorating events of the Boer War.

Kiran *m.*

An Indian name deriving from the Sanskrit for 'ray of light, sunbeam'.

Kirk *m.*

A Scandinavian name for 'church', brought to

prominence as a first name by the actor, Kirk Douglas. It would originally have been the surname of someone who was connected with the church, or lived near one.

Kirsty, Kirsten *f.*

Both forms of the name **CHRISTINE**. Kirsty was originally a Scottish pet form, while Kirsten comes from Scandinavia. **Ki(e)rsten** is also found.

Kishen *see* **Krishna**

Kissie, Kissy *see* **Kezia(h)**

Kistna *see* **Krishna**

Kit *see* **Christopher**

Kitty *see* **Katharine**

Kizzie *see* **Kezia(h)**

Kodey, Kody *see* **Cody**

Korey, Korrie, Kory *see* **Corey**

Krishna *m.*

The name of a popular Hindu god, a partial incarnation of Vishnu, and deriving from a Sanskrit word for 'black'. In northern India it occurs as **Kishen**; other regional forms include **Kishan**, **Krishan** and **Kistna**.

Krista, Kristin, Kristina, Kryssa, Krystyna *see* Christine

Klaus *see* Nicholas

Kumar *m.*, Kumari *f.*
The boy's name derives from the Sanskrit for 'boy', but it is usually taken to mean 'prince'. The feminine form means 'girl' or 'daughter'.

Kurt *see* Conrad

Kushal *m.*
An Indian name meaning 'clever'.

Kyle *f. and m.*
This is a Scottish place and surname meaning 'a strip of land'. It is more usual as a name for boys than girls, for whom *Kyla* is also used.

Kylie *f.*
Originally an Australian Aboriginal word for a 'curled stick' or 'boomerang', it was this name's pleasant sound rather than its meaning which appealed to parents. It first became familiar to white Australians through the

novelist Kathleen Tennant, whose nickname and pen-name were both Kylie. Its use spread slowly from Australia throughout the English-speaking world, and it is best known in this country through the actress and singer, Kylie Minogue.

Kym *see* **Kim**

L

Lacey *f.*
Although this is on the surface the surname, which comes from a French place name, used as a first name, the recent popularity of this name in the USA probably owes much to its associations with 'lace'.

Lachlan *m.*
From Gaelic **Lachlann** or **Lochlann**. Primarily a Highland name, it was introduced as a term for Viking settlers there, but was taken by Scots emigrants to Australia and Canada where it flourished. Short forms are **Lachie** and **Lochie** and there is an occasional feminine form **Lachina**.

Laeta, Laetitia *see* **Letitia**

Laila *see* **Leila**

Lakeisha *f.*
An adaptation of the name **KEISHA** used by Afro-American parents. The prefix 'La-' became fashionable in the early 1970s in names such as **LATASHA** and **LATOYA**, and was popular until the '90s when it began to be replaced by 'Sha-'. Other frequently used names

with this prefix include **Laquisha**, **Lashay**, **Lashonda**, **Latisha**, **Latrice** and **Latonya**.

Lakshmi *f.*

The name of the Hindu goddess of wealth and good fortune. Lakshmi derives from the Sanskrit for 'mark', referring to a lucky birthmark.

Lal *m.*, Lalita *f.*

An Indian name and endearment. As a Hindi term of address the male form, Lal, means 'darling boy', though it derives from a Sanskrit word meaning 'caress'. Lalita, the feminine form, means 'playful' or 'charming'. The name has been in use since the Middle Ages.

Lalage *f.*

From the Latin for 'one who prattles'. Short forms are **Lal** and **Lally**.

Lana *see* Alan

Lancelot *m.*

A name of disputed meaning, possibly from the Old French for 'servant'. It can also be spelt **Launcelot**, and was used in Britain from the 13th century due to the popularity of Sir Lancelot, the knight without equal, in stories of King Arthur. The short form **Lance** is more common today.

Laquisha *see* **Lakeisha**

Lara *f.*

A short form of the Russian name **Larissa**, the meaning of which is uncertain, although it may well be used by some parents as a variation of **LAURA**. Lara came into general use in the 1960s after the success of the film of Pasternak's *Dr Zhivago*, with its tragic heroine of this name.

Laraine *see* **Lorraine**

Larissa *see* **Lara**

Lark *see* **Raven**

Larrie, Larry *see* **Laurence**

Lashay, Lashonda *see* **Lakeisha**

Latasha, Latisha *f.*

There is a strong tradition of name-creating among certain sections of American society, which goes back to at least the last century. These two names and **LATOYA** are among the commonest of a large group of names which have grown up in the American Black community over the last forty years. They are mostly blends, or combinations of syllables taken from different names,

L

which work because they sound right at the time, echoing the sounds from other popular names. Many of them start with 'La' and particularly 'Lat'. Since names such as **Laverne** (with the option of **Leverne** for boys) were popular with an earlier generation, it may be that the French influence found in place and surnames in the southern USA is the source, although it could just as well come from the many girls' names which begin with these letters.

Latrice, Latonya *see* Lakeisha

Latoya *f.*
A name introduced to Afro-Americans by the well-known singer LaToya Jackson. Her mother invented the name, making use of the fashionable prefix 'La-'. **LaToy** and **Toya(h)** are also used.

Launcelot *see* Lancelot

Laura, Lauren *f.*
Laura is derived, like **Laurel**, from the Latin for 'laurel', a symbol in the classical world of victory and poetic genius. **Lauretta** is the diminutive form. Together with **Laurencia** and **Lora** these names were common from the 12th century. Lauren or **Loren** (also used for boys) and **Lori** are popular variants. Other diminutives which are sometimes used are **Laureen**, **Laurene**, and **Laurissa**, **Loretta** and **Lolly**. Laurel, the plant name, sometimes spelt **Lorel**, is also found (see also **LARA**).

Lauraine *see* **Lorraine**

Laurel, Lauren *see* **Laura**

Laurence, Lawrence *m.*
From the Latin meaning 'of Laurentium', a town which
took its name from the laurel plant, symbol of victory.
It became common in the 12th century. St Laurence, the
3rd-century Archdeacon of Rome, was a favourite
medieval saint. The name was popular in Ireland because
of St Laurence O'Toole, a 12th-century Archbishop of
Dublin, whose real name was **Lorcan** (Irish for 'fierce').
Larrie or **Larry** is the usual abbreviation in England,
while **Laurie** or **Lawrie** is used in Scotland. **Loren** is a
form of the name used for both boys and girls.

**Laurencia, Laureen, Laurene, Lauretta,
Laurissa** *see* **Laura**

Laurie *see* **Laurence**

Laverne *see* **Latasha**

Lavinia *f.*
The meaning of this name is unknown, but in classical
legend it was the name of Aeneas' wife, for whose hand
in marriage he fought and defeated a rival suitor. The
town of Lavinium, originally called Latium, was renamed

after her. The name was very popular for a while during the Renaissance, but then faded out, only returning to fashion in the 18th century. **Lavina** is probably a variant.

Lawrence, Lawrie *see* Laurence

Lea *see* Leah, Lee, Leo

Leah *f.*
A Hebrew name, probably meaning 'cow'. In the Bible, Leah was the sister of Rachel and the first wife of Jacob. **Lea** and **Lia**, the Italian form of the name, are sometimes used, although they can also be a short form of a number of names ending in the sound.

Leanne *see* Lianne

Leanora, Leanore *see* Leonora

Lee, Leigh, Lea *f. and m.*
From the various forms of the surname meaning 'meadow'. It may have spread from the southern US, and probably owes its popularity there to the Confederate general, Robert E. Lee (1807–70). See also **KAYLEIGH**.

Leena *f.*
An Indian name which means 'devoted'. In some cases it may be a form of the Arabic name **LINA**.

Leigh Ann *see* Lianne

Leila *f.*

A Persian name meaning 'night', probably indicating 'dark-haired'. Byron started the fashion for it in the 19th century by using it in a poem with an oriental setting called *The Giaour*. The name also appears in the Persian romantic legend of **Leilah** and Mejnoun, the Persian equivalent of the Greek story of Cupid and Psyche. **Laila** is also used.

Len *see* Leonard

Lena *see* Helen

Lennie, Lenny, Lennard *see* Leonard

Lenore *see* Leonora

Leo *m.,* Leonie *f.*

From the Latin for 'lion'. Six emperors of Constantinople and thirteen popes were named Leo. **Leon** is the French form, from which the feminine **Leonie** comes. Other versions used for girls include **Lea**, **Leola**, **Leona** and **Leontine**.

Leolin(e) *see* Llewelyn

Leon *see* Leo, Lionel

Leona *see* Leo

Leonard *m.*

From the Old German meaning 'brave as a lion'. The
6th-century St Leonhard was a Frankish nobleman who
was converted to Christianity. He became a hermit and
devoted his life to helping prisoners, of whom he is the
patron saint. His popularity made the name common in
medieval England and France and it was revived in the
19th century. The usual shortened forms are **Len**, **Lennie**
and **Lenny**. It is sometimes spelt **Lennard**.

Leonie *see* Leo

Leonora, Lenore, Leonore *f.*

These names are European forms of **ELEANOR**, all of
which have been used from time to time in Britain,
although none of them appeared there before the
19th century and their introduction was probably due
to contemporary literary and musical influences.
The spellings **Leanore** and **Leanora** are also found.
A short form which all these names share is **NORA**.

Leontine *see* Leo

Leopold *m.*

From the Old German words meaning 'people' and
'bold'. This name came to Britain through Queen

Victoria's uncle, King Leopold of Belgium, after whom she named her fourth son. It has not been used much in the 20th century.

Leroy *m.*

A surname from the Old French meaning 'the king' which was probably given to royal servants. It has been very popular as a first name in the US, particularly among Black Americans in recent years.

Leslie, Lesley *m. and f.*

These were respectively the usual masculine and feminine spellings of the name, although they are both now used for girls. It is a Scottish surname, perhaps meaning 'garden of hollies', used originally by the Lords of Leslie in Aberdeenshire. It was taken into general use as a first name in the late 19th century.

Lester *m.*

This is a form of the town name Leicester used as a first name. The town is an ancient one, and its name indicates that it is a Roman town in the territory of the Ligore clan.

Letitia *f.*

From the Latin meaning 'gladness'. **Lettice** was the usual form of this name from the 12th to the 17th centuries, during which time it was very popular. In the 18th century the Latin **Laetitia** superseded it, now more frequently spelt Letitia. The phonetic form **Leticia** has recently become quite popular in the USA, giving a short form **Tiesha**, used independently. **Laeta** is also found. None of these names is common at present, though Lettice did return briefly in the late 19th and early 20th century. The short forms **Lettie** and **Letty** are sometimes used independently.

Leverne *see* **Latasha**

Levi *m.*

This is a Hebrew name, meaning 'associated', which has recently become more popular in the USA, possibly due to familiarity with the word as a brand name. It is occasionally given to girls, and has been elaborated into **Levon**.

Lewis, Louis *m.*

From Old German Chlodowig, meaning 'famous warrior', and latinized into Ludovicus from which **Ludovic** derives. **Clovis**, the Old French form, was the name of the founder of the French monarchy. His name later became Louis, the name of eighteen other French kings. The Normans brought the name to England where it became Lewis. Use in the UK of the French form, Louis, is comparatively recent, with Robert Louis Stevenson an early example; this form is quite common in the Scottish lowlands and the usual form in the USA. Short forms are **Lou** and **Louie**, **Lew** and **Lewie**.

Lex *see* **Alexander**

Lia *see* Leah

Liam *see* William

Lianne, Leanne *f.*

A pet form of the name JULIANA, via the French
Julianne, which has become popular as an independent
name. It can also be spelt **Liane** and occurs in such forms
as **Leigh Ann**.

Libby, Liese, Liesel *see* Elizabeth

Lilian, Lily *f.*

Originally these names may have been pet forms of
ELIZABETH. **Lillian** is found in Shakespeare's time but
the name was probably associated with the lily flower
even then. In the 19th century Lily was definitely given
as the name of the flower, which is a Christian symbol of
purity. **Lil** is the usual abbreviation. Other forms of the
name include **Lillah** or **Lila**, and, in Scotland, **Lillias**.

Lilith *f.*

From the Hebrew meaning either 'serpent' or 'belonging
to the night'. In mythology Lilith was an evil spirit who
haunted the night and who had been Adam's rejected
wife before Eve. It has been used very rarely.

Lillah, Lillian, Lillias, Lily *see* Lilian

Lin *see* **Linda, Lyn**

Lina *f.*

A short form of names ending in '-lina', such as **Angelina** and **Carolina**, used as an independent name. It can also be used as a pet form of these names. In the Arab world it derives from a word meaning 'tender'. Some Arabic experts refer the name to a type of palm tree.

Linda *f.*

This was a common ending for girls' names in Old German, and comes from the word for a snake, an animal which was held in great reverence by primitive German tribes. It represented wisdom and suppleness, and the names derived from it were therefore complimentary. In Spanish *linda* means pretty, and this may also have had some effect on the use of Linda as an English first name, which dates only from the 19th century. It is also used as a contraction of **BELINDA**. Linda is also spelt **Lynda**, while **Lindy**, **Lindi(e)**, **Lin** and **LYN** are pet forms.

Lindsey *f. and m.*

From the Scottish surname meaning 'pool island'. Together with its other forms, **Lindsay**, **Linsey** and **Linsay**, this name is used for both boys and girls. The form Lindsay tends to be the more usual one for boys. At the moment all forms of the name are used more frequently for girls than for boys and can then take the form **Linzi**.

Lindy *see* **Linda**

Linet, Linette, Linnet *see* **Lynette**

Linn, Linne *see* **Lyn**

Linsay, Linsey, Linzi *see* **Lindsey**

Lionel *m.*

This name means 'young lion'. A French diminutive of
Leon, it thus derives from the same root as **Leo**. It was
the name of one of King Arthur's knights and was given
by Edward III of England to his third son, later Duke of
Clarence. The name was very popular in the Middle
Ages and survived into more recent times, particularly in
the north of England, where it has come back into
general, though infrequent, use.

Lisa, Lisette, Liz, Liza, Lizzy
see **Elizabeth**

Llewellyn *m.*

This name derives from Welsh. The original form was
Llywelyn and its meaning is doubtful but the form
Llewellyn suggests that users thought it was connected
with the Welsh word for 'lion'. It is an old Welsh name
which was anglicized into **Leolin(e)** as early as the
13th century. This form was used at least until the
17th century. **Lyn** is a short form.

Lloyd *m.*

A Welsh name meaning 'grey'. **Floyd** is a variant form
which has arisen due to the difficulty of pronouncing the
Welsh 'll', and which appears to come from the USA.

Llywelyn *see* **Llewellyn**

Lo *see* **Dolores**

Lochie, Lochlann *see* **Lachlan**

Logan *f. and m.*

This Scottish place name, meaning 'little hollow',
became a surname, which led in turn to its use in
Scotland as a first name. Since 1990 the name has
surprisingly become one of the top fifty names for boys
in several western American states, but its popularity
has not yet spread from Scotland and the USA to other
English-speaking countries.

Lois *f.*

In the New Testament Lois was the grandmother of
TIMOTHY. As the rest of the family had Greek names,
Lois is probably Greek also, but its meaning is not
known. Like many obscure biblical names, it was
adopted in the 17th century by Puritans. It fell out of use
but was revived at the beginning of the 20th century.

Lola *f.*

This was originally a diminutive of the Spanish **DOLORES**

and of **Carlotta** (see **CHARLOTTE**). The pet form, **Lolita**, has become well known in the 20th century through Vladimir Nabokov's novel of that name.

Lolly, Lora, Lorel, Loretta *see* **Laura**

Loraine *see* **Lorraine**

Lorcan *see* **Laurence**

Loren *see* **Laura, Laurence**

Lori *see* **Laura, Lorraine**

Lorna *f.*
This name was created by R.D. Blackmore for the heroine of his novel *Lorna Doone*, published in 1869. He may have had in mind both the Marquis of **Lorne** and the old English word meaning 'lost, forsaken'.

Lorraine *f.*
This is the French district, whose name derives from the Old German place name Lotharingen, meaning 'Lothar's place'. Lothar was an Old German warrior name meaning 'famous army'. Lorraine is the form used in France. In Britain and North America it sometimes takes the forms **Loraine**, **Laraine** or **Lauraine**. **Lori** is a pet form.

Lottie, Lotty *see* **Charlotte**

Lou, Louie *see* **Lewis, Louisa**

Louella *see* **Luella**

Louis *see* **Lewis**

Louisa, Louise *f.*
Louise is the French, and Louisa the Latin female form of **Louis** (see **LEWIS**). Though common much earlier in France, Louise did not come to Britain until the 17th century when Louise de Keroual became Charles II's mistress. It was popular for about a century until Louisa replaced it but nowadays Louise is once more the popular form. Pet forms are **Lulu**, **Lou** and **Louie** (see also **LUELLA**).

Loveday *f.*
This name was common in the Middle Ages, but is now mainly restricted to those of Cornish descent. It used to be used for both sexes, but is now rarely used for boys. In the past a loveday was a day when members of a community who had had a quarrel were called to meet to see if they could sort things out without going to law. **Lowdy** is an old pet form.

Lowena *f.*
Lowena is an old Cornish name meaning 'joy', which can

also be spelt **Lowenna**. Its popularity has been growing rapidly in Cornwall, and it is beginning to spread to other areas. The name **Lowenek**, 'joyful', can also be used. Both names are stressed on the second syllable.

Lucas *see* Luke

Lucasta, Lucette, Lucia *see* Lucy

Lucille *f.*, Lucius *m.*

From the Latin word *lux*, meaning 'light' (see **LUCY**). **Lucilla** retains the Latin form, and Lucille is French. The male form Lucius and its variants **Lucien** and **Lucian** are much less common than the feminine names.

Lucina *see* Lucy

Lucinda *f.*

Originally a poetic form of **LUCY**, this name is now given independently, and has recently become quite popular. The short forms **CINDY**, **Cindi** or **Cindie** are sometimes used as names in their own right.

Lucretia *f.*

This is a Roman family name. Its use as a first name in Renaissance Europe was due to the story of the Roman matron, Lucretia, who was raped by Tarquin and committed suicide as a result. This incident led to the expulsion of the ruling Tarquin family from Rome and the foundation of the Roman republic. Shakespeare's poem, *The Rape of* **Lucrece**, spread the use of the name in this form. It was common in Britain between the 16th and the 18th centuries and has never quite died out.

Lucy *f.*

Lucy is the usual English form of the Latin **Lucia** from *lux*, 'light'. In Roman times the name was often used for a child born at dawn; the goddess **Lucina** was the patroness of childbirth, bringing children into the light of day. St Lucy was a Sicilian martyr who was much beloved in the Middle Ages, and the name became well established after the Norman Conquest. Other forms are **Lucette**, LUCINDA, **Lucasta** and **Lulu**.

Ludovic *see* Lewis

Luella *f.*

A blend of the names LOUISE and ELLA. Today the name is most popular in North America. **Louella** is an alternative spelling.

Luke *m.*

A Greek name, latinized as **Lucas**, meaning 'a man of Lucania' in southern Italy. St Luke the Evangelist is the patron saint of doctors and also of painters, and the name was often given by a craftsman to his son. The name appeared in the 12th century as **Lucas** but a century later it was well established in the English form, Luke.

Lulu *see* **Louisa, Lucy**

Luned *see* **Eluned, Lynette**

Luther *m.*

From the Old German, meaning 'people's warrior'.
The modern use of Luther as a first name is entirely due
to Martin Luther, the German leader of the Reformation,
and to the American civil rights campaigner Martin
Luther King, named after him.

Lydia *f.*

From the Greek meaning 'a Lydian girl'. Lydia was a
district of Asia Minor where the people were famous
merchants, and were said to have invented coinage. In
the Acts of the Apostles, Lydia was a widow of Philippi
who was converted by St Paul when he stayed at her
house. The name was not used in this country before the
17th century.

Lyn *f. and m.*

A short form of such names as **LINDA**, **LYNETTE** and
Carolyn (see **CAROLINE**) when used for girls. It can also
take the form **Lin**, **Linne**, **Linn**, **Lynn** and **Lynne.** As a
boy's name it can take the form Lyn or Lynn and is
derived either from a surname or from a short form of
LLEWELLYN.

Lynda *see* **Linda**

Lynette *f.*

From the Welsh name **ELUNED** via its short form, **Luned**.
The form Lynette was introduced by the poet Tennyson
in the story of 'Gareth and Lynette' in his *Idylls of the
King*. It is also spelt **Linet**, **Linnet**, **Linette** and **Lynnette**,
and **LYN** is used as a short form.

Lynn, Lynne *see* Lyn

M

Mabel *f.*

Mabel is a shortening of **AMABEL**, with **Mabella** as the Latin form. Both were current from the 12th to the 15th century, but were rare thereafter until Mabel was revived in the 19th century and became very common. It then suffered another fall from favour. The pet form often used is **MAY**. **Maybelle** and **Maybelline** are developments of the name.

Mackenzie *f.*

As a Scottish surname, this refers to a 'son of Coinneach', a Gaelic name which usually takes the anglicized form **KENNETH**. It was popularised as a girl's name by the actress Mackenzie Phillips who appeared in a 1970s American TV series. Although the name was chosen by parents because it was unusual, if its use continues to spread at the present rate it will soon be familiar to everyone.

Macsen *see* **Maximilian**

Madel(e)ine *f.*

Magdalene, the original form of the name, is Hebrew and means 'woman of Magdala', a town on the Sea of Galilee which was the birthplace of St Mary Magdalene.

From about the 12th century the name was used in England in the French form Madeline, often abbreviated to Maudlin and Madlin. **Magdalen**, the biblical form, was adopted after the Reformation. It was usually pronounced Maudlin, but because the meaning of this word developed the sense of 'weak and sentimental', this form was replaced by the current pronunciation. It shares the short form **Madge** with MARGARET. **Maddie** or **Maddy** is also used. A Continental short form is **Magda**, which has also been given as an independent name.

Madge *see* **Madeline, Margaret**

Madison *f.*
Use of Madison as a first name derives ultimately from the surname, which means 'son of MAUD or **Magdalen**'. The name was used by a character in the 1984 film *Splash*, sparking its real-life use as soon as the film was released. It continues to grow in popularity.

Madoc, Madog *m.*
A Welsh name meaning 'fortunate'. It is rarely used outside Wales (see also MARMADUKE).

Madonna *see* **Donna**

Mae *see* **May**

Maegan *see* **Margaret**

Maeve *f.*

The more usual phonetic form of the Irish name
Meadhbh, meaning 'she who makes drunk'. It was the
name of a famous queen in Irish legend. A diminutive
is **Meaveen**, and the name is occasionally spelt **Meave**
or **Mave**.

Magda, Magdalen(e) *see* Madeline

Maggie *see* Margaret

Magnus *m.*

This is a Latin adjective meaning 'great'. The spread
of this name was due to the Emperor Charlemagne,
Carolus Magnus in Latin. Some of his admirers took
Magnus for a personal name, and among those who
christened their sons after him was St Olaf of Norway.
The name spread from Scandinavia to Shetland and
Ireland. From Shetland the name became well
established in Scotland. In Ireland it became **Manus**,
hence the common Irish surname McManus.

Mahalia *f.*

A form of the Hebrew **Mahala** meaning 'tenderness'.
No longer a very unusual name, it is best known from
the singer, Mahalia Jackson.

Mai *see* May

Maia *see* **Maya**

Mair, Maire *see* **Mary, Moira**

Mairead *see* **Margaret**

Mairi *see* **Mary**

Mairin *see* **Maureen**

Maisie *see* **Margaret**

Maja *see* **Maya**

Malcolm *m.*

From the Gaelic *mael Colum*, 'follower of St Columba'.
This was a very popular Scottish name, borne by
four kings of Scotland. It was used very occasionally
in medieval England, but only became common in
this century. Short forms are **Mal** and **Col(u)m**
(see **Callum**).

Mallory *f.*

This name has a pleasant sound, but a less pleasant
meaning: as a surname it derives from the French and
means 'ill-omened' or 'unfortunate'. It is nevertheless
being well used by American parents in the 1990s,
having been launched in its first-name role by a
character in the TV series *Family Ties*.

Malvina *f.*

A name invented by the Scottish poet, James
Macpherson (1736–96). He may have taken it from the
Gaelic meaning 'smooth brow'. The form **Melvina** is
also found.

Manish *m.*, Manisha *f.*

An Indian name which refers to 'intellect' or
'intelligence'.

Manju *f.*

An Indian name derived from the Sanskrit for
'beautiful'. Similar names are **Manjubala** and **Manjulika**,
both meaning 'beautiful girl'.

Mamie *see* Mary

Mandy *see* Amanda

Manny *see* Emanuel

Manon *see* Mary

Manuel *see* Emanuel

Manus *see* Magnus

Maol Mhuire *see* **Miles**

Marc, Marcel *see* **Marcus**

Marcia *f.*

The feminine form of the Latin Marcius, a Roman clan name which probably was derived from Mars, the god of war. St Marcia was an early Christian martyr. The name can be pronounced with either three syllables, or with two, reflected in the alternative spelling **Marsha**. **Marcy** is used as a short form. **Marcella**, **Marcelle**, **Marcelline** and **Marcine** are all developments of the name.

Marcus, Mark *m.*

These names are probably derived from Mars, the Roman god of war, and were used as Roman family and personal names. Although it occurs from the Middle Ages in Britain, Mark has only become common since the 1950s. The Latin form, Marcus, is the less common of the two, but has recently had a certain popularity with parents. The French forms **Marc** and **Marcel**, the latter derived from the Latin diminutive of the name, Marcellus, are also used in Britain today.

Marcy *see* **Marcia**

Maredudd *see* **Meredith**

Margaret *f.*

From the Latin *margarita*, derived from the Greek word meaning 'a pearl'. However, the ultimate origin is said to be Persian for 'child of light', the ancients believing that pearls were formed when oysters rose from their beds at night to look at the moon, and trapped a drop of dew in their shells which was then transformed into a pearl by the moonbeams. The name first appears in Scotland in the 11th century, thanks to St Margaret, wife of Malcolm III. She was born in Hungary where the name had spread through respect for St Margaret of Antioch, a 3rd-century martyr. The name became very common in medieval England and, after a decline, regained popularity in the 19th century. The most common pet forms are **Maggie**, **Madge**, **Meg** and **Peg(gy)**. **Maisie** was a particularly Scottish variant, and **MEGAN**, Welsh. The Irish form is **Mairead** ('mar-ed'). Other diminutives sometimes used are the Swedish **GRETA**, French **Margot** (now also spelt **Margaux**) and **Marguerite**, and **RITA**, from **Margarita**, which is also the source of the Scandinavian pet form **Meta**. Other forms include **Marghanita**, **Margaretta** and **Margoletta** (see also **DAISY**, **MARGERY**, **MAY**, **PEARL**).

Margery, Marjorie *f.*

Margerie was originally a pet form of the French **Marguerite** (see **MARGARET**), but it became established in England as early as the 12th century. Marjorie is the spelling in Scotland, where the name was popular from the late 13th century after Robert the Bruce gave it to his daughter, founder of the **Stewart** or STUART dynasty through her marriage to Walter the Steward. **Marge** and **Margie** are pet forms.

Marghanita, Margot, Margoletta
see **Margaret**

Marguerite *see* **Margaret, Margery**

Mari, Maria(h) *see* **Mary**

Mariam, Mariamne *see* **Miriam**

Marian *f.*

Marian or **Marion** was originally a diminutive of the French **Marie** (see **MARY**), which was early established as an independent name and was common on both sides of the Channel in medieval times. Marian was later extended to **Marianne**, giving rise to the double name **Mary Anne** in the 18th century. **Marianna** is the Spanish equivalent, which is sometimes given in England. In the USA **Marion** is occasionally found as a boy's name, as in the case of Marion Morrison, the real name of actor John Wayne (1907–79). In such cases it uses the surname Marion as a first name, possibly influenced by Francis Marion who played an important part in the American War of Independence.

Marie, Mariel(la), Marielle, Marietta, Mariette *see* **Mary**

Marigold *f.*

This name, borrowed from the flower, was adopted with others in the late 19th century, but has never been common.

Marilyn *f.*

This diminutive of **MARY** is now used independently. Its popularity was heightened by the film actress, Marilyn Monroe (1926–62).

Marina *f.*

From the Latin *marinus*, meaning 'of the sea'. The name has been used occasionally from at least the 14th century, probably on account of St Marina of Alexandria, a martyr of the Greek church. The name became more popular in Britain in 1934, when Prince George married Princess Marina of Greece, who later became Duchess of Kent.

Mario *see* Marius

Marion *see* Marian

Marisa, Marise, Marissa *see* Mary

Marius *m.*

From a Roman family name which was adopted as a first name during the Renaissance. It has never been common in this country, although **Mario** is very popular in Italy. The name is probably derived from Mars, the Roman god of war.

Marjorie *see* **Margery**

Mark *see* **Marcus**

Marlene *f.*

This is a German shortening of Mary Magdalene
(see **MADELEINE**). It was introduced to English speakers
by the song *Lili Marlene* and by the actress Marlene
Dietrich (1901–1992). **Marlena** is a form which reflects
the German pronunciation of the name, but a two
syllable pronunciation, the second half of the name
sounded as in the word 'lean' as opposed to the
German 'lane', is common in this country (see also
ARLENE). A shortening, **Marlee**, is also used.

Marlon *f. and m.*

A name of unknown origin, brought into use through
the fame of the actor, Marlon Brando (b. 1924). **Marlin**
and **Marlo** have also been used for both sexes in the
United States.

Marmaduke *m.*

From the Irish *mael Maedoc*, meaning 'servant of
MADOC'. The name is mainly confined to Yorkshire,
where Celtic civilization lingered after the Norse
invasions of northern England. **Duke** is sometimes used
as an abbreviation, but in America its use usually
derives from the title.

Marsha *see* **Marcia**

Martha *f.*

From the Aramaic, meaning 'lady'. In the New Testament Martha was the sister of Mary and Lazarus. The name was common in France in the Middle Ages where there was a legend that Martha had come to France after the Crucifixion. It was not adopted in Britain until after the Reformation. Variants include **Marta** and **Martella**. **Martie** is the commonest pet form.

Martin *m.,* Martina *f.*

From the Latin Martinus, a diminutive of Martius meaning 'of Mars', the Roman god of war. According to popular legend, St Martin was a 4th-century soldier who cut his cloak in half to share it with a beggar one winter's night; he later became Bishop of Tours in France. Martin has been used more or less without a break since the 12th century. **Martyn** is the Welsh spelling, and **Marty** a short form. **Martina** and **Martita** are the female forms of the name. **Martinella** and the French feminine **Martine** are also found for girls.

Marvin *see* Mervyn

Mary *f.*

A biblical name, traditionally meaning 'dew of the sea', but possibly going back to an ancient Egyptian name. The earliest form of the name was MIRIAM which later translations of the Bible changed to **Mariam** and **Maria** (now also spelt **Mariah**), and finally Mary. The name was held to be too sacred for general use until about the 12th century when the French form, **Marie**, and the diminutive, **MARIAN**, were common. The Scots kept the French Marie and used the Gaelic **Mairi** and **Mhairi** or **Mhari**. **Maire** is the Irish form, and **Mair** or **Mari** the Welsh. The latinized Maria was adopted in the 18th century, giving a pet form of **Ria**. **Marise** and **Maris(s)a** are Continental forms of the name. Other elaborations are **Mariel(le)**, **Marietta**, **Mariette**, and **Mariella**. Pet forms of Mary are **Molly**, currently a popular choice, **Polly**, **Mimi**, **Mamie** and **MAY**, with **Manon** a French pet form (see also **MARIAN**, **MARILYN**, **MAUREEN**, **MAYA**, **MIA**, **MIRIAM**, **MOIRA**). A recent trend has been to adopt the Continental habit of linking Marie with another name, to produce names such as **Marie-Rose** and **Marie-Louise**.

Maryann, Maryanne, Mary Anne
see **Marian**

Mason *m.*
The surname, which comes from the occupation, used as a first name.

Matilda *f.*
From the Old German meaning 'mighty in battle'. This name was particularly popular in medieval court circles, introduced by William the Conqueror's wife who bore the name. Later, their granddaughter, sometimes known

as **MAUD**, fought her cousin Stephen for the throne. The name fell into disuse but returned to favour in the 18th century. **Matty** and **Tilly** are pet forms. Although by no means common, there has been a recent increase in the the use of this name.

Matthew *m.*

From the Hebrew meaning 'gift of God', and the name of one of the Evangelists. The name was particularly popular from the 12th to the 14th centuries. After the Reformation the Greek form, **Matthias**, was adopted. In the Bible it is used for the name of the apostle chosen to succeed Judas Iscariot. Today the English form is popular, and the usual short form is **Matt**.

Matty *see* **Matilda**

Maud *f.*

The Old French form of the name **MATILDA**. This name was popular in Britain after the Norman Conquest, but fell out of use about the 15th century. It was revived in the 19th century by Tennyson's well-known poem *Maud* (1855). It is also spelt **Maude**, and **Maudie** is sometimes used as a pet form.

Maura *see* **Moira**

Maureen *f.*

A phonetic form of the Irish **Mairin**, meaning 'little

MARY'. The variant forms in Britain are **Moreen** and **Moira**. The Irish also have a name **Mor** meaning 'tall', with a pet form **Moirin**, which can be anglicized as **Moreen**.

Maurice, Morris *m.*

From the Latin *Mauritius*, meaning 'a Moor'.
The spread of the name was due to St Maurice, a 3rd-century martyr in Switzerland, after whom the town of St Moritz was named. The Normans brought the name to England as Meurisse, which was soon anglicized to Morris. The more modern French form, Maurice, has now to a large extent replaced the English form, although it is usually pronounced the same way. There is a Welsh equivalent, **Meurig**, which occurs from the 5th century. Short forms are **Morrie** and **Maurie**.

Mave *see* Maeve

Mavis *f.*

From the old word for song thrush. It was first used by Marie Corelli in her novel *The Sorrows of Satan* (1895). See also **THELMA**.

Max *see* Maximilian, Maxwell

Maximilian *m.*

Maximus in Latin means 'greatest'. Two 3rd-century saints bore its derivative, Maximilian, yet it is popularly thought to have been invented by German Emperor

Frederick III, combining the last names of Quintus
Fabius Maximus and Scipio Aemilianus, two Roman
generals. His son, later Emperor Maximilian I, was a
huntsman and fighter, and the name became very
popular in German-speaking countries. It has recently
become more popular in this country, particularly in
its short form, **Max**. **Macsen** is the Welsh form of
Maximus. **Maxime** is used in France for both sexes,
but in Britain this, or **Maxine**, tends to be used for girls,
keeping **Maxim**, also a Russian form of the name,
for boys.

Maxwell *m.*

From a Scottish surname, which derives from a place
name meaning 'Mac's well'. It has been given as a first
name since the end of the last century. **Max** is the short
form.

May *f.*

This was originally a pet form of **MABEL**, **MARGARET**
or **MARY** but it has more recently been associated with
the month (see **JUNE**), and it is now a separate name.
Variants are **Mae**, as in the actress Mae West
(1892–1980), and **Mai** (see also **AVRIL**).

Maya *f.*

In India this name derives from a Sanskrit word
meaning 'illusion', an important word in Hindu
philosophy. In Europe Maya usually refers to the Roman

goddess Maia, whose name probably meant 'great', or else is a form of **MARIA** (see **MARY**).

Maybelle, Maybelline see **Mabel**

Meadhbh, Meave, Meaveen see **Maeve**

Meera f.

An Indian name which means 'saintly woman'.

Megan f.

Megan started life as a Welsh pet form of **Meg**, itself a pet form of **MARGARET**. It is currently very popular throughout the English-speaking world. In Australia, Canada and the USA it is quite often spelt as **Meghan**, as if it were an Irish name, and Americans also use forms such as **Maegan** and **Maygen**.

Mehul f.

This Indian name refers to 'rain-clouds'.

Mel see **Melvin**

Melanie f.

From the Greek for 'black' or 'dark-skinned'. Melania is an ancient name used by both the Greeks and the Romans. It came to England from France in the mid-17th century in its French form, Melanie, which also became **Melony** or **Mel(l)oney** and **Melany** in Britain.

Melicent, Melisenda, Melisande, Melisent *see* Millicent

Melissa *f.*

From the Greek meaning 'a bee' and the name of a nymph in Greek mythology. It was used occasionally in the 18th century, and has been quite popular in recent years. Other names with the sense of 'bee' or 'honey' that are used are **Melinda**, sometimes shortened to **Mindy**, and **Melita**.

Melloney, Meloney, Melony *see* Melanie

Melody *f.*

This vocabulary word has come into first-name use in recent years.

Melvin, Melvyn *m.*

Various theories have been put forward as the source of this name. It seems likely that it comes from a surname, which can come from a variety of sources, several of them Scottish. **Mel** is the short form.

Melvina *see* Malvina

Mercedes *see* Dolores

Mercy *f.*

This is the virtue used as a first name, in the same way

as HOPE. The pet form is **Merry**, which is also used as an independent name. The old-fashioned **Mercia** can either be a form of this or be from the Anglo-Saxon kingdom of Mercia, which covered the Midlands.

Meredith *f. and m.*

From the surname from the ancient Welsh **Maredudd** or **Meredydd**, 'great chief'. It can be spelt **Meridith** and shares **Merry** as a short form with **MERCY**. Use of the name for girls is a 20th-century innovation.

Meriel *see* Muriel

Merle *f.*

This is the French for 'blackbird' originally derived from Latin. It was adopted as a first name in the 19th century. It became well known as the name of the film actress, Merle Oberon (1911–79). In the USA it is used sometimes as a boy's name.

Merlene, Merlin, Merlyn *see* Mervyn

Merlin *see* Raven

Merrill *see* Muriel

Merry *see* Mercy, Meredith

Mervyn *m.*

From the Welsh name **Myrddin** ('sea fort'), which is the

true form of **Merlin**, the name of King Arthur's legendary magician. It is also spelt **Mervin**. Merlin has recently come to be used for girls, sometimes in the forms **Merlene** or **Merlyn**. **Marvin**, also a common surname, is probably a form of Mervyn, although some would dispute this.

Meryl *see* **Muriel**

Meta *see* **Margaret**

Meurig *see* **Maurice**

Mhairi, Mhari *see* **Mary**

Mia *f.*

A Scandinavian pet form of **MARY**, although some associate it with the Italian and Spanish word for 'my'. The actress Mia Farrow brought the name into more general use.

Michael *m.,* Michelle *f.*

From the Hebrew meaning 'who is like the Lord?' In the Bible Michael was one of the seven archangels and their leader in battle, and he therefore became the patron saint of soldiers. The variant form **Micah**, the name of a minor prophet in the Old Testament, was used in the 17th century among Puritans and can now be found used for both sexes, sometimes as **Mica** or

Myka. Michael has pet forms **Mike**, **Mick** or **Micky**. The surname **Mitchell**, derived from Michael, is also used as a boy's name, with the short form **Mitch**. **Michelle** is the French female form of the name, also found as **Michele**, which can be shortened to Shelley. **Michaela** is another feminine form of the name. **Misha** or **Mischa** is in Russia a pet form of Michael, but because of the 'a' ending is sometimes thought of as a girl's name. Spanish forms are **Miguel** and **Miguela**.

Milan *m.*

In Europe this name usually derives from the Czech for 'grace'. As an Indian name the derivation is from a word meaning 'union'.

Mildred *f.*

The 7th-century King Merowald of the Old English kingdom of Mercia had three daughters: Milburga ('gentle defence'), Mildgyth ('gentle gift'), and Mildthryth ('gentle strength'). It was from the last of these that Mildred was derived and the popularity of the three sisters, all of whom became saints, led to the name's becoming common in the Middle Ages. It was revived in the 19th century.

Miles *m.*

An old name of unknown meaning. The Normans brought to Britain the forms Miles and **Milo**. It has also been used to transliterate the Irish **Maol Mhuire**

('devotee of Mary') and its Gaelic form **Mael Moire**.
A variant spelling is **Myles**.

Milla *see* Camilla

Millicent *f.*

From the Old German meaning 'strong worker'. This
name was common in France about a thousand years
ago, when it had the form **Melisenda**, now also
Melisande. The French brought it to England in the late
12th century in the form **Melisent**, and it survived with
minor changes of spelling such as **Melicent** well into the
17th century. In the 19th it was revived. **Millie** or **Milly**
is a common abbreviation.

Millie, Milly *see* Amelia, Camilla, Emily, Millicent

Milo *see* Miles

Milton *m.*

From the Old English surname derived from a place
name meaning 'mill-enclosure'. Initial use as a first name
may have been due to the poet, John Milton (1608–74).
It has been particularly popular in the US.

Mima *see* Jemima

Mimi *see* Mary

Mindy *see* **Melissa**

Minna, Minnie *see* **William**

Minta, Minty *see* **Araminta**

Mira *see* **Myra**

Mirabel, Mirabelle *f.*

From the Latin for 'admirable, wonderful'. The Latin form **Mirabella** was used in the last century, but it was later anglicized to Mirabel.

Miranda *f.*

From the Latin meaning 'deserving admiration'. This name was coined by Shakespeare for the heroine of *The Tempest* (1612), a young woman blessed with many admirable qualities. Like other Shakespearian names it has come into use in the 20th century.

Miriam *f.*

This is the old form of **Mary**, and in the book of Exodus in the Old Testament it was the name of the sister of **Moses** and **Aaron**. It is traditionally interpreted as meaning 'dew of the sea', but possibly, like Miriam's brothers' names, goes back to ancient Egyptian sources. It first became common in Britain in the 17th century. **Mariam** and **Mariamne** are variant forms which have recently gained popularity. **Mitzi** can be a short form of Miriam or **Maria**.

Mischa, Misha, Mitch, Mitchell
see **Michael**

Mitzi *see* **Miriam**

Mohammad, Mohammed
see **Muhammad**

Mohan *m.*, Mohana *f.*
In early times a name of **Krishna**'s; from the Sanskrit for 'attractive'.

Moira, Moyra *f.*
Moira or **Maura** is an English phonetic spelling of **Maire**, the Irish form of **Mary**. **Maureen** has the same origin, but has developed as a separate name, though Moira is occasionally used as its short form.

Moirin *see* **Maureen**

Molly *see* **Mary**

Mona *f.*
This name is derived from a diminutive of the Irish **Muadhnait** ('mooa-nid'), meaning 'noble, good'. It came

into use in the late 19th century along with other Irish
names which spread throughout Britain at that time,
during a general revival of interest in Celtic culture.
It can also be a short form of **MONICA**.

Monica *f.*

The etymology of this name is uncertain, but it could be
connected with Greek *monos* meaning 'alone' or Latin
monere meaning 'to advise'. St Monica was the mother
of St Augustine and was a paragon of motherly virtues.
MONA is sometimes used as a short form, and there are
French and Scandinavian forms, **Monique** and **Monika**.

Montagu(e), Montgomery *m.*

Founder of this ancient noble family was Drogo de
Montacute, William the Conqueror's companion who
received estates in Somerset. He took his name from
Mont Aigu, a 'pointed hill' in Normandy. Montagu(e)'s
first-name use dates from the 19th century, when many
aristocratic surnames, e.g. **CECIL**, **HOWARD**, **DUDLEY**,
MORTIMER, **PERCY**, were adopted by the public. It shares
Monty as a short form with Montgomery, from the Old
French meaning 'mountain of the powerful one'.

Montserrat *see* **Dolores**

Monty *see* **Montague**

Mor *see* **Maureen, Morag**

Morag *f.*
A Scottish name from the Gaelic and Irish name **Mor** meaning 'great' or 'tall'.

Moray *see* **Murray**

Morcant *see* **Morgan**

Moreen *see* **Maureen**

Morgan *f. and m.*
In its earliest form, **Morcant**, this name meant 'sea-bright' (see **MURIEL**), but it later absorbed another name, **Morien**, meaning 'sea-born'. Its earliest celebrated male bearer was the first recorded British heretic, who was known as Pelagius, a Greek translation of the name. It was almost always a male name until this century, but now seems to have become part of the modern trend to use traditional boys' names for girls. The most famous female precedent for the name was Morgan(a) le Fay, King Arthur's wicked half-sister.

Morna, Myrna *f.*
Both these names come from the Gaelic name **Muirne**, which means either 'gentle', the traditional interpretation, or possibly 'high-spirited'.

Morrie, Morris *see* **Maurice**

Mortimer *m.*

An aristocratic surname adopted as a first name in the 19th century. The surname was derived from a French place name meaning 'dead sea'. The Mortimer family connect it with the Dead Sea in Palestine, where their ancestors fought in crusading times. The pet form **Morty** was also used independently in Ireland as a form of the Irish name **Murtaugh** or **Murty** ('skilled sailor'). The short form **Mort** is also used.

Morven *f.*

A Scottish name, from an old name for the northwest of the country. In legend it is the name of the kingdom of **FINGAL** and means 'high mountains'.

Morwenna *f.*

Morwenna comes from Welsh and probably means 'maiden'. There was a 5th-century saint of this name about whom little is known, and the name used to be confined to Wales and Cornwall but now seems to be spreading. It is also found as **Morwen**.

Moses *m.*

The meaning of this name is uncertain and it is possibly Egyptian rather than Hebrew. It became common among Jews after their return from captivity in Babylon. In Britain it first appears in the Domesday Book as Moyses, which became Moyse or **Moss** in general use. The present form, Moses, which was not used until the

Reformation, is the form used in the Authorized Version of the Bible.

Moyra *see* **Moira**

Muadhnait *see* **Mona**

Muhammad *m.*

The name of the Prophet of Islam, which comes from the word 'praise'. It is probably the most popular Islamic name and is spelt in various ways, **Moham(m)ed** and **Moham(m)ad** being the common variants.

Muhsin *m.*, Muhsina *f.*

A popular name in the Arab world, derived from an Arabic word meaning 'charitable' or 'benevolent'.

Muirne *see* **Morna**

Muneer *see* **Munir**

Mungo *m.*

This name was originally a term of affection given to St **Kentigern** by his followers, and in Gaelic means 'beloved'. Kentigern was a 6th-century Bishop of Glasgow and is generally known as St Mungo. The name is confined to Scotland and the most famous bearer was Mungo Park, the 18th-century explorer of the River Niger.

Munir *m.*, Munira *f.*

From the Arabic for 'brilliant' or 'illuminating'. The name has the alternative male form **Muneer**.

Murad *m.*

This Arabic name means 'desired' or 'wanted'.

Murali *f.*

From the Sanskrit word for 'flute'. The reference is to the young Krishna, who played the flute to attract female cowherds to his side.

Murdo, Murdoch *m.*

This Scottish name is derived from the Gaelic meaning 'seaman', and is equivalent to the Irish **Murtaugh** (see **MORTIMER**).

Muriel, Meriel *f.*

A Celtic name meaning 'sea-bright'. It came to England at the time of the Norman Conquest, via the many Celts who had settled in Brittany and Normandy in earlier centuries. Both forms were in common use until the mid-14th century. Muriel was revived in the 19th century and Meriel came back into use at the beginning of this century. Other forms such as **Meryl** and **Merrill** have appeared more recently.

Murray *m.*

From the Gaelic meaning 'sea'. The Scottish clan of

Murray, or Moray, probably took its name from the Moray Firth in the northeast of Scotland. James Stewart, Earl of Moray, was half-brother of Mary, Queen of Scots, and he acted as Regent when she was imprisoned in Lochleven Castle. His fame gave rise to the use of **Moray** as a first name in Scotland, but today the form Murray is more common, with **Murry** a variant.

Murtaugh, Murty see Mortimer

Mustafa *m.*

From the Arabic meaning 'chosen'. It is one of the names used to describe the Prophet Muhammad.

Myfanwy *f.*

A well-known Welsh name meaning 'my fine one'. The commonest short forms in Wales are **Fanny** and **Myfi**.

Myles see Miles

Myra *f.*

This name appears to have been invented in the 16th century by Fulke Greville, Lord Brooke, for the heroine of his love poems, and until the 19th century it was used exclusively by poets and novelists. He may have wanted to echo the sound of 'admired'. The variant form **Mira** is found but this can also be a short form of MIRABEL or MIRANDA.

Myrddin see Mervyn

Myrna *see* **Morna**

Myron *m.*

The Greek word for 'fragrant'. It was the name of a famous sculptor in the 5th century BC.

Myrtle *f.*

One of the flower names which has been used as a name since the 19th century. The name is Greek, and in Ancient Greece the myrtle was a symbol of victory, while in the last century, myrtle was a traditional element in a bride's bouquet. The variant form **Myrtill(a)** is also found occasionally.

N

Nadim *m.*
This Arabic name refers to a 'drinking companion' or 'friend'. It is also spelt **Nadeem**.

Nadine *f.*
A French name, derived from the Russian for 'hope'. Variants are **Nada** and **Nadia**.

Naeem, Naeema *see* Naim

Nafisa(h) *f.,* Nafis *m.*
From the Arabic for 'precious, delicate'. It is more commonly used for girls and has other spellings, such as **Nafeesa**.

Naim *m.,* Naima *f.*
From the Arabic word meaning 'comfortable', 'contented' or 'tranquil'. Some families prefer to spell the names **Naeem** and **Naeema.**

Nan *see* Anne

Nancy *f.*
This was originally a pet form of **ANNE**, but has long been established as a name in its own right. **Nancie** is occasionally found, and **Nanette** and **Nana** are French forms.

Nandy *see* **Ferdinand**

Nanette, Nanny *see* **Anne, Nancy**

Naomi *f.*

From the Hebrew meaning 'pleasant'. In the Old Testament Naomi was the mother-in-law of Ruth, and loved her daughter-in-law so much that when their menfolk died, she left her home to travel back to Israel with Ruth. The name was adopted by the Puritans in the 17th century and has recently increased in popularity.

Nastasia *see* **Anastasia**

Nat *see* **Nathan, Nathaniel**

Natalie, Natasha *f.*

These names come from the Latin *natale domini*, meaning 'the birthday of the Lord', and were originally restricted to children born around Christmas. The name comes from Russia where it is spelt **Natalya**, and has the pet form Natasha, both popular choices in recent years. This is sometimes spelt **Natacha** or **Natasja**, and can have the short form **Tasha**. **Natalia** or Natalie can be shortened to **Talia**, **Talya** or **Tally**.

Nathan *m.*

From the Hebrew meaning 'gift'. It was the name of the prophet in the Old Testament who condemned King

David for putting Uriah in the front line of battle to get him killed, so David could marry his widow, Bathsheba. It has recently become more popular. The name shares the short form **Nat** with NATHANIEL.

Nathaniel *m.*

From the Hebrew meaning 'gift of God'. It was the name of the apostle who was better known by his second name, BARTHOLOMEW. It was rare in Britain until after Shakespeare's use of it in *Love's Labour Lost* (1594) but it is more common in North America today than in Britain. **Nat**, the short form, is shared with NATHAN.

Nayan *m.,* Nayana *f.*

An Indian name derived from the Sanskrit for 'eye'. The feminine form refers to a girl with lovely eyes.

Neal, Neil *see* Nigel

Neelofar *see* Niloufer

Ned, Neddy *see* Edward

Neha *f.*

This Indian name means 'rain'.

Neirin *see* Aneurin

Nell, Nelly *f.*

These are pet forms of **HELEN** and **ELEANOR**. They were already in use in Britain in the Middle Ages. A famous holder of the name was Nell (Eleanor) Gwyn, the mistress of Charles II.

Nelson *m.*

A surname meaning 'Neil's son' (see **NIGEL**). It is used as a first name in memory of Horatio Nelson (1758–1805).

Nerissa *f.*

This is one of the less common names taken from Shakespeare, in this case **PORTIA**'s witty maid from *The Merchant of Venice*. It is not clear what Shakespeare meant by the name, but he may have taken it from *nereis*, the Greek word for a sea-nymph.

Nerys *f.*

An unusual Welsh name, meaning 'lady', which has become widely known through the actress, Nerys Hughes.

Nessa, Nessie, Nest, Nesta *see* Agnes

Net, Netta, Nettie *see* Anthony, Janet

Neville *m.*

From the French surname Neuville, meaning 'new town'. It was introduced into England at the time of the Norman Conquest, when the Neville family, which came

over with William the Conqueror, was very powerful.
Their influence continued, but the name was not
adopted as a first name until the 17th century. **Nevil** is
a variant spelling.

Niall *see* **Nigel**

Niamh *f.*

This name, pronounced 'nee-av' or 'neev', is currently
very popular in Ireland. It means 'radiance, brightness'
and was originally the name of a pagan goddess. In Irish
legend Niamh was a fairy woman who fell in love with
OSSIAN and carried him off to the magical Land
of Promise.

Nichola, Nichole *see* **Nicola**

Nicholas *m.*

From the Greek meaning 'victory of the people'.
The name was common in the Middle Ages as a result
of the popularity of St Nicholas, the patron saint of
children and sailors. The usual form then was **Nicol.**
In Latin the name is Nicholaus and the use of **Claus** in
'Santa Claus' is taken from **Klaus,** the modern German
development of the Latin. **Nick(o)** and **Nicky** are the
pet forms. (See also **COLIN, NICOLA.**)

Nicola, Nicole *f.*

Nicola is one of the Italian forms of **NICHOLAS**, others
being Nocolo and Niccolo. The feminine Italian form is

Nicoletta, but in Britain Nicola has wrongly been assumed to be feminine because of the '-a' ending. American and Australian parents have always used **Nicole**, the French feminine form of Nicholas. The names are also spelt **Nichola** and **Nichole,** and **Nicolette** is also used. **Nickie**, **Nikki** and **Nicci** are short forms shared with Nicholas (see also COLETTE).

Nigel, Niall, Neal, Neil m.

The origin of these names goes back to an Irish name, the meaning of which could be 'champion', 'cloud' or 'passionate'. Niall is the Irish spelling of the name, but it early on developed different spellings. When medieval scribes wanted to write the name in Latin documents they gave it the form *Nigellus*, as if it were a name which came from the Latin *niger* meaning 'black'; and when interest was strong in all things medieval in the 19th century, this Latin form was adopted as Nigel. Nigel has rare girls' forms, **Nigella** and **Nigelia**.

Nikhil m.

An Indian name derived from the Sanskrit for 'entire', 'complete'.

Nik(h)ita f.

An Indian name derived from a word meaning 'the earth'.

Nikki, Nicci, Nickie *see* Nicola

Niloufer *f.*

An Indian name which means 'celestial being'. It occurs in various spellings, such as **Neelofar.**

Nina *f.*

A pet form of various Russian names ending '-nina', which is now established in this country as a name in its own right.

Ninian *m.*

The name of a 5th-century saint who converted the Picts in the south of Scotland to Christianity. It is mainly found in Scotland.

Nisha *f.*

An Indian name meaning 'night'.

Nishant *f.*

This Indian name refers to 'dawn', the end of the night.

Nita *see* **Joan**

Noah *m.*

Despite the wide fame of Noah and his Ark, this Hebrew name meaning 'rest' has been quite rare, but its use is now increasing, particularly in the USA.

Noel *f. and m.*

This is an old French name derived from the Latin *dies natalis*, meaning 'birthday'. The name refers to

Christmas Day and was often given to children born then. **Nowell** is an English spelling which is also used and **Noelle** is an alternative girl's form. **Christmas** is also found occasionally as a first name.

Nola *see* Fenella

Nona *see* Anne

Nora(h) *f.*

An Irish abbreviation of **HONORIA**, now used as a separate name. It is also found as a short form for **ELEANOR** and **LEONORA**. In Ireland the pet forms **Noreen** and **Nonie** are used.

Norm *see* Norman

Norma *f.*

Possibly from the Latin meaning 'rule' or 'precept'. The great success of Bellini's opera *Norma* (1831) brought the name into popular favour. It has been used as a feminine counterpart of **NORMAN**.

Norman *m.*

From the Old English for 'Northman', used first of all for the Vikings, and then for the descendants of the Viking settlers in France who were known as 'Normans'. It was popular in Scotland, and for a while was considered a purely Scottish name, being used as a

substitute for the Gaelic **Tormod** ('protected by Thor'),
itself originally a Viking name. **Norm** and **Norrie** are
short forms.

Nowell *see* **Noel**

Nuala *see* **Fenella**

Nye *see* **Aneurin**

O

Oberon *see* **Aubrey**

Octavia *f.,* **Octavius** *m.*

A Roman family name derived from the Latin meaning 'eighth'. It was also used as a given name for an eighth child in the 19th century, but now that such large families are rare it is used without regard to its original sense. **Octavian** is an alternative masculine form.

Odette, Odile *see* **Ottilie**

Odysseus *see* **Ulysses**

Oengus *see* **Angus**

Oisin *see* **Ossian**

Ol, Ollie *see* **Oliver**

Olaf *see* **Oliver**

Olga *f.*

From the Norse word *helga*, meaning 'holy'. The founder of the Russian monarchy is supposed to have been a Scandinavian traveller, and it was in Russia that Olga evolved from the Scandinavian form, **HELGA**.

St Olga was the wife of the Duke of Kiev in the 10th century, and she helped spread Christianity in Russia.

Oliva, Olive *see* Olivia

Oliver *m.*

In Old French legend Oliver was one of Charlemagne's greatest knights. Since these knights were of Frankish origin – that is to say of Germanic ancestry – their names are likely to be from Old German. Thus it is thought that this name goes back to the same source as the Scandinavian **Olaf** ('heir of his ancestors'). However, users probably associate it with the more obvious source of the olive tree, symbol of peace. Oliver was popular until the parliamentary revolt led by Oliver Cromwell in the 17th century, after which the name fell out of favour. It was revived in the 19th century and is now very popular. **Ol** and **Ollie** are short forms. **Havelock** is said to be the name's Welsh form.

Olivia *f.*

The female form of **OLIVER**, but even more strongly associated with the Latin *oliva*, meaning 'olive'. St **Oliva** was venerated as the protectress of the olive crops in Italy. Olivia was first found in England in the early 13th century, was used by Shakespeare in *Twelfth Night*, and is currently very popular. **Olive** is a rarer form, although well-known as the name of the cartoon character Olive Oyl, Popeye's girlfriend.

Olwen, Olwyn f.

From the Welsh, meaning 'white foot-print'. The name
first occurs in an old Welsh legend in which Olwen, a
giant's daughter, is wooed by a prince, who has to get
help from King Arthur to do the tasks that are set him.
She was named Olwen because white clover sprang up
wherever she trod. The name became very popular in
Wales and spread to England in 1849 when a new
translation of the story was published.

Omar see Umar

Oona, Oonagh see Una

Ophelia f.

From the Greek meaning 'help'. Its use is due to
Shakespeare's *Hamlet* (1601). In the play, Ophelia is
Hamlet's lover but goes mad after he murders her father
and abandons her, and is finally drowned.

Oprah f.

This name is well known through the talk show host
Oprah Winfrey, but perhaps because of this close
association with one person, it has not yet come into
general use in either the USA or Britain. Oprah Winfrey
has explained that her parents intended to call her
Orpah, a biblical place name which possibly means
'gazelle'. The registrar misspelt the name as Oprah,
which her parents then preferred.

Oriel, Oriole *see* **Aurelia**

Orla *f.*

An Irish name meaning 'golden princess'. It also occurs as **Orlagh** and in the Old Irish spelling **Orlaith**, and is currently popular in Ireland.

Orlando *m.*

This is the Italian form of **ROLAND**. Italian names were fashionable in the 16th century and Shakespeare used this one in his play *As You Like It* (1600). It has become rather more common recently.

Orpah *see* **Oprah**

Orson *m.*

From the Old French *Ourson*, meaning 'little bear'. This is not a common name, though it is familiar through Orson Welles (1915–85), the American actor and director.

Orville *m.*

A name invented by the 18th-century novelist, Fanny Burney, for the hero of her novel *Evelina*. It is fairly rare in Britain. A famous American example was Orville Wright, aviation pioneer and brother of **WILBUR**.

Osbert *m.*

From the Old English, meaning 'bright god'. It shares **Oz** and **Ozzy** as pet forms with **OSWALD**.

O

Oscar *m.*

In the 1760s James Macpherson gave the name to
OSSIAN's warrior son in his poems on the legendary past
of Scotland, and Napoleon's enthusiasm for the Ossianic
legend caused him to give the name Oscar to his godson,
later King of Sweden. It became widespread on the
Continent, and was regularly used in England and
Ireland. The trial of Oscar Wilde in 1895 for
homosexuality caused an abrupt fall in the name's
popularity in Britain, but it remained in use in the US,
where it is found as **Oskar**, the Scandinavian spelling.
It probably means 'deer-lover'.

Osman *see* Uthman

Ossian *m.*

In legend Ossian ('little deer') is the son of **FINN** and
father of **OSCAR**. It is spelt **Oisin** in Irish, while **Osheen**
reflects the Irish pronunciation, although it is usually
pronounced as it is spelt in England. A female form
Ossia also exists.

Oswald *m.*

From the Old English meaning 'god power'. Oswald,
King of Northumbria in the 7th century, was killed
fighting the Welsh at Oswestry. He was later canonized,
and the place is said to take its name from him. A second
St Oswald helped St **DUNSTAN** with his church reforms
in the 10th century. Because of these two saints, the

name was popular in the Middle Ages and has never entirely died out. **Oz** and **Ozzy** are used as pet forms shared with **OSBERT**.

Ottilie *f.*

This is a modern form of **Ottilia**, which comes from the Old German meaning 'prosperity'. St Ottilie is the patron saint of Alsace. **Ottoline** is another form of the name, and the French **Odette** and **Odile** have also been used in Britain. The Continental male form, **Otto**, is less common in this country.

Owen, Owain *m.*

This is one of the most popular of all Welsh names, but its origin is uncertain. It may well have come from the Greek name **EUGENE** meaning 'well-born', or from Welsh *oen*, meaning 'lamb'. There are many bearers of the name in Welsh history and legend, but the best known is Owen Glendower, who fought for Welsh independence in the 15th century. The name has spread to the rest of Britain and to North America.

Oz, Ozzy *see* Osbert, Oswald

P

Paayal *see* **Payal**

Padma *f. and m.*
This Indian name, usually identified with the goddess Sri or Lakshmi, derives from a Sanskrit word meaning 'lotus'. Other forms are **Padmal, Padmini** and **Padmavati**. In some parts of India **Padma** and **Padman** are used as boys' names.

Paddy, Padraig *see* **Patrick**

Paige *f.*
The surname, originally given to someone who acted as a page, used as a first name. It has been popular for some time in the USA, and has recently become very popular in the UK, probably because of the name's prominent use in several imported television series.

Paloma *f.*
This means 'dove', the symbol of peace. Its use by the artist, Pablo Picasso, for his daughter made the name more widely known.

Pamela *f.*
From the Greek meaning 'all honey'. This name dates from the late 16th century when it was coined by

Sir Philip Sydney for his romance *Arcadia*. It did not come into general use until the publication of Samuel Richardson's novel *Pamela* (1740). It has been most used in the 20th century, and **Pam(mie)** is the usual pet form.

Pandora *f.*

In Greek legend Pandora ('all-giving') is a beautiful but foolish woman created by the gods to plague mankind. She opened the box that contained all the ills that afflict us. After their escape, only hope, which had been sealed up with them, was left to help mankind.

Pansy *f.*

The flower name deriving from the French *pensée*, 'a thought'.

Parvati *f.*

An Indian name, from the Sanskrit meaning 'of the mountain', a reference to the wife of **SHIVA**.

Pascal *m.,* Pascale *f.*

A French name meaning 'Easter', which has come into general use since the 1960s.

Pat *see* Patricia, Patrick

Patience *f.*

This name was fashionable in the 17th century when girls were named after abstract virtues and Sir Thomas Carew could call his four daughters Patience, Temperance, Silence and **PRUDENCE**.

Patricia *f.*

The feminine of Latin *patricius*, meaning 'nobleman'. It was originally only used in Latin records to distinguish a female bearer of the name **PATRICK** then used for both sexes, but it was used independently from the 18th century. It has become common only in the last hundred years, possibly encouraged by the popularity of Queen Victoria's granddaughter Princess Patricia of Connaught. Current abbreviations are **Pat**, **Patsy**, **Patti(e)**, **Patty** and **Tricia**.

Patrick *m.*

From the Latin *patricius*, meaning 'nobleman'. St Patrick adopted this name at his ordination. He was born in Britain in the late 4th century, captured by pirates when still a boy and sold as a slave in Ireland. Although he escaped, he wished to convert the Irish to Christianity, so after training as a missionary in France, he returned to devote his life to this cause. **Pat** and **Paddy** are short forms, and **Padraig** the Irish form.

Patsy, Patti, Pattie, Patty *see* Patricia

Paul *m.*

From the Latin *paulus*, meaning 'small'. The New Testament tells how **SAUL** of Tarsus adopted this name after his conversion to Christianity. The name was not

common until the 17th century. It was often coupled
with the name **PETER**, as the saints Peter and Paul share
the same feast day.

Paula, Paulina, Pauline *f.*

The female forms of **PAUL**. The 4th-century St Paula
founded several convents in Bethlehem, and thus
established the name in the Middle Ages. Paulina and
Pauline or **Paulette** are respectively the Latin and
French forms. **Polly** is sometimes used as a pet form.

Payal *f.*

An Indian name meaning 'anklet'. It is also spelt **Paayal.**

Pearl *f.*

This name first became common in the 19th century,
with other gem names such as **BERYL** and **RUBY**. It has
also been used as a pet name for **MARGARET**, which is
derived from the Greek for 'pearl'.

Peg, Peggy *see* **Margaret**

Penelope *f.*

In Greek legend Penelope was the name of Odysseus's
faithful and astute wife, who waited ten years for her
husband to return from the Trojan Wars. The name has
been used regularly since the 16th century. It is often
abbreviated to **Pen** or **Penny**.

Perce *see* **Perceval, Percy**

Perceval, Percival *m.*

The name Percival first occurs in the Old French
Arthurian romances of Chrétien de Troyes in the 12th
century, where it is the name of a successful seeker of the
Holy Grail. Chrétien interprets the name as *perce-val*,
'one who pierces the valley'. However, when used as a
surname, Perceval probably refers to Percheval, a place
in Normandy. The name has been used in the UK since
the 14th century. The short forms are **Perce** or **Percy**,
and sometimes **Val**.

Percy *m.*

This famous northern family is descended from William
de Perci, one of William the Conqueror's companions
who took his name from a Norman village. Initially its
use as a first name was confined to those connected with
the Percy family, but in the 19th century it came into
general use, partly due to the poet, Percy Bysshe Shelley.
It shares the short form **Perce** with **Perceval** and is also
a short form of this name.

Perdita *f.*

This is from the Latin meaning 'lost'. It was coined by
Shakespeare for the heroine of *A Winter's Tale*, who was
lost at birth.

Peregrine *m.*

From the Latin *peregrinus*, meaning 'stranger' or
'traveller' and hence 'pilgrim'. There was a 7th-century
saint of this name who was a hermit near Modena in

Italy. The name has been used in the UK since about the 13th century, but it has always been rather uncommon. PERRY is used as a short form.

Perry *m.*

This name sometimes occurs as an abbreviation of PEREGRINE, but it is also a surname used as a first name. It was the surname of two 19th-century American admirals, one of whom inflicted a defeat on the British while the other led the expedition that opened up Japan to the west. Their exploits probably encouraged the use of the name in the US. The singer Perry Como, who helped spread the popularity of the name, was born Pierino, a pet form of PETER.

Persephone *see* Corinna

Peter *m.*

From the Greek *petras*, meaning 'rock'. *Cephas* is the Aramaic equivalent which Jesus gave as a nickname to Simon bar Jonah, to symbolize steadfastness in faith. Peter was chief of the Apostles and became the first Bishop of Rome. He was a favourite saint of the medieval church and his name was very popular throughout Christendom. In England the name is first recorded in the Domesday Book in the Latin form, Petrus. The Normans brought over the French form, **Piers** (or **Pierce**), which was usual until the 14th century, when Peter became predominant, although Piers is now quite fashionable once again. The name was unpopular after

the Reformation because of its association with the
Papacy and did not return to fashion until 1904, when
James Barrie's *Peter Pan* was published. A short form is
Pete. **Peta**, **Petra** and **Petrina** are modern female forms
of the name.

Petronella, Petronilla *f.*

These are derived from Petronius, a Roman family
name. Petronilla, a 1st-century martyr, came to be
connected with St **PETER**, and was even thought by
some to be his daughter; because of this the name was
popular in the Middle Ages and used as Peter's female
equivalent.

Petula *f.*

Possibly from the Latin term meaning 'seeker'. It is a
very rare name but the singer Petula Clark has made it
well known.

Phebe *see* Phoebe

Phelim *see* Felix

Philip *m.*

From the Greek meaning 'lover of horses'. It was
common in the Middle Ages on account of the Philip the
Apostle. However, in Elizabeth I's reign Philip of Spain
was the arch enemy of England, and the name suffered
accordingly. It was revived in the 19th century. **Phil** is
now the most usual short form, although **Pip** and **Flip**

are sometimes used. **Phillip** is a variant spelling reflecting the form usually found in surnames.

Philippa *f.*

This is the female form of **PHILIP**, but originally was only used to distinguish women (who shared the name Philip with males in the Middle Ages) in Latin records. Its use as a separate name dates from about the 19th century and is now quite popular. Often abbreviated to **Pippa**, an Italian form, it can be found as **Phillippa** and **Philipa**. **Philippine** is a much rarer female form of Philip.

Phillip *see* Philip

Phillippa *see* Philippa

Phillis *see* Phyllis

Philomena *f.*

This name comes from the Greek for 'beloved'. It used to be a popular name in Ireland, but is now rather out of fashion. It was thought that there were two saints of this name, but when it was realized that the word Philomena on the inscription on their graves was an address to the reader and not their names the cult was suppressed; hence the name's fall from favour.

Phoebe *f.*

From the Greek meaning 'the shining one'. It is one of the titles given to the Roman moon goddess, **DIANA**. It occurs as a personal name in St Paul's Epistle to the Romans and, perhaps for this reason, was adopted after the Reformation, reaching its peak of popularity in the 17th century. It is currently enjoying another rise in popularity and sometimes spelt phonetically **Phebe**. It can be used as a pet form of **EUPHEMIA**.

Phyllis, Phillis *f.*

From the Greek meaning 'leafy'. In legend it was the name of a girl who died for love and was transformed into an almond tree. **Phyllida** is an alternative form which is sometimes found.

Pia *f.*

From the Latin meaning 'pious'. It was not used by English speakers until well into this century.

Pierce, Piers *see* **Peter**

Pip *see* **Philip**

Pippa *see* **Philippa**

Polly *see* **Mary, Paula**

Pooja *f.*, Poojan *m.*

This Indian name, which can also be spelt **Puja** and **Pujan**, means 'worship'.

Poojit *m.*, Poojita *f.*

An Indian name which means 'worshipped'. It also occurs as **Pujit** and **Pujita**.

Poonam *f.*

An Indian name which refers to the 'full moon'. The spelling **Punam** is also used.

Poppy *f.*

The flower used as a name. It was particularly popular at the end of the 19th century and the beginning of the 20th, and is once again becoming fashionable.

Portia *f.*

Portia is an old Roman family name with the unfortunate meaning of 'pig'. However, Portia, wife of Brutus, became famous for her stoicism and bravery, which probably inspired Shakespeare to choose this name for the heroine of *The Merchant of Venice*. This Portia is beautiful, rich, wise, witty and charming, and it is thanks to her that the name has come into use as a modern girl's name.

Pratik *m.*

An Indian name which means 'a symbol'.

Primrose *f.*

This flower name was popular at the beginning of the 20th century. **Primula** is a rare variant.

Priscilla *f.*

The Latin diminutive of *prisca*, meaning 'ancient'. It was the name of a woman mentioned in the Acts of the Apostles and as with other New Testament names it was a favourite with the 17th-century Puritans. It also appears as **Prisca** but this form is very rare. **Pris** and **Prissy** are sometimes found as short forms, but **Cilla** is the most used form.

Priya *m.,* Priyal *f.*

An Indian name which means 'beloved'. The girls' versions also include **Priyam, Priyanka** and **Priyasha.**

Prudence *f.*

Prudence first appears as a name in Chacer's books, and it was one of the first abstract virtues to be adopted by the Puritans. It is usually abbreviated to **Prue** or **Pru** (see also **PATIENCE**).

Prunella *f.*

Probably from the Latin *prunus*, meaning 'little plum'. It is also the name of a kind of silk and the Latin name for a wild flower, the self-heal, and a bird, the hedge sparrow or dunnock. The actress Prunella Scales has made the name more widely known. It shares short forms with **PRUDENCE**.

Puja, Pujan *see* **Pooja**

Pujit, Pujita *see* **Poojit**

Punam *see* **Poonam**

Punit *m.,* **Punita** *f.*
An Indian name which means 'pure'.

Q

Qasim *m.*

The name of a son of the Prophet Muhammad, this comes from the Arabic and refers to a 'distributor', one who distributes food and money among the people.

Quanisha *see* Kanisha

Queenie *f.*

This name is sometimes given independently, but it is really a pet name for **Regina**, which is Latin for 'queen'. Regina was used from the Middle Ages, possibly with reference to the Virgin Mary, Queen of Heaven. Queenie was also used as a nickname for girls christened **VICTORIA** during Queen Victoria's long reign.

Quentin, Quintin *m.*

From the Latin for 'fifth', originally a name for a fifth son. Quentin was the French form which the Normans introduced to England. It became obsolete after the Middle Ages except in Scotland, although it revived in the 19th century, possibly due to Walter Scott's historical romance *Quentin Durward* (1823). **Quinton** is another form of the name.

Quincy _m._

A surname taken from a French place name. Its use
in the US may have been due to the prominent
New England family of that name in colonial times.
John Quincy Adams (1767–1848), the 6th President,
may have received his middle name in honour of this
family or it may have been taken from Quincy,
Massachusetts, where he was born. It can also be found
as **Quincey**.

R

Rab, Rabbie *see* **Robert**

Rabiah *f.*
An Arabic name which means 'garden'.

Rachel *f.*
From the Hebrew for 'ewe', a symbol of gentleness and innocence. In the Book of Genesis, Rachel was 'beautiful and well-favoured', and **JACOB** laboured seven years to win her (Gen. XXIX, 20). In Britain the name was adopted after the Reformation and was very popular in the 17th and 19th centuries and is popular today. The usual pet forms today are **Rach**, **Rachie**, **Rae**, **Rai** and **Ray**, and it can be spelt **Rachael**. The actress **Raquel** Welch shows the Spanish form of the name. From Rachel have developed the forms **Rachelle** (sometimes pronounced with a 'sh' sound) and **Rochelle**, the French for 'little rock', a place name taken from Brittany to the US where the name is popular. **SHELLEY** is a short form.

Radha *f.*
The name of the cowherd loved by Krishna. It derives from the Sanskrit for 'success'. Another form of this Indian name is **Radhika.**

Radhakrishna *m.*

This Indian name is a blend of **RADHA** and **KRISHNA**, and is meant to symbolize the male and female nature of the supreme god.

Rae, Rai *see* Rachel, Raymond

Raelene *see* Darlene

Raheel *see* Rahil

Raheem, Raheema, Raheemah *see* Rahim

Rahil *f.*

An Arabic form of **RACHEL**. It is also found as **Raheel** and **Raheela.**

Rahim *m.*, Rahima(h) *f.*

From the Arabic meaning 'merciful' and 'compassionate'. The fuller form of the male name is AbdurRahim 'servant of the Merciful', a reference to one of the attributes of Allah. The spellings **Raheem**, **Raheema** and **Raheemah** are also found.

Raja *m.*

An Arabic name which means 'hope'.

Rajan *m.*

An Indian name derived from the Sanskrit word for 'king'. Similar names include **Rajesh** and **Rajendra**.

Rajani *f.*

From the Sanskrit meaning 'the dark one' or 'night'. This is one of the names of the Hindu goddess **DURGA**.

Rajendra, Rajesh *see* **Rajan**

Rajni *f.*

An Indian name from the Sanskrit for 'queen', this name can also be a contracted form of **RAJANI**.

Rajnish *m.*

This Indian name derives from the Sanskrit words meaning 'ruler of the night', the reference being to the moon. **Rajneesh** is a variant spelling of the name.

Ralph *m.*

From the Old Norse words meaning 'counsel' and 'wolf'. In its earlier form, Radulf, this name was fairly common in England before the Norman Conquest, and it was reinforced by French use. The medieval spellings were **Ralf** and **Rauf** which were pronounced with the same vowel sound as the word 'ray'. **Rafe** was the common form in the 17th century and Ralph appears in the 18th century. The current usual pronunciation with a short 'a' and pronouncing the 'l' is 20th-century practice. **Raoul** is the French form of the name, and **Raul** the Spanish.

Rama _m._

From the Sanskrit for 'pleasing'. As the seventh incarnation of Vishnu, Rama is widely worshipped in India. Rama's full name is **Ramachandra**, or **Ramachander** in southern India.

Ramona _see_ Raymond

Ranald _see_ Ronald

Randolph _m._

From the Old English Randwulf, meaning 'shield wolf', which in the Middle Ages became **Ranulf** and **Randal(l)**. The short form, **Randy**, has been used as a name in its own right, particularly in the USA, where it can also be a short form of the girl's name, **Miranda**.

Raqib _m._

A Muslim name from an Arabic word meaning 'guardian' or 'supervisor', especially in religious matters.

Raquel _see_ Rachel

Rashad _m._

This Arabic name means 'integrity' or 'maturity'.

Rastus _see_ Erasmus

Rauf *see* **Ralph**

Raul, Raoul *see* **Ralph**

Raven *f.*

The name of this large, sleek black bird has been intensely used by Afro-American parents since 1989, when an actress of that name appeared in TV's *The Cosby Show*. Other bird names such as **Finch**, **Lark**, **Merlin** and **Swan** have occasionally been used in the past. **MAVIS**, a poetical name for the song thrush, enjoyed a spell of popularity, and **Robin** has long been in use. **JAY** can also be interpreted as a bird name. With Raven the colour of the bird is clearly felt to be an important factor, as use of the name is restricted to Black Americans.

Ravi *m.*

The Indian name of the sun god, from the Sanskrit for 'sun'. **Ravindra** is another boy's name based on the same word.

Ray *see* **Rachel, Raymond**

Raymond *m.*

From the Old German meaning 'counsel protection'. The Normans brought the name to Britain and it was particularly popular in crusading times. Two 13th-century saints bore the name. One of them spent much of his life rescuing Spaniards captured by the Moors.

Redmond or **Redmund** is a form of the name which developed in Ireland. The short form, **Ray**, is sometimes given independently. There is a feminine form **Raymonde** which also has the short forms **Ray**, **Rai** and **Rae**. The Spanish female form is **Ramona**.

Razina *f.*

A Muslim name from the Arabic for 'contented'.

Rebecca *f.*

In the Old Testament **Rebekah** (the name's Hebrew form) was the wife of **ISAAC** and was famous for her beauty. It was a favourite name among Puritans, who took it to North America. It is occasionally spelt **Rebekka** and is currently very popular. **Becky** is the short form.

Redmond, Redmund *see* **Raymond**

Reece *see* **Rhys**

Reg, Reggie *see* **Reginald**

Regina *see* **Gina, Queenie**

Reginald *m.*

From the Old English Regenweald, meaning 'power force'. It was not a common Anglo-Saxon name but was reinforced at the time of the Norman Conquest by the French equivalent **Reinald** or **Reynaud**, and developed into **Reynold**. It can be abbreviated to **Reg**, **Reggie** or **REX** (see also **RONALD**).

René, Renée *m. and f.*

These are the French boys' and girls' names derived from the Latin *renatus*, meaning 'reborn'. The Latin form was sometimes used by Puritans in the 17th century, and the French forms have been used in Britain in the 20th century. The Latin feminine form, **Renata**, is also used occasionally.

Renie *see* Irene

Reshma *f.*

An Indian name which means 'silken'.

Reuben *m.*

From the Hebrew meaning 'behold a son', it appears in the Bible as the name of a son of Jacob, the founder of one of the tribes of Israel. The form **Ruben** is also found.

Rex *m.*

This is the Latin for 'king' which has been used as a first name only in recent times. It is also found as an abbreviation of **REGINALD**.

Reynard *m.*

From the Old German, meaning 'mighty and brave'. This and Rainard were the Norman French forms, but they never became as common as **Reynold** (see **REGINALD**), with which they were often confused. It is very rare today, except as a term for a fox, taken from one of the characters in Aesop's fables with this name.

Reynaud, Reynold *see* Reginald

Rhiannon *f.*

The name of an important figure in medieval Welsh literature. There is evidence that she was originally a Celtic goddess connected with horses. The name means 'great queen, goddess' and is spreading outside Wales. The old form was **Riannon**, and a new form **Rhianna** is also found.

Rhoda *f.*

Derived from the Greek for 'rose', this is a New Testament name (see Acts X, 11-13) that was taken into use in the 17th century. It was popular in the early years of this century.

Rhodri *see* Roderick

Rhona *see* Rowena

Rhonda *f.*

This is a simplified spelling of the Welsh place name, Rhondda, which has been used as a first name since the early part of this century.

Rhonwen *see* **Rowena**

Rhydderch *see* **Roderick**

Rhys *m.*

An old Welsh name meaning 'rashness, ardour'. It has
had many famous bearers, including a Prince Rhys who
checked the Norman advance into Wales. The name's
popularity is increasing rapidly in the mid 1990s, with
the alternative spelling **Reece** overtaking Rhys itself.

Ria *see* **Mary**

Rian *see* **Ryan**

Riannon *see* **Rhiannon**

Richard *m.*

This name first appears in Anglo-Saxon as Ricehard
meaning 'strong ruler', which was later developed into
Ricard. It was the Normans who spread the present
form of the name, the softer, French Richard. The short
form **Dick** appears as early as the 13th century, and this
is still very common, though **Rich(ie)**, **Dickie**, **Rick(ie)**,
Ricky and **Dickon** have been used at various times.
Female forms of the name include **Richelle**, **Richenda**
and **Ricarda**.

Rick, Rickie, Ricky *see* **Derek, Eric,
Richard**

Riona *see* **Catriona**

Rishi *m.*

An Indian name which means 'sage' or 'wise man'.

Rita *f.*

This is an abbreviation of **Margarita** (see **MARGARET**). However, it is used much more often as a separate name, and some of its popularity in the present century may have been due to its use by the film star, Rita Hayworth (1918-87).

Robert *m.*

This name is derived from the Old German meaning 'famous and bright'. Although there was an equivalent Anglo-Saxon name, it was the French form which took hold in Britain after the Norman Conquest. King Robert the Bruce popularized the name in Scotland where it has the local short forms **Rab** and **Rabbie**. **Rob**, **Robbie**, **Bob**, **BOBBIE** or **Bobby** and **BERT** are used in England. **Robin** or **Robyn**, a French pet form of Robert, is now popular in its own right (see also **RUPERT**).

Roberta, Robina *f.*

These are female forms of **ROBERT** and **Robin**. Both have been popular, particularly in Scotland. **BOBBIE** and **Robin** or **Robyn** are also used.

Robin, Robyn *see* **Robert, Roberta**

Rochelle *see* **Rachel**

Rod, Roddy *see* **Roderick, Rodney**

Roderick *m.*

From the Old German meaning 'famous rule'. The
Goths took the name to Spain where it became Rodrigo,
and it was established there at least as early as the 8th
century. In Britain the name is commonest in Scotland
where it was first used to transliterate the Gaelic name,
Ruairi. In Wales it is used as **Rhodri**, meaning 'crowned
ruler' or **Rhydderch** ('reddish-brown'). Short forms are
Rod, **Roddy** and **Rory**.

Ro(d)ge *see* **Roger**

Rodney *m.*

This means 'reed island', and was originally a surname.
It was not used as a first name until Admiral George
Rodney gave it heroic associations in the 18th century.
Short forms are **Rod** and **Roddy**.

Roger *m.*

Hrothgar, meaning 'famous spear', was an Anglo-Saxon
form of this name. It became famous as the name of a
legendary king, but it was the Normans who gave us the
present form, which was derived from Old German.
Roger was a favourite name in the Middle Ages, but
from the 16th to the 19th centuries it was thought of as
a peasant name and consequently fell from esteem.

The ancient short form Hodge, once a type-name for a farm labourer, has been replaced by **Ro(d)ge**.

Roisin *see* **Rose**

Roland, Rowland *m.*

From the Old German *Hrodland*, meaning 'famous land'. Roland was the most famous of Charlemagne's warriors, and the Normans brought the name to England. **Rowland**, currently a popular variant, is both the medieval spelling and the form of the surname which comes from this name. They are shortened to **Roly** or **Rowley**. ORLANDO is the Italian version of the name.

Rolf *m.*

From the Old German meaning 'famous wolf'. **Rollo** is a Latin form and Rollo the Ganger ('Walker') was a 9th-century Norwegian exile who, with his followers, founded the Norman race. Rolf developed in Normandy and came to Britain at the time of the Norman Conquest. It was soon absorbed into RALPH, but revived in the late 19th century.

Roly *see* **Roland**

Romey, Romy *see* **Rosemary**

Rona *see* **Rowena**

Ronak *m.*

This Indian name is from a Sanskrit word meaning 'embellishment'.

Ronald *m.*

Ronald and **Ranald** are Scottish equivalents of Reynald and **REGINALD**, but they are from the Norse (Viking) not the Old English forms. Ranald is still almost exclusively Scottish but Ronald is now widespread. Short forms commonly used are **Ron** and **Ronnie**.

Ronan *m.*

An Irish and Scottish name meaning 'little seal', borne by a number of early saints. **Ronat** is the feminine form, although **R(h)ona** (see **ROWENA**) is also used.

Rory, Rorie *m.*

From the Irish and Gaelic **Ruairi**, meaning 'red-haired'. The name became popular in Ireland due to the fame of the 12th-century King Rory O'Connor. It is also widely used in the Scottish Highlands, and is sometimes found in England as an abbreviation of **RODERICK**. It can also be spelt **Ruari** and **Ruaridh**.

Rosa, Rosabel, Rosabella, Rosalba
see **Rose**

Rosalie *f.*

From Latin *rosalia*, the name of a Roman festival when garlands of roses were draped on tombs. Its use as a first name is due to St **Rosalia**, a 12th-century hermit, the patron saint of Palermo in Sicily. Rosalie is the French form.

Rosalind *f.*

The origin of this name is the Old German Roslindis, either made from elements meaning 'horse and serpent' or 'fame and shield' – the experts disagree. When the Goths took it to Spain it was interpreted as *rosa* and *linda*, 'pretty rose', and it was with this meaning that it came to England in Elizabeth I's reign. It was used by Shakespeare for the heroine of *As You Like It* and in another form, **Rosaline**, in two other plays. Largely due to this literary association it has been popular ever since. It developed a number of different forms such as **Rosalyn**, **Rosalin**, **Rosalinda**, **Roslyn** and **Rosaleen**, which is used in Ireland as an alternative form of **Roisin** (see **ROSE**). A short form is **Roz**.

Rosamund, Rosamond *f.*

This comes from the Old German words meaning 'horse' and 'protection', but it has generally been associated with the Latin *rosa munda*, meaning 'pure rose' or *rosa mundi*, 'rose of the world'. The Normans brought the name to England. A short form is **Roz**.

Rosanna(h), Rosanne *see* **Roseanne**

Rose *f.*

This flower, the symbol of the Virgin Mary, has been the most popular of all flower names which are used as personal names. The Normans brought the name to England and it has been consistently popular, giving rise to many derivatives, like **Rosalba** ('white rose'), **Rosetta**, ('little rose'), and **Rosabel(la)** ('beautiful rose'), as well as **Rosina**, **Rosita** and the pet form **Rosie** or **Rosy**. **Rosa** is a Latin form which has been used occasionally since the 19th century. In Ireland **Roisin**, sometimes spelt **Rosheen** to reflect its pronunciation, is popular. It means 'little rose'. Rose is used as a short form of all the girls' names which begin with its sound.

Roseanne *f.*

This is one of the many developments of **ROSE**, here combined with **ANNE**. Variants include **Roseanna**, **Rosanna**, **Rosanne** and **Rosannah**, as in Rose + **HANNAH**.

Rosemary *f.*

This is generally considered to be a plant name, although it is sometimes analyzed as a combination of **ROSE** and **MARY**. The plant name is derived from the Latin *ros marinus*, meaning 'dew of the sea' which describes the misty blue-green of its leaves. It can be spelt **Rosemarie**, and **Romy** or **Romey** and **Rosie** are short forms.

Rosetta, Rosheen, Rosina, Rosita
see **Rose**

Roshan *m.*, Roshni *f.*

A Muslim name from the Persian for 'shining' or
'famous'. ROXANA is the English form of the name.

Rosie *see* **Rose, Rosemary**

Roslyn *see* **Rosalind**

Ross *m.*

From the Gaelic for 'of the peninsula', and the name of
a Scottish clan. It has been most used in Scotland and
Ireland, Canada and Australia.

Rosy *see* **Rose**

Rowan *f. and m.*

From the Irish **Ruadhan**, meaning 'little red-(haired)
one'. It was the name of an Irish saint. Once used
exclusively for boys, it is now also found as a girl's
name, in which case it can take the form **Rowanne**.

Rowena *f.*

Probably best thought of as a form of the Welsh
Rhonwen, meaning 'fair (woman) slender as a lance'.
Rowena was the daughter of the Saxon chief Hengist
and her beauty bewitched the British king Vortigern,
bringing about his downfall; she may have had a truly

Saxon name, but her story is transmitted through Welsh-speaking British writers and seems to have taken on a Welsh form. Its modern use is due to Sir Walter Scott, who gave this name to the heroine of his novel *Ivanhoe* (1819). **Rowina** is another spelling. **Rhona** or **Rona** has been claimed as a short form of Rhonwen, although it is also the name of a Scottish island.

Rowland, Rowley *see* Roland

Roxana *f.*

The English form of a Persian name meaning 'dawn, light'. Roxana was the name of one of Alexander the Great's wives, and the marriage was said to be a love-match. **Roxane** and **Roxanne** are variants. Muslims use the form **RASHAN**.

Roy *m.*

From the Gaelic *ruadh*, meaning 'red'. A well-known example of the name is the famous Highlander Robert Macgregor, commonly known as Rob Roy because of his red hair, who was involved in the Jacobite Rising of 1715. Walter Scott's novel about him may have contributed to the name's popularity.

Roz *see* Rosalind, Rosamund

Ruadhan *see* Rowan

Ruairi, Ruari, Ruaridh *see* Roderick, Rory

Rohan *f. and m.*

This name comes from a Sanskrit word which can mean either 'ascending' or 'medicine', although some like to interpret the meaning as 'sandalwood'. In Sri Lanka it is the name of a sacred mountain, also known as Adam's Peak, which has on its summit a mark like a footprint which features, with different interpretations, in the legends of all three of the island's great religions – Muslim, Hindu and Buddhist.

Ruben *see* Reuben

Ruby *f.*

This is one of many jewel names introduced during the 19th century.

Rudolf, Rudolph *m.*

From the Old German Hrodulf, meaning 'famous wolf', the same name that gives us **ROLF**. Rudolf is the Modern German form of the name. The spread of this name was undoubtedly helped by the widespread adoration of Rudolf Valentino (1895–1926), the American film star. Another American, the singer **Rudy** Vallee (1901–86) made the pet form, found in Germany as **Rudi**, well known.

Rufus *m.*

This is a Latin word meaning 'red-haired'. William Rufus was the second son of William the Conqueror, and became King William II of England. It gained popularity as a given name during the 19th century.

Rupak *m.*, Rupli *f.*

An Indian name from a Sanskrit word meaning 'beautiful'. Other boys' names based on the same word are **Rupesh, Rupchand** ('as beautiful as the moon') and **Rupinder** ('of the greatest beauty'). Names for girls which have a basic meaning of 'beauty' include **Rupashi** and **Rupashri.**

Rupert *m.*

This name has the same origin as **ROBERT** and means 'bright fame'. In Germany it became Rupprecht, and Rupert is an English form of this. Prince Rupert of the Rhine was the nephew of Charles I, and a brilliant general. He came to England to support the Royalist cause during the Civil War, and was much admired for his dashing bravery. It was because of him that the English form of the name was coined and became popular.

Rupesh, Rupinder *see* **Rupak**

Russell *m.*

This is primarily a surname and is derived from the Old French *rousel*, which means 'little red (haired) one'.

It was a surname which came into use as a first name
along with other family names in the 19th century.
Rus(s) and **Rusty** are pet forms.

Ruth *f.*

A biblical name which came into common use just after
the Reformation on account of the Old Testament
heroine who gave her name to the Book of Ruth. The
name is also associated with the abstract noun, ruth,
meaning 'sorrow' or 'pity'. **Ruthie** is a pet form.

Ryan *m.*

A common Irish surname meaning 'little king', now used
as a first name. Its spread was greatly helped by the
success of the film star Ryan O'Neal (b. 1941). It is also
found as **Rian**.

S

Saagar *see* **Sagar**

Sabah *f.*

An Arabic name which means 'morning' or 'dawn'. The Lebanese singer of this name has made it well known in the Arab world.

Sabina *f.*

A Latin name meaning 'a Sabine woman'. It has been used in Ireland for the Irish **Sadhbh**; **Sive** in its phonetic spelling, meaning 'sweet'. There is also a French form, **Sabine**.

Sabrina *f.*

This is a very ancient name, used for the River Severn before the Romans came and probably the name of the goddess of the river. The poet John Milton (1608–74) used it as the name of the nymph of the Severn in his masque *Comus*, and subsequent uses of it as a first name probably stem from this.

Sacha *f. and m.*

A Russian short form of **ALEXANDER**. Although originally a man's name, the 'a' ending has led to its use for girls. **Sasha** is an alternative form.

Sadie *see* **Sarah**

Saffron *f.*
The name of the golden-yellow crocus pollen used as a spice, which has come to be given as a first name in modern times.

Sagar *m.*
An Indian name meaning 'ocean'. The spelling **Saagar** is also used.

Sahil *m.,* Sahila *f.*
An Indian name which means 'guide'.

Sajad *see* **Sajjad**

Sajan *m.*
This Indian name means 'beloved'.

Sajjad *m.*
This Muslim name refers to one who 'prostrates' himself, or worships God. The name is sometimes spelt **Sajad.**

Salah *m.,* Saliha(h) *f.*
A popular Muslim name from the Arabic for 'goodness, righteousness'.

Salima *f.*, Salman *m.*

An Arabic name which means 'safe' or 'unharmed'.

Sally *f.*

Originally a pet name for **SARAH**, but one that is nowadays used independently. It is shortened to **Sal**.

Salma *f.*

From an Arabic word meaning 'peaceful'. The word for 'peace' is much used as a greeting in the Middle East, as the Arabic salaam or the Hebrew shalom. The latter forms the basis of names like **Salome** and **Solomon**, both of which mean 'peaceful'.

Salome *f.*

The Greek form of an Aramaic name meaning 'peace'. In the New Testament Salome was one of the women at Jesus' tomb on Easter Sunday. However, the story of the Salome who danced the dance of the seven veils and, at her mother's insistence, asked Herod for John the Baptist's head as a reward, has given the name a bad reputation.

Sam, Sammy *see* Samantha, Samuel

Samantha *f.*

Probably an 18th-century coinage, meant to be a feminine version of **SAMUEL**. It first became popular in the 1950s, when it appeared in the film *High Society* and in the title song, *I Love You, Samantha*, and is well used once again. It shares short forms **Sam** and **Sammy** with SAMUEL.

Samimah *f.*

From the Arabic for 'true' or 'sincere'. The name is also spelt **Sameema** and **Sameemah.**

Samir *m.,* Samira(h) *f.*

An Arabic name which means 'one whose conversation in the evening or at night is lively'. The spellings **Sameer, Sameera** and **Sameerah** are also used.

Samuel *m.*

From the Hebrew meaning 'heard by God'. The Old Testament tells how the prophet Samuel was the leader of the Israelites and how he chose Saul and later David as their kings. In Scotland and Ireland it was for a long time used to transliterate the Gaelic **Somhairle**, a name anglicized as **Sorley**; this derives from the Old Norse term meaning 'summer wanderer', that is, 'Viking'. Currently a popular choice, it shares short forms **Sam** and **Sammy** with SAMANTHA.

Sana *f.*

This Arabic name means 'resplendence' or 'brilliance'. **Saniyya** has the same meaning.

Sanchia *f.*

A Provençal and Spanish name derived from the Latin

sanctus, meaning 'holy'. The name came to England in the 13th century when the Earl of Cornwall married Sanchia, daughter of the Count of Provence.

Sandip *f.*

This Indian name means 'beautiful'.

Sandra *f.*

This is a short form of Italian **Alessandra**, now used as a name in its own right (see **ALEXANDRA**). **Sandie** or **Sandy** (also used for **CASSANDRA**) are pet forms. It also appears as **Sondra**, and the designer **Zandra** Rhodes uses an unusual alternative form.

Saniyya *see* **Sana**

Sanjay *m.*

From a Sanskrit word which means 'triumphant', but referring specifically to the charioteer of King Dhritarashtra in classic Hindu epics. The name was made familiar by Sanjay Ghandi, son of the former Indian Prime Minister, and, more recently, through a character in the TV series *EastEnders*.

Sandy *see* **Alexander, Sandra**

Sara(h) *f.*

Sarah comes from the Hebrew, meaning 'princess', and was the name of Abraham's wife in the Old Testament. Sara is the Greek form found in the New Testament.

SALLY, **Sal** and **Sadie** started life as pet forms. In Ireland Sarah has been used to render the Irish **Sorcha** ('sorr-ha', the 'h' as in Scottish 'loch') meaning 'bright', and **Saraid** ('sahr-it') meaning 'excellent'.

Sarika *f.*

An Indian name which refers to the 'koel' or 'black cuckoo'.

Sasha *see* Sacha

Saskia *f.*

This was the name of the wife of the Dutch artist Rembrandt (1606–69), whose paintings of her introduced the name to this country. It may be connected with the word for Saxon.

Saul *m.*

From the Hebrew meaning 'asked for (child)'. The name occurs in the Old Testament as that of the first King of Israel, and in the New Testament as St **PAUL**'s name before his conversion to Christianity. It was initially used as a first name in Britain in the 17th century.

Savannah *f.*

The name of a river and city in the state of Georgia. American parents are making increasing use of the name.

Scarlett *f.*

The use of Scarlett as a first name is due entirely to the success of Margaret Mitchell's *Gone with the Wind*. In the novel, Scarlett O'Hara is given her grandmother's maiden name as a middle name, but always called by it. **Scarlet** is also used.

Scott *m.*

This is a surname, meaning 'a Scot', used as a first name.

Seamas *m.*

This is an Irish form of **JAMES**. It is also spelt **Seamus** and the Gaelic form is **Seumas** or **Seumus**. **Shamus** is a modern phonetic version of the name (see also **HAMISH**).

Sean *f. and m.*

The Irish form of **JOHN**, developed from the French Jean. It is also spelt as it is pronounced, **Shaun** or **Shawn**. **Shane** is a variant form. Shawn and Sean are used now for girls, along with **Shawna** and **Shawndelle**.

Sebastian *m.*

From the Latin *Sebastianus*, meaning 'man of Sebasta'. The name of this town in Asia Minor was derived from the Greek meaning 'majestic' or 'venerable'. St Sebastian was executed by being shot with arrows, and his martyrdom was a particularly popular subject for paintings. The name took hold in Spain and in France, where it was shortened to **Bastien**, and taken by fishermen across the Channel from Brittany to the West Country, where the form **Bastian** took root. The name did not spread to the rest of Britain until modern times, but Sebastian is now reasonably common, having the short forms **Seb** and **Sebbie**.

Seeta, Seetha *see* Sita

Sejal *f.*

This Indian name means 'river' or 'water'.

Selina *f.*

The etymology of this name is disputed. One possible derivation is from **Selene**, the Greek moon goddess; another is from the Latin name Coelina from *caelum*, meaning 'heaven', through the French form **Céline**. **Celina** and **Selena** are also found.

Selma *f.*

Selma is the name of a castle in James Macpherson's 18th-century poems about Scottish legendary heroes. When the poems were translated into Swedish the translator failed to make the meaning clear, and it was understood by many Swedish readers to be a personal name; some then used it for their children. Immigrants took the name to the US, where it is still more common than in Britain.

Seonaid *see* Sheena

Serena *f.*

This is a Latin word meaning 'calm, serene (woman)'.

Seth *m.*

This is a biblical name meaning 'appointed' which was given to the third son of Adam and Eve. It was popular with the Puritans who took it to America, where it has returned to popularity.

Seumas, Seumus, Shamus *see* Seamas

Shahid *m.*, Shahida(h) *f.*

An Arabic name which means 'witness' or 'martyr'.

Shahin *m.*

An Arabic name which means 'falcon'. **Shaheen** is a variant spelling.

Sham *see* Shyam

Shamina(h) *f.*

An Arabic name from a word meaning 'scent' or 'flavour'.

Shanae *f.*

An Afro-American name, making use of the now fashionable prefix 'Sha-'. It seems to be an invented name of no special meaning, its sound being more important. It is also spelt **Shanay** and **Shanaye**.

Shane *see* **John, Sean**

Shanel(le), Shannel *see* **Chanel**

Shani *see* **Sian**

Shanice *f.*

An Afro-American blend of the fashionable 'Sha-' prefix and Janice. The name has been given publicity by singer Shanice Wilson, who uses only her first name as her stage name.

Shaniqua *f.*

Currently the most frequently used Afro-American name which uses the popular 'Sha-' prefix. It adapts a name like **Monique** or **Monica**. It is also spelt **Shanika**.

Shannon *f. and m.*

This is the Irish river and place name, meaning 'the old one', which has become a popular first name in recent years. It is less common for boys.

Sharad *m.,* Sharada *f.*

From an Indian word for 'autumn'. An alternative feminine form is **Sharadini**.

Sharadchandra *m.*

From the Indian for 'autumn moon'. **Sharadindu**, also for boys, has a similar meaning.

Sharadini *see* Sharad

Sharif *m.,* Sharifa(h) *f.*

This Arabic name means 'eminent' or 'honourable'.
It is also used as a title for descendants of the Prophet
Muhammad.

Sharlene *see* Charlene

Sharlott *see* Charlotte

Sharmaine *see* Charmaine

Sharon *f.*

In the Bible Sharon, which means 'the plain', is an area
of rich natural beauty and to compare a woman to it
came to be a great compliment. It has been used as a
first name only this century, but has been very popular.
It is occasionally spelt **Sharron**. **Shari** is a pet form.

Shaun(a), Shawndelle, Shawn *see* Sean

Shayla, Sheela *see* Sheila

Sheba *see* Bathsheba

Sheena *f.*

This is a phonetic form of **Sine**, the Gaelic for **JANE**.
An alternative form of Jane is **Siubhan**, which in Irish
becomes **Siobhan**, with phonetic spellings **Shevaun** and

Chevonne. Shona, the Scottish form of **JANET**, comes from the same root and is a phonetic form of **Seonaid,** in Irish **Sinead** (shin-aid).

Sheila *f.*

A phonetic spelling of **Sile**, the Irish form of **CECILIA**. It can also be spelt **Shelagh**, **Shiela** and **Sheela**. In the USA it has developed the form **Shayla**.

Shelby *f.*

An English place name and surname now frequently used in the USA as a girl's name. The original meaning was probably 'settlement with willow trees'. Its use as a first name was sparked by a character in the film *Steel Magnolias*.

Shelley *f.*

This is a pet form of **MICHELLE** and **RACHEL** as well as being a variant of the name **SHIRLEY**. From the 1940s the name was brought to public attention by the actress Shelley Winters.

Sheree, Sherrie, Sherry *see* Cherie

Sheril, Sheryl *see* Cheryl

Shevaun *see* Sheena

Shiela *see* Sheila

Shirley *f.*

This was originally a place name meaning 'shire meadow'. From this it became a surname in Yorkshire and elsewhere. It was primarily a boy's name until Charlotte Brontë started the fashion for it as a girl's name in 1849, when her novel *Shirley* appeared (see also SHELLEY).

Shiva *m.*

The name of the Hindu god, from the Sanskrit meaning 'benign'. Similar names are **Shivaji**, **Shivesh**, **Shivlal**, **Shivraj** and **Shivshankar**, which mean 'Lord Shiva'.

Shona *see* Sheena

Shree, Shri *see* Sri

Shrikant *see* Srikant

Shyam *m.,* Shyama *f.*

From the Sanskrit for 'dark', but identified with KRISHNA. In some parts of India the male form becomes **Sham**. The feminine form, **Shyama**, is a name of the goddess DURGA. Similar names for girls, with a basic meaning of 'dusky', include **Shyamal**, **Shyamala**, **Shyamalendu**, **Shyamali**, **Shyamalika**, **Shyamalima**, **Shyamari** and **Shyamasri**.

Shyann *see* Cheyenne

Sian *f.*

This is the Welsh form of **JANE**, properly spelt **Siân**.
Siani is a pet form which may appear as **Shani**.

Sibyl, Sibylla *see* **Sybil**

Sidney, Sydney *f. and m.*

This is a surname used as a first name from at least the
beginning of the 18th century. The spelling Sydney did
not appear until the 19th century, and the city in
Australia was named after Viscount Sydney, who was
then Secretary of State. The short form is **Sid**. In the
18th century girls were given surnames as first names
more often than was usual until very recently, and
Sydney as a girl's name may date from this. Alternatively,
it may be a form of the Latin name **Sidonia** ('woman of
Sidon'), which became **Sidonie** in French and **Sidony** in
English. In the US Sydney is regarded primarily as a
female name.

Sierra *f.*

The Spanish word for a mountain range used as a first
name in the USA, although possibly, because of its
association with automobiles, not destined to spread to
the UK. The situation is complicated in the USA by the
fact that **Ciara**, a feminine form of **KIERAN**, is a brand
of perfume there which is used as a first name and
pronounced in the same way as Sierra.

Silas *see* **Silvester**

Sile *see* **Sheila**

Silvester, Sylvester *m.*

The Latin for 'wood-dweller'. There have been three popes of this name, which was quite common in both forms in the Middle Ages. The New Testament name **Silas** is probably a form of Silvester. Like so many names popular with the Puritans, Silas is showing signs of coming back into fashion. **Sylvestra** and **Sylvana** are rare female forms.

Silvia, Sylvia *f.*

This is the Latin word meaning '(woman) of the wood'. Rhea Silvia was the mother of Romulus and Remus, the founders of Rome. This may have been the reason why the name was adopted during the Renaissance in Italy. Like other classical names, it came to England in Elizabethan times. Shakespeare used it in *Two Gentlemen of Verona*, and this probably gave rise to its use in Britain. The diminutive form is **Silvie** or **Sylvie**.

Simon *m.,* Simone *f.*

This is the better-known English form of the New Testament **Simeon**, the name of the man who blessed the baby Jesus in the Temple. The popularity of Simon in the Middle Ages was due to Simon **PETER**, the Apostle, whose popularity was great at that period. The short form is **Sim**. Simone is the feminine form taken from the French.

Sine, Sinead, Siobhan *see* **Sheena**

Sion *see* **John**

Sis, Sisley, Sissy *see* **Cecilia**

Sita *f.*
From the Sanskrit for 'furrow', the reference being to the goddess who personifies agriculture and is wife to Rama. **Seeta** and **Seetha** are other spellings of the name.

Siubhan *see* **Sheena**

Sive *see* **Sabina**

Skye, Skyler *f. and m.*
Skye is the name of the Scottish island used as a fashionable name, comparable to the older use of IONA. The name's associations with the word 'sky' may have helped its rise, and it is sometimes found as **Sky**. The same sound may have helped make the Dutch surname **Skyler**, 'scholar', a popular first name in the USA, for it is often shortened to **Sky**.

Sneha(1) *f.,* **Snehin** *m.*
From a Sanskrit word which originally meant 'oil', but later came to mean 'friendly affection'. **Snehal** is another form with the meaning 'friendly'. The male form, **Snehin**, means 'friend'.

Somhairle *see* **Samuel**

Sonal *f.*

An Indian name meaning 'golden'. **Sonali** and **Sonika** are variants.

Sondra *see* **Sandra**

Sonia *f.*

This is a Russian pet form of **SOPHIA**, and its use in Britain is modern, perhaps a result of the novel of this name by Stephen McKenna, published in 1917. **Sonya** and **Sonja** are other spellings of the name.

Sonika *see* **Sonal**

Sophia, Sophie *f.*

From the Greek meaning 'wisdom'. *Hagia Sophia* ('Holy Wisdom') is a common dedication for Orthodox churches as in the case of the great cathedral at Constantinople. This led to Sophia's use as a name in Greece. The name spread through Hungary to Germany and then to England when George I became king. Both his mother and his wife had the name. Sophie is the anglicized form which is currently the more popular. The form **Sophy** is also used (see **SONIA**).

Sorcha *see* **Sarah**

Sorley *see* **Samuel**

Spencer *m.*

This name, originally a surname given to the steward of a great household, but later an aristocratic name, was made famous by the actor Spencer Tracy. It has recently been popular with American parents.

Sri *f.*

This Indian name is from the Sanskrit meaning 'light' or 'beauty', later developing into 'majesty' and used as a title as well as a name. Sri is one of the names of Lakshmi, goddess of prosperity and beauty. **Shree**, **Shri** and **Sree** are variants.

Srikant *m.*

From the Sanskrit words meaning 'beautiful throat', a name applied to the god Shiva. **Shrikant** is an alternative spelling.

Stacey, Stacy *f. and m.*

This is a pet form which has become popular as an independent name. For men it was a short form of EUSTACE; as a woman's name it was originally short for ANASTASIA.

Stanley *m.*

This was originally a surname derived from an old Anglo-Saxon place name meaning 'stony field'. It was used as a first name from the mid-19th century partly because of its association with Sir Henry Morton Stanley, the famous explorer. It has the short form **Stan**.

Stefan, Steffan *see* Stephen

Stella *f.*

This is the Latin word for 'star'. Its use stems from its literary associations. An early use was in Sir Philip Sidney's *Astrophel and Stella* (1591). Then, in the early 18th century, Jonathan Swift used it as a pet name in letters to Esther Johnson. Other forms are ESTELLA and **Estelle.**

Stephen, Steven *m.*, Stephanie *f.*

From the Greek *stephanos* meaning 'crown' or 'wreath'. The laurel wreath was the highest honour a man could attain in the classical world. Stephen was a common personal name in Ancient Greece, and was borne by the very first Christian martyr. Steven is the alternative spelling. **Steve** and **Stevie** are the modern pet forms. There is a Welsh form, **Steffan**, and also a Continental form, **Stefan**. The female form, Stephanie, currently seems to be a more popular choice than Stephen.

Stuart *m.*

From the Old English *sti weard*, an official who looked after animals kept for food. Though it has changed its meaning somewhat, it survives as 'steward' today. The co-founder of the Scottish royal house of Stewart or Stuart in the 14th century was William the Steward who married the king's daughter and whose son later became king. **Stewart** is a common alternative and **Stuert** is also used.

Suhayl *m.*

An Arabic name which refers to a bright star, Canopus, in the southern constellation Carina. **Suhail** is a variant.

Sujan *m.*

An Indian name which means 'honest'.

Sumayyah *f.*

A Muslim name of uncertain meaning, borne by the first martyr in the cause of Islam. It also occurs as **Sumaya, Sumayah** and **Sumayya.**

Sunil *m.*

This is a rather puzzling name, as it comes from an obscure, ancient Sanskrit word meaning 'very dark blue'. Its use as a first name is modern. It has become a popular choice for parents in India and is sometimes interpreted as 'sapphire'. The form **Sunila** can be used for girls.

Sunila *see* Sunil

Sunita *f.*

This name comes from the Sanskrit for 'of good conduct' or 'righteous' and was the name of a princess in epic poetry who was the daughter of the King of Bengal. **Suniti** is another form of the name.

Sunni *see* Surinder

Suraj *m.*

This Indian name means 'the sun'.

Surinder *f. and m.*

This is a development of the name **INDRA**, and can be interpreted as meaning 'mightiest of the gods'. It is also found in the form **Surendra**. It is less often found used for girls than for boys, and as a boy's name can be shortened to **Sunni**.

Susan, Susanna(h) *f.*

Shushannah is Hebrew for 'lily' and Susanna(h) was the earliest form of this name in England, occurring in the Middle Ages and becoming quite common after the Reformation. Susan was adopted in the 18th century. In the 20th century the French forms, **Suzanne** and **Suzette**, have also been used in Britain, and spellings such as **Susana** and **Suzanna** have been found. **Sue**, **Sukey**, **Susie** and **Suzy** are pet forms.

Swan *see* **Raven**

Sybil *f.*

In classical times the Sibyls were prophetesses, and some of them were supposed to have foretold the coming of Christ. Because of this, **Sibylla** came to be used as a first name, the Normans bringing it with them to England. Sybil or **Sibyl** had a revival in the second half of the 19th century after Disraeli had published his political novel of that name (1845). The actress **Cybill** Shepherd has introduced another form of the name.

Sydney *see* **Sidney**

Sylvana, Sylvester, Sylvestra *see* **Silvester**

Sylvia, Sylvie *see* **Silvia**

Syril *see* **Cyril**

T

Tabitha *f.*
This name derives from the Aramaic word for 'gazelle'. In the New Testament it is the name of a Christian woman of Joppa who showed great charity towards the poor, and was raised from the dead by St Peter. The Greek form of her name was DORCAS. **Tabatha** is a modern spelling of the name.

Tadhg *see* Timothy

Taffy *see* David

Tahir *m.*
An Arabic name which means 'pure' and 'virtuous'.

Talia *see* Natalie

Taliesin *see* Ceridwen

Talitha *f.*
From an Aramaic word meaning 'girl'. It has very occasionally been used in the 20th century.

Tallulah *f.*
This name is well known from the American actress

Tallulah Bankhead (1903–68). She was named after her grandmother, who was in turn named after a place, Tallulah Falls in Georgia. The place name is said to come from a Native American word meaning 'terrible'. The name was given further publicity by a character in the film and musical *Bugsy Malone*, and while still rare, is beginning to be chosen by parents.

Tally, Talya *see* Natalie

Tam *see* Thomas

Tamara *f.*
Tamara is the Russian form of the biblical name **Tamar**, which means 'date palm'. Tamara was the name of a famous Russian queen, and remains a popular name in Russia. A pet form is TAMMY.

Tammy *f.*
A pet form of TAMARA and TAMSIN, now used as an independent name. In 1957 a film called *Tammy* and a song of that name, which was the bestselling record in the USA, started a vogue for the name's use. It is also a Scottish form of **Tommy** (see THOMAS).

Tamsin *f.*
This is a West Country female form of THOMAS. It can also be found as **Tamsine**, **Tamzin** and **Tamzen**. It

comes from **Thomasin** or **Thomasine** which have been
used since the Middle Ages. **Thomasina** is an old
latinized version which was revived in the 19th century.
TAMMY is a short form of these names.

Tania *see* **Tanya**

Tanisha *f.*
This name is used almost exclusively by Afro-Americans
and seems to be a Hausa name from West Africa,
meaning 'girl born on Monday'. It comes in a variety of
forms, including **Taneisha**, **Tanesha**, **Taniesha**, **Tenecia**,
Tenesha and **Tenisha**.

Tanith *f.*
The name of a Phoenician goddess of love that has
recently come into occasional use as a first name. It can
also take the form **Tanit**.

Tanner *m.*
A surname, from the job, used as a first name.

Tansy *f.*
The name of a yellow wild flower used as a first name.
It can also be a pet form of **ANASTASIA**.

Tanya *f.*
Tanya or **Tania** is a pet form of **Tatiana**, which has been

popular in Russia for many years, inspired by St Tatiana, a martyr revered by the Orthodox Church. **Tonya** is also found although, properly, this is the Russian pet form of **ANTONIA**.

Tara *f.*

Tara is the name of the hill where the ancient High Kings of Ireland held court and which plays an important part in Irish legend. It has been used as a first name only since the end of the last century.

Tasha *see* Natalie

Tasnim *f.*

An Arabic name meaning 'fountain of paradise'. It is also found as **Tasneem.**

Tatiana *see* Tanya

Tatum *f.*

This name, which seems to have been coined for the actress Tatum O'Neal, comes from a surname which in turn comes from an Old English place name meaning 'homestead of a man named Tata'.

Taylor *f. and m.*

This English surname, indicating an ancestor who was a tailor, has been made familiar as a first name by the American author (Janet Miriam) Taylor Caldwell, who chose to use it as her pen name in order to obscure her gender. That confusion continues today, with use of the name in the USA being almost equally divided between girls and boys.

Tecla *see* Thecla

Ted, Teddy *see* Edmund, Edward, Theodore

Tegan *f.*

This is an old Cornish name meaning 'lovely little thing' or 'ornament'. The name first got more general exposure in the 1980s in the television series *Dr Who*, when it was used for an Australian air hostess who became involved in the doctor's adventures. The name seems to have reappeared in the form **Tiegan** in the Australian soap *Home and Away*. Tegan is pronounced with a short 'e' sound, but Tiegan with the sound of 'tea'. The word 'teg', meaning 'pretty, fair', is found in Welsh as well as Cornish, for they are closely related, and there are a number of Welsh names that use it, of which **Tegwen**, 'pretty and fair', is the most common.

Tejal *f.*

An Indian name meaning 'lustrous'.

Tekla *see* Thecla

Tenecia, Tenesha, Tenisha *see* **Tanisha**

Terence *m.*

This is from the Latin Terentius, the name of a famous Roman comic playwright. Short forms are **Terry** and **Tel**. It is now also found in the forms **Terance**, **Terrance**, **Terrence** and **Terrell** (although this could also be from the name of an American city). It is a comparatively modern name, having come from Ireland, where it was used to transliterate the native **Turlough** ('tar-loch', pronounced as if Scottish), meaning 'instigator' (see also **THEODORIC**).

Teresa, Theresa *f.*

The meaning of this name is obscure. The first recorded Theresa was the wife of the 5th-century St Paulinus, and was responsible for his conversion. The name was for a long time confined to Spain until the fame of St Teresa of Avila (1515–82) spread the name to all Roman Catholic countries, but it did not become common in this country until the 18th century. It is often abbreviated to **Tess**, **Tessa** or **Tessie**. The form **Teri** or **Terry**, shared with some boys' names, is also found. A variant is **TRACY**. The French form, **Thérèse**, is also found occasionally.

Terrance, Terrell, Terrence *see* **Terence**

Terry *see* **Terence, Teresa, Theodoric**

Tess, Tessa, Tessie *see* Teresa

Thea *see* Dorothy, Theodora

Thecla *f.*

St Thecla, whose name means 'God's glory', was the first female martyr, just as St Stephen was the first male one. The name was popular in the Middle Ages, but is now an unusual choice. It can also be spelt **Tecla**, **Tekla** and **Thekla**.

Thelma *f.*

Like **MAVIS**, this name was introduced in the 19th century as a character in a novel by the writer Marie Corelli, and spread quickly throughout the country. There is a Greek word *thelema* meaning 'will', which may have had some influence on its development.

Theo *f. and m.*

This is a short form of **Theobald**, a Germanic name made up of elements meaning 'people' and 'bold', and of names such as **THEODORE**; but it is increasingly being used as an independent name. If used for girls it comes from **THEODORA**.

Theodora *f.*

This is the feminine form of **THEODORE**, which has been used since the 17th century. It is usually abbreviated to

Theo (sometimes used as an independent name), **Thea** and **Dora**. The rarer **Theodosia** has a similar meaning.

Theodore *m.*

From the Greek meaning 'gift of God'. There are 28 saints of this name in the Church Calendar. In England the name did not become general until the 19th century, but in Wales it has long been used as a form of **Tudur** or **Tudor**, which in fact probably comes from a Celtic name. The usual abbreviation in North America is **Ted** or **Teddy**, as in the case of President Theodore Roosevelt who gave his name to the teddy bear. In England **Theo** (sometimes used as an independent name) is a more common abbreviation.

Theodoric *m.*

From the Old German meaning 'people's ruler'. The Old English form of the name was Theodric which in medieval times became **Terry**, and in French **Thierry**. Theodoric became the most common form in the 18th century, but it is rare in Britain today (see also **Derek**, **Terence**).

Theodosia *see* Theodora

Theophania *see* Tiffany

Theresa, Thérèse *see* Teresa

Thierry *see* **Theodoric**

Thomas *m.*

From the Aramaic nickname meaning 'twin'. It was first given by Jesus to an Apostle named Judas to distinguish him from Judas Iscariot. The abbreviation **Tom** appears in the Middle Ages. **Tam** and TAMMY are the Scottish pet forms. The use of **Tommy** as a nickname for a British private soldier goes back to the 19th century, when the enlistment form had on it the specimen signature 'Thomas Atkins'. Thomas has been one of the three top boys' names for some years.

Thomasin, Thomasina, Thomasine *see* **Tamsin**

Thora *f.*

From the Norse meaning 'Thor-battle'. Its earlier form was **Thyra**. Thor was the god of thunder in Norse mythology, and he also gave his name to 'Thursday'. Thora is a rare name in Britain, but well known from the actress, Thora Hird.

Thurstan *see* **Dustin**

Thyra *see* **Thora**

Tiesha *see* **Letitia**

Tiffany f.

Originally a pet form of the name **Theophania**, from the Greek meaning 'the manifestation of God'. Tifainé was the Old French form, and this name was given to girls born at the time of the Epiphany, the words having the same meaning. These names were rare until recently when Tiffany became popular.

Tiegan see Tegan

Tilak m.

An Indian name which refers to the *tika* or *tilak*, the red mark worn as a caste-mark or decoration by Hindus. It is also placed as a blessing on the forehead of an honoured guest.

Tilly see Matilda

Timothy m.

Timotheos is an old Greek name meaning 'honouring God'. Its use as a first name is due to Timothy, the companion of St **PAUL**. It was not used widely until the 16th century when many classical and biblical names were introduced. **Tim** and **Timmy** are the abbreviations. **Timothea** is a rare female form. In Ireland Timothy has long been used as an equivalent for the native **Tadhg** ('tieg') which means 'poet'.

Tina f.

Originally a short form for girls' names ending in '-tina',

commonest of which is **Christina** (see **CHRISTINE**). It is now used in its own right.

Titus *m.*

This is a Latin name of unknown meaning. Two well-known holders of the name were a follower of St Paul and, in contrast, the infamous Titus Oates, an English conspirator and perjurer in the 17th century. It is probably best known today as the name of the hero of Mervyn Peake's *Gormenghast* books.

Toby *m.*

Toby is the English form of the Greek **Tobias**, itself derived from the Hebrew name which means 'the Lord is good'. The story of *Tobias and the Angel*, which is told in the Apocrypha was a favourite one in the Middle Ages. Punch's dog Toby is named after the dog that accompanied Tobias on his travels.

Tod, Todd *m.*

Originally a surname meaning 'fox', now used as a first name.

Toinette *see* **Anthony**

Tolomey *see* **Batholomew**

Tom, Tommy *see* **Thomas**

Toni, Tonio, Tony *see* **Anthony**

Tonya *see* **Antonia, Tanya**

Torcall *see* **Torquil**

Toria *see* **Victoria**

Tormod *see* **Norman**

Torquil *m.*

This is the English rendering of the Norse name, Thorketill ('Thor's cauldron'). The first element is the name of the Norse thunder god, Thor. The original became **Torcall** in Gaelic, which was anglicized into Torquil. It is used in Scotland, especially in the Outer Hebrides and among the Macleod family, and it has occasionally been given in England.

Totty *see* **Charlotte**

Toyah *see* **La Toya**

Tracy *f. and m.*

This popular girl's name seems to have started life as a pet form of TERESA. It is also found as **Tracey** and **Tracie**. Its beginnings as an independent name were probably helped by the use of the surname Tracy (from a French place name) as a boy's name, particularly as at the time when it first became popular Spencer Tracy (1900–67) was a well-known film star.

Travis *m.*

A surname used as a first name. It comes from the French word *traverser*, meaning 'to cross' and would have been given originally to a toll-collector.

Trevor *m.*

From the Welsh **Trefor**, meaning 'great homestead'. Trevor is the English spelling. **Trev** is the short form.

Tricia *see* **Patricia**

Triss *see* **Beatrice**

Tristan, Tristram *m.*

This is a name of obscure origin, possibly Pictish. It appears as the name of the noble hero of the medieval love stories of Tristram and **Isolda**. When Tristram is escorting Isolda to be married to his uncle they unknowingly drink a magic love-potion intended for the newly-weds, and are doomed to adulterous love until their tragic deaths. **Tristran** is also found.

Trixie *see* **Beatrice**

Troy *m.*

Troy was the ancient city in Asia Minor besieged by the Greeks for ten years. Its use as a first name was boosted in the 1960s by the actor Troy Donahue. It has been popular in Australia and is well used in the USA.

Trudi, Trudie, Trudy *see* Gertrude

Tudor, Tudur *see* Theodore

Tulsi *m.,* Tulasi *f.*

This Indian name is from the Sanskrit word meaning 'sacred basil', a plant which symbolizes Vishnu. Tulasi, the girls' form, is also the name of a goddess based on the same word.

Turlough *see* Terence

Tyler *f. and m.*

A surname, from the job, used as a first name. It is currently very popular in the USA and can be shortened to **Ty**.

Tyrone *m.*

The name of the Irish county, which means 'Eoghan's land', used as a first name. It was used in the past by the actor, Tyrone Power (1913–58) in the USA and by the British theatre director, Sir Tyrone Guthrie (1900–71). **Ty** is the short form, although Guthrie was known to his friends as Tony. **Tyree**, another Celtic district name, is also used.

U

Ulick *see* **Ulysses, William**

Ulysses *m.*

This is the Latin name for the Greek hero **Odysseus**, whose tale is told in Homer's *Odyssey*. Though little used in England, Scotland or Wales, it has been used in Ireland as an equivalent for **Ulick**, an Irish form of **WILLIAM**. James Joyce's most famous novel bears this name.

Umar *m.*

A popular Muslim name from the Arabic for 'flourishing'. It was the name of the Prophet Muhammad's lifetime companion and supporter. Another form of the name is **Omar**.

Una *f.*

The etymology of this ancient Irish name is obscure. It is also found in the forms **Oonagh** or **Oona** (pronounced 'oo-na'), both of which are also found in Scotland. **Juno**, influenced by the name of the Roman queen of the gods, is another Irish form, best known from Sean O'Casey's play *Juno and the Paycock* (1924). The Elizabethan poet Edmund Spenser took the Irish name Una and gave it its Latin sense, 'one, unity', in his epic poem *The Faerie Queene*.

Unice *see* **Eunice**

Unity *f.*

This is one of the abstract virtue names that became quite common among Puritans after the Reformation. It is rarely found today.

Ursula *f.*

From the Latin meaning 'little she-bear'. The name was fairly common in the Middle Ages on account of St Ursula, a 5th-century Cornish princess who, along with her companions, was murdered near Cologne while on a pilgrimage. The name had a revival after Mrs Craik chose it for her heroine in her popular novel, *John Halifax, Gentleman* (1856).

Uthman *m.*

A Muslim name from an Arabic word meaning 'baby bustard'. Uthman was the son-in-law of the Prophet Muhammad. The Turkish form of the name, **Usman**, is also much used, though often westernized as **Osman**. The name of the Ottoman Empire derived from this name's Latin and Italian plural form.

V

Val *see* **Perceval, Valentine, Valerie**

Valentine *f. and m.*

From the Latin *valens*, 'strong' or 'healthy'. St Valentine was a 3rd-century Roman priest martyred on February 14th, the eve of the celebrations of the pagan goddess Juno, when lots were drawn to choose lovers. The feast was absorbed into the Christian calendar. **Valentina** is an alternative girl's form. **Val** is a common diminutive, shared with **VALERIE**.

Valerie *f.*

This is the French form of the Roman family name **VALERIA**, and was taken into use in Britain in the late 19th century. It comes from a word meaning 'to be in good health'. It has the short form **Val**.

Vanda *see* **Wanda**

Vanessa *f.*

A name invented in the early 18th century by the writer Jonathan Swift as a pet name for **ESTHER** Vanhomrigh. He took the first syllable of her surname and added Essa, which was probably a pet form of Esther.

Vanna *see* **Gianna**

Vaughn, Vaughan *m.*

From the Welsh *fychan*, meaning 'small one'.

Velma *f.*

A name of unknown origin, first used in the 1880s in the United States.

Venetia *f.*

The Latin name for the Italian city of Venice, used as a first name. It was previously thought to have a connection with **Venus**, the Roman goddess of love, which is very occasionally used as a first name.

Vera *f.*

This name has two possible derivations. One source is the Russian for 'faith', another is the Latin meaning 'true'. It was used in English literature in the 19th century, and became popular in Britain at the beginning of the 20th. It is sometimes used as an abbreviation of **VERONICA** (see also **VERENA**).

Verena *f.*

The name of a rather obscure 3rd-century saint. Its meaning is not known, but may well come from the same source as **VERA**. St Verena lived in Switzerland and her name is popular there, but use among English speakers probably owes something to the name's prominence in Henry James's novel *The Bostonians*.

Vergil *see* **Virgil**

Verity *f.*

From the old English word for 'truth'. It was first used by the Puritans in 17th century, and has been quite common ever since. The variant **Verily** ('truly') is also found occasionally.

Vernon *m.*

Richard de Vernon was a companion of William the Conqueror. The surname comes from a French place name which means 'alder grove'. It was not used as a first name until the 19th century, when many such aristocratic names were taken into general use.

Veronica *f.*

Traditionally, this name is thought to derive from the Latin *vera icon*, meaning 'a true image'. St Veronica wiped the sweat from Christ's face on his way to Calvary, and a 'true image' of his face was said to have been left on the cloth. It is more likely, however, that the name is a form of **BERENICE**. **Véronique** has long been popular in France, and from here it reached Scotland in the late 17th century. It does not appear much in England before the late 19th century (see also **VERA**).

Veva *see* **Genevieve**

Vic *see* **Victor**

Vickie, Vicky, Vikki *see* **Victoria**

Victor *m.*

This is the Latin for 'conqueror'. Although it occurs in medieval England it was not common until the 19th century when it was used as a boy's form of **VICTORIA**. The commonest short form is **Vic**.

Victoria *f.*

From the Latin for 'victory'. This name was hardly used in Britain until the reign of Queen Victoria, who was named after her German mother. In the recent past the name has been very popular and is often found in one of its short forms, **Vicky**, **Vickie**, **Vikki** and **Tori** or **Toria**. **Vita** and **Viti** and the nickname **QUEENIE** are also found.

Vida *see* **Davida**

Vijay *m.*, Vijaya *f.*

This Indian name is from a Sanskrit word meaning 'victory'. The feminine form, Vijaya, is also applied to the goddess **DURGA**, wife of Shiva.

Vikesh *m.*

An Indian name which means 'the moon'.

Vilma *see* **William**

Vina *see* Davida

Vinay *m.*, Vinaya *f.*

An Indian name which means 'educating to act in a proper way'. For Buddhists it suggests the modest behaviour appropriate to a monk.

Vincent *m.*

From the Latin for 'conquering'. There was a 3rd-century Spanish martyr of this name and it occurs in English records from the 13th century. But the 17th-century St Vincent de Paul popularized the name when he founded the Vincentian Order of the Sisters of Charity. It became quite common in the 19th century. Its usual short form is **Vince**.

Viola, Violet *f.*

Viola is Latin for 'violet'. Although it does occur in the Middle Ages, the modern use of this name comes from Shakespeare, who gave it to the heroine of *Twelfth Night*. **Violette** and **Violetta** have also been used.

Viral *m.*

This Indian name means 'priceless'.

Virgil *m.*

The name of the great Roman poet. The original spelling of his name was **Vergil**. The name has been more used in the USA than in Britain.

Virginia *f.*

Although there was a Roman family called Virginus,
the modern use of this name dates only from 1587.
Sir Walter Raleigh had called his newly founded colony
in North America Virginia, after Elizabeth I, the 'Virgin
Queen', and the name Virginia was given to the first
child born to the settlers there. **Ginny**, **Gini** or **Jinny** is
a common pet form.

Vishal *m.*, Vishala *f.*

An Indian name which means 'immense, spacious'.
For girls **Vishalakshi** is also used, with the meaning
'wide-eyed'.

Vita, Viti *see* Victoria

Vitus *see* Guy

Vivian, Vivien *f. and m.*

From the Latin *vivianus*, which means 'lively'. Vivian
is now used for both sexes, but was originally the
masculine form, with Vivien, **Vivyan** or **Vyvyan** mostly
used for girls. The French **Vivienne** is always female.
Viv is used for short.

Vonda *see* Wanda

Vyvyan *see* Vivian

W

Wal, Wally *see* Wallace, Walter

Wallace *m.*

From the surname of Sir William Wallace, the great Scottish patriot of the 13th century. The use of his surname as a first name started about a hundred years ago. The surname comes from the same root that gives us the word 'Welsh', but which was once used of the British in the north as well. Another spelling of the name is **Wallis**, found in North America where it is used for both sexes. The short forms, **Wal** and **Wally**, are shared with **WALTER**.

Walter *m.*

From the Old German Waldhar, meaning 'army ruler'. The name was very popular among the Normans, and quickly became established in England. Sir Walter Raleigh is a very well-known later example and he used the short form **Wat** for his son. **Walt**, **Wal** and **Wally** are more popular short forms in use today, and Walt is used as an independent name in North America.

Wanda *f.*

This is a Polish girl's name which is probably connected with the word 'vandal'. Its wider use may have started when a novel of the same name by Ouida was published in 1883. **Vanda** and **Vonda** are both variants.

Waqar *m.*

This Arabic name means 'dignity' or 'soberness'.

Warren *m.*

From the surname, which can either be from an old German tribe name, Varin, or from a Norman place name meaning 'a game-reserve'. The Normans introduced the forms Warin and Guarin to England and these led to the surnames Warren, Waring and Garnet.

Warwick *m.*

The name of the English town which means 'houses by the weir', used as a surname and then as a first name. **Warrie** is a pet form.

Wasim *m.,* Wasimah *f.*

An Arabic name which means 'handsome' or 'graceful'. The feminine form, **Wasimah**, also means 'pretty'.

Wat *see* Walter

Wayne *m.*

This is a surname meaning 'cart' or 'cart-maker'. Its use as a first name is mainly due to the popularity of actor John Wayne (1907–79).

Wendy *f.*

This name was first used by James Barrie in *Peter Pan* (1904). The name started as 'Friendy-Wendy', a pet

name for Barrie used by a child friend of his, Margaret
Henley. **Wenda** has been described as a variant of
Wendy, but is more probably a form of **Gwenda** (see
Gwen).

Wenonah *see* **Winona**

Wesley *m.*

John and Charles Wesley were the founders of
Methodism, and the name came to be used as a first
name in their honour. As a surname it means 'west
meadow'. **Wes** is a short form.

Whitney *f. and m.*

This name, made famous by the singer Whitney
Houston, was originally a surname meaning '(living) at
the white island'. Its use as a first name in the USA may
be due to its being the surname of both a wealthy family
prominent in national politics and arts, and of Josiah
Dwight Whitney (1819–96), geologist and surveyor,
after whom the USA's highest mountain outside Alaska,
Mount Whitney in south California, is named.

Wilbur *m.*

This name is used in North America but is practically
unknown in Britain. The most famous example was
Wilbur Wright, who, with his brother **Orville**, made
the first successful powered flight in 1903.

Wilfred, Wilfrid *m.*

From the Old English Wilfrith, meaning 'desiring peace'.
St Wilfrid was an important figure in the 7th century,
and his name was particularly popular in Yorkshire
where he preached and founded the bishoprics of Ripon
and Hexham. The name did not survive the Norman
Conquest but was revived by high-church Anglicans in
the 19th century. It has the pet form **Wilf**.

William *m.*, Wilma *f.*

From the Old German, meaning 'desiring protection'.
William was always a popular name with the Normans,
who brought it to England, and, until the 13th century
when it was ousted by JOHN, it was the commonest of all
names in England. **Will** or **Willie** are the old short forms
but **Bill** and BILLIE are more usual today. **Gwilym**,
shortened to **Gwill**, is the Welsh form of the name, and
Liam a short form which has spread from Ireland; **Ulick**
is another Irish form. Feminine forms which have been
used occasionally are **Wilhelmina** and Wilma. Their pet
forms include **Willa** or **Vilma**, **Minnie** and **Minna** and
Elma (see ELMER). These feminine forms are more
popular in America where German immigrants have
spread their use.

Winifred *f.*

From the Welsh feminine name **Gwenfrewi**, anglicized
as Winifred and later confused with the Old English
male name **Winfrith**, meaning 'friend of peace'.
St Winifred, a 7th-century saint, is said to have been

decapitated by a Welsh prince when she rejected his advances, but then was restored miraculously to life. Although she was a popular saint in the Middle Ages, her name was not used much until the 16th century. It was a very popular name at the turn of the century. **Win**, **Winnie** and, less often, **Freda** are short forms. **Winifrid** is also used.

Winona *f.*

This is a Sioux word meaning 'eldest daughter'. It is also the name of a city in Minnesota. The name occurs as **Wenonah** in Longfellow's poem *Hiawatha* (1855), and can also be found as **Wynon(n)a**.

Winston *m.*

This is the name of a small village in Gloucestershire, which became a surname. The name has been used in the Churchill family since 1620, when Sir Winston Churchill, father of the 1st Duke of Marlborough, was born. His mother was Sarah Winston. It has come into use in honour of Sir Winston Churchill (1874–1965) to mark his contribution to world affairs.

Wyn, Wynfor, Wynne *see* Gwyn

Wynona *see* Winona

X

Xan, Xander *see* **Alexander**

Xanthe *f.*
From the Greek meaning 'yellow'. It has occasionally been used in Britain.

Xara *see* **Zahra**

Xavier *m.*
The surname of St Francis Xavier (1506–52) used as a first name. It is also occasionally spelt **Javier** or **Zavier** and there are rare feminine forms, **Xavia**, **Zavia**, **Xaviera** and **Xaverine**.

Xenia *f.*
The Greek word for 'hospitality'. It is only occasionally found. **Xena** is also used (see also **Zena**).

Y

Yasin *m.*

A name formed by the names of Arabic letters from an important passage in the Koran. Yasin features in a well-known Egyptian tale fighting social injustice.

Yasmin, Yasmina, Yasmine *see* **Jasmine**

Yehudi *see* **Jude**

Yolanda *f.*

From the Greek meaning 'violet flower'. The Gilbert and Sullivan opera IOLANTHE comes from the same root. **Yolande** is the French form.

Yseult(e), Ysolde *see* **Isolda**

Yves *see* **Ivo, Ivor, Yvonne**

Yvonne, Yvette *f.*

These are French names meaning 'yew'. They are female pet forms of the Breton boy's name, **Yves**. The boy's name has never been common in Britain, but the girls' versions are quite popular.

Z

Zachary *m.*

The English form of **Zacharias**, the Greek for the Hebrew **Zachariah** or **Zechariah**, meaning 'the Lord has remembered'. Zachary was used occasionally in the Middle Ages, but did not become at all common until the Puritans adopted it in the 17th century. They took it to America where it has recently become popular, together with the short form **Zak** or **Zack**. It is now spreading to this country. **Zacchaeus** and **Zakki** are other forms of the name.

Zahid *m.*

An Arabic name which means 'abstinent'.

Zahra, Zara *f.*

A Muslim name which means 'to flower' or 'to achieve splendour'. It was the family name of the Prophet's mother and is traditionally used in her honour. The English form came to the attention of the British public in 1981 when Princess Anne, the Princess Royal, used it as her daughter's name. It is occasionally found as **Xara**.

Zainab *see* Zaynab

Zak *see* Zachary, Isaac

Zake *m.*, Zakiya *f.*

An Arabic name meaning 'pure, chaste'. The feminine form can also be spelt **Zakiyah** and **Zakiyya**.

Zakki *see* Zachary

Zandra *see* Sandra

Zara *see* Zahra

Zavia, Zavier *see* Xavier

Zaynab *f.*

A popular Muslim name, of uncertain meaning. Some scholars link it with a fragrant plant, and it was borne by several members of the Prophet Muhammad's family. It is frequently found as **Zainab.**

Zeb *m.*

This can be a short form of such Hebrew names as **Zebulun** ('exaltation') or **Zebedee** ('my gift'), or can simply be an attempt by parents to find an unusual name. Similarly **Zed** can be seen as a short form of **Zedekiah** ('justice of the Lord').

Zechariah *see* Zachary

Zed, Zedekiah *see* Zeb

Zeke *see* Ezekiel

Zelda *see* **Griselda**

Zena *f.*

One theory is that this name comes from a Persian word meaning 'woman'. Another makes it a pet form of various other names such as **Zinaida** which comes from Zeus, the Greek king of the gods, it is the name of two Russian saints; and another a variation of **XENIA**. It is also found as **Zina**.

Zenobia *f.*

This was the name of a great Queen of Palmyra (modern Syria) in the 3rd century AD. She was seen as a threat to the Eastern Roman Empire, and her aggressive foreign policy forced the Emperor Aurelian to invade. This he did successfully and put an end to her power, though he spared her life. The name appears in Cornwall from the 16th century but the reason for this is unknown.

Zillah *f.*

From the Hebrew for 'shade'. The name occurs in the Old Testament (Genesis IV, 19-23) and was used occasionally after the Reformation.

Zina, Zinaida *see* **Zena**

Zita *f.*

The name of the last Empress of Austria who, although deposed just after the end of the First World War, died only in 1989. It comes from an Italian word for 'little girl' and was the name of a humble but good maid who became the patron saint of domestic servants.

Zoe, Zoë f.

This is the Greek word for 'life'. The Alexandrian Jews used it to translate the Hebrew equivalent for **EVE** into Greek. The name spread throughout the Eastern Church but has been used only in Britain in the last hundred years.

Zola f.

The name of the French novelist Emile Zola (1840–1902) used as a first name. Although best known from the runner Zola Budd, the name has been used before. The lead singer of the 1950s pop group The Platters was Zola Taylor.

Zuleika f.

From the Persian meaning 'brilliant beauty'. The name is known from Max Beerbohm's satirical novel *Zuleika Dobson* (1911), whose heroine is so beautiful that all the young men at Oxford University kill themselves for love of her.

Most popular girls' and boys' names

The following lists are based on the Registrar General's Indexes of Births for England and Wales. They show the names which are currently the most popular in England and Wales.

Girls

1	Chloe	+2
2	Emily	+2
3	Sophie	-2
4	Jessica	-2
5	Megan	+5
6	Hannah	+2
7	Rebecca	-1
8	Lauren	-3
9	Charlotte	-2
10	Georgia	+7
11	Amy	-2
12	Lucy	+3
13	Emma	
14	Bethany	
15	Katie	-3
16	Shannon	-5
17	Laura	-1
18	Olivia	+5
19	Eleanor	+3

20	Courtney	+34 New entry
21	Sarah	-3
22	Molly	+6
23	Abigail	-3
24	Jade	-5
25	Alice	-1
26	Ellie	+6
27	Holly	+2
28	Rachel	-2
29	Danielle	-8
30	Elizabeth	-5
31	Zoe	-1
32	Paige	-5
33	Georgina	+6
34	Chelsea	-1
35	Victoria	+2
36	Leah	
37	Samantha	-6
38	Nicole	-4

39 Anna	+6	45 Louise	+2
40 Amber	+1	46 Melissa	+3
41 Natasha	−6	47 Caitlin	+21 New entry
42 Grace	−2	48 Jasmine	+7 New entry
43 Alexandra	−5	49 Kayleigh	+4 Re-entry
44 Ella	+13 New entry	50 Natalie	−7

Boys

1 Jack		19 William	
2 James	+2	20 Adam	−4
3 Thomas		21 Lewis	+3
4 Daniel	−2	22 Jake	−5
5 Joshua		23 Michael	−3
6 Matthew		24 Oliver	−1
7 Samuel	+1	25 Nathan	+5
8 Joseph	+1	26 Christopher	−1
9 Ryan	−2	27 Kieran	−1
10 Jordan	+2	28 Bradley	+4
11 Luke		29 Ben	+5
12 Connor	+1	30 Jacob	+5
13 Liam	−3	31 Jamie	−2
14 Benjamin	+1	32 Aaron	+1
15 Callum	+7	33 Mohammed	+3
16 Alexander	−2	34 Robert	−7
17 Harry	+1	35 Cameron	+7
18 George	+3	36 David	−5

37	Andrew	−9	44	Charles	+1
38	Kyle	−1	45	Jonathan	−6
39	Charlie	−1	46	Ashley	−6
40	Brandon	+13 New entry	47	Sam	+2
41	Reece	+3	48	John	−7
42	Alex	+1	49	Joe	+2 New entry
43	Edward	+3	50	Scott	−3

+/− indicates movement since 1996

COLLINS GEM — BABIES' names

COLLINS GEM — BEER

COLLINS GEM — BIRDS

COLLINS GEM — CALORIE Counter

COLLINS GEM — FACT FILE

COLLINS GEM — FENG SHUI

COLLINS GEM — FLAGS

COLLINS GEM — Healthy EATING

COLLINS GEM — QUOTATIONS

COLLINS GEM — SAS Self-Defence

COLLINS GEM — SAS Survival Guide

COLLINS GEM — SEASHORE

COLLINS GEM — TREES

COLLINS GEM — Understanding DREAMS

COLLINS GEM — WILD flowers

COLLINS GEM — WINE Dictionary